LATIN AMERICAN ECONOMIC INTEGRATION

THE PRAEGER SERIES
ON
INTERNATIONAL ECONOMICS
AND
DEVELOPMENT

ISAIAH FRANK

CONSULTING EDITOR

LATIN AMERICAN ECONOMIC INTEGRATION

Experiences and Prospects

EDITED BY
MIGUEL S. WIONCZEK

FREDERICK A. PRAEGER, *Publishers*
New York • Washington • London

FREDERICK A. PRAEGER, *Publishers*
111 Fourth Avenue, New York, N.Y. 10003, U.S.A.
77–79 Charlotte Street, London, W.1, England

Published in the United States of America in 1966
by Frederick A. Praeger, Inc., Publishers

Library of Congress Catalog Card Number: 65–24948

Printed in the United States of America

Preface

This volume represents the outcome of a coordinated effort of a number of economists and social scientists of many different nationalities, working in four continents, on problems of economic developments. The common denominator for this rather heterogeneous group of contributors is their preoccupation with the stagnation of the economies of the underdeveloped world; their intellectual dissatisfaction with orthodox formulas for achieving economic development, still fashionable in the industrial countries and defended with arguments based upon the traditional theory of international trade; and finally, their belief that economic regional integration programs implemented slowly—against overwhelming odds—in Latin America and in other less developed areas might represent a major defense against the slow but continuous disintegration of the world economy, in which prosperous groupings of the developed countries of the Northern Hemisphere would be confronted by a myriad of unviable small national economic units in the southern portion of the globe.

This volume, written originally in 1964 and published in Spanish in Mexico by Fondo de Cultura Económica under the title *Integración de América Latina—Experiencias y Perspectivas,* has been revised and brought up to date by its editor to give the English-speaking reader a general survey of the main problems faced by Latin American Free Trade Association (LAFTA) and Central American Common Market (CACM) during their early years of existence. The purpose of the book is to weight achievements against failures of both integration schemes and to outline major issues on which collective action must be taken by the member countries within the near future to avoid the transformation of LAFTA and CACM into ineffective preferential trade agreements. Both schemes make sense in the longer run only if they achieve the objective of dynamizing the economic growth and industrialization of Latin America.

The editor would like once again to express his deep appreciation to all the contributors to this symposium and to thank Mr. Plácido García Reynoso, Deputy Secretary of Industry and Commerce of Mexico, and Dr. Arnaldo Orfila Reynal, Director of Fondo de Cultura Económica in Mexico City, for their moral support in this enterprise. Professor Raymond Vernon, Harvard University, who offered extremely useful comments on the content of the original volume and Professor Isaiah Frank, Johns Hopkins University, who helped to bring about the English-language edition, deserve the editor's gratitude as well.

MIGUEL S. WIONCZEK

Mexico City
October, 1965

Foreword

The Final Act of the United Nations Conference on Trade and Development of 1964 establishes the principle that in international economic relations,

> regional economic groupings, integration or other forms of economic cooperation should be promoted among developing countries as a means of expanding their intra-regional and extra-regional trade and encouraging their economic growth and their industrial and agricultural diversification with due regard to the special features of development of the various countries concerned as well as their economic and social systems.[1]

In other words, world opinion finally arrived at a consensus to the effect that economic-integration programs, such as the Latin American Free Trade Association (LAFTA) and the Central American Common Market, constitute an important instrument for economic development, provided they ensure an equitable distribution of the benefits of integration and do not entail elements of discrimination against other areas in process of development. The general principle recognized by the 120 countries that met in Geneva tacitly admits that these economic integration programs are essentially aimed at granting reciprocal preferences not intended for extension to the already developed sector of the world economy.

[1] *Proceedings of the United Nations Conference on Trade and Development, I: Final Act and Report* (New York: United Nations, 1964), 11.

Anyone undertaking a study of the major economic problems of our time must conclude that the lack of close coordination of national efforts in behalf of development in each of the so-called peripheries—Latin America, Africa, and Asia—is responsible in large measure for the difficulties presently faced by the underdeveloped world. On the other hand, the lengthy discussions and negotiations conducted during the first Geneva UNCTAD conference in 1964 incontrovertibly proved that we are living in an age of growing economic regionalism.

An analysis of the world-trade trend in the last ten or fifteen years clearly points up this phenomenon. While commercial interchange among the three large sectors of the world economy (the free-enterprise industrialized countries, the planned-economy bloc, and the underdeveloped regions) is expanding at an extremely sluggish pace, trade flows *within* each of the first two groups have proved to be extraordinarily dynamic. Between 1950 and 1962, intraregional commerce among the industrial countries of the West expanded at an annual rate of nearly 10 per cent, while that of the Soviet bloc increased even more rapidly. Today, intraregional trade represents approximately three-fourths of the first group's over-all trade, as against two-thirds of that of the second. In contrast, intraregional interchange in the three large underdeveloped areas—Latin America, Africa, and Asia—has never reached even 10 per cent of total trade transactions by those regions, if, in the case of Asia, both Japanese commerce and Hongkong and Singapore entrepôt trade are excluded. These correlations are far from accidental: they reflect, respectively, the presence and absence of a causal process in which the evolution of a complex of interrelated economies fosters reciprocal trade, and the latter, in turn, stimulates the growth process.

The present work could scarcely be published at a more helpful and opportune moment, for it provides a detailed inventory of the experience of the two Latin American economic-integration programs and, in addition, evaluates their outlook and potential. This newest effort by the editor, Miguel S. Wionczek, in behalf of Latin American economic cooperation is indeed praiseworthy. In line with a duly formulated program, he has elicited a cohesive series of essays from a group of economists of a dozen different nationalities, living on four continents. Prepared in the exercise of full intellectual freedom in every case, all these papers concur in deeming it imperative to accelerate and broaden economic-integration and economic-cooperation programs in Latin America.

Mexico's is one of the few instances in which the process of sustained development in recent decades supports an optimistic view of the future. Moreover, as substantiated by documentation and analyses prepared on the occasion of the UNCTAD Geneva conference, it is indisputably true that the long-term prospects for the traditional commodity trade of the developing regions are not encouraging. Even assuming that on some not far-distant day—in response to demands made by the underdeveloped world—the industrialized countries of West and East were to eliminate all barriers and practices that presently obstruct or distort international trade in primary goods and were, further, to offer preferential market access for the manufactures and semifinished goods exported by countries in process of development, Latin America, Africa, and Asia would still not have a capacity to import that would be consistent with their growing development needs. It is true that a part of the resources needed for tangibly increasing the per capita income and the welfare of these regions, which are characterized by accelerated demographic growth, could be supplied by external economic assistance. Aid programs, however, are encountering resistance on the part of large sectors of opinion in the industrial countries of the West. In view of such opposition, which has picked up particular momentum in the United States and France, funds for aid—in the true sense of the term—can hardly be expected to make up the future deficit between the import needs of the underdeveloped areas and the income they will derive from their exports to industrial centers. It is estimated, for example, that the increase in economic aid to a net 1 per cent of the national income of the developed countries, as recommended in Geneva, would raise the flow of such financial assistance to some $9 billion yearly. However, by 1970, the joint trade deficit of Latin America, Africa, and Asia, assuming a 5 per cent annual rate of economic growth, is forecast at some $20 billion. Obviously, then, there will be no way to mobilize sufficient resources to make up the difference between the two figures mentioned, unless integration and intraregional trade programs are actively promoted in areas in process of development.

Because of its relative degree of development, its history and cultural traditions, and the existence of institutional instruments (the Montevideo and Managua treaties), Latin America faces an easier task in promoting integration and intraregional trade than do the other underdeveloped areas. However, although the enhanced trade flows within LAFTA and the Central American Common Market, in recent years, are definitely worthy of note, certain statistics should be taken into account. Intrazonal exports of the nine signatories to the Montevideo Treaty amounted to $361 million in 1961 and rose to $638 million in 1964. The latter figure, however, represented only 10 per cent of those nations' total export trade. For that matter, intrazonal trade has only by 1964 been restored to the levels of interchange reached in the mid-1950's. In Central America, regional trade is increasing at a more forceful pace, but still does not exceed 15 per cent of the area's over-all trade. Assuming that LAFTA and Central American intraregional commerce expands at similar rates in the future, several decades will elapse before any decisive effects are produced on the economic development of Latin America.

In company with the majority of contributors to this book, I believe that, in the case of the Latin American Free Trade Association, present integration mechanisms are not strong enough to launch an adequate and expedite program. This affirmation should not be interpreted as a criticism of the Montevideo Treaty, signed in 1960, for, at that time, a more vigorous agreement would not have been feasible. However, this does not mean that the twelve years stipulated in the treaty must, of necessity, be waited out before taking greater advantage of the experience gained and finding more thoroughgoing solutions to the problems that have arisen, not only as a result of extraregional economic difficulties, but from the very fact that in February, 1960, the Latin American republics formally decided to follow the path of economic cooperation as a means of accelerating their development.

The introductory chapter of this work outlines the conditions necessary to the viable integration of an underdeveloped region, and the remaining pages contain essays prepared by the eminent economist Raúl Prebisch, by Gustavo Magariños of the LAFTA secretariat, and by many other distinguished experts from within and without Latin America. In combination, these studies provide a clear and detailed insight into what remains to be done in Latin America to enable its integration program to gather the strength it needs and to save this regional economic-cooperation endeavor from frustration. As expressed by the editor at the conclusion of his essay on the history of the Montevideo Treaty, "If the integration program does not soon pick up speed and breadth, but degenerates into a preferential trade zone of very limited scope, the blame can hardly be placed on the existence of unfavorable circumstances or the action of external forces." The last three essays in this volume, which analyze the impressive progress made to date by the Central American Common Market, completely refute the arguments of those who, in the name of misguided nationalism, blind conservatism, or, more seriously still, the defense of vested interests, maintain that unambitious, isolated development is to be preferred, and who do what they can to block efforts aimed at establishing intercommunication among the Latin American economies.

At the UNCTAD Geneva conference, Latin America, perhaps for

the first time in its history, managed to speak with a single voice both in its relations with the economically advanced regions and in those with the country groupings from other underdeveloped continents. It appears to have been demonstrated that it is far easier for a region to join in the defense of its interests over against the rest of the world than to unite in solving internal problems with a practical approach and in a spirit of compromise. Be that as it may, it should be emphasized once again that Latin America cannot wait a quarter of a century to become economically integrated, and such integration will not be achieved if efforts are limited to a mere continuance of trade-barrier reductions at a timid rate.

There is a need—as underscored by Dr. Raúl Prebisch in his essay—for far-reaching political decisions that will endow the instruments of integration with the efficacy needed to withstand elements of possible stagnation in the near future. These decisions obviously cannot be taken by technicians, intellectuals, and businessmen, despite the ample evidence that these groups are impressively intensifying their support of, and participation in, the integration program. It is incumbent on the various governments to shoulder the task of strengthening the Montevideo Treaty and accelerating its operations.

Plácido García Reynoso

Contents

LATIN AMERICAN ECONOMIC INTEGRATION

I

MIGUEL S. WIONCZEK

Introduction: Requisites for Viable Integration

The main body of what might be called the doctrine of regional economic integration in Latin America was built, although not systematically, on the writings of Dr. Raúl Prebisch and certain studies of the U.N. Economic Commission for Latin America (ECLA) published during the course of the last ten years. Unfortunately, none of this material is very well known outside the confines of the Latin American economic profession. The integration doctrine elevates to the multinational plane the thesis that economic development is impossible without industrialization. According to this thesis, the sustained growth of an underdeveloped economy depends on the degree to which an active process of substitution of imports by domestic production can be promoted, so as to extend the country's capacity to import to cover the acquisition of an optimum volume of capital goods and technology.

At the beginning of the 1950's, the process of import substitution in the field of consumer manufactures in the larger countries of Latin America had just about reached its limit, and the import capacity of almost all the republics in the region ceased to grow at the rate needed to finance the expanding cost of industrialization. This last phenomenon is owing, among other causes, to the exceedingly rapid technological progress made by the industrially advanced countries. In addition, the development problem became complicated by the population explosion and the social tensions common to backward economies having an extremely inadequate distribution of income—tensions that have been brought to an even higher pitch because of the demonstration effect that the levels of welfare in world economic centers exert on the peripheral societies.

As an alternative to stagnation, it was logical that the idea of economic integration should arise. Its authors maintain that the creation of a regional market in response to the liberation of trade currents among the nations in the area, the subsequent advantage taken of economies of scale, and the coordination of national industrialization policies would enable a more rational mobilization of unemployed production factors and lead to an acceleration of Latin America's economic growth. According to the same school of thought, the principal obstacles that, in the recent past, have kept these potentially available production factors from being incorporated into the development process are the limitations of the national markets and external bottlenecks.

As affirmed in one of the ECLA studies preceding the signing, in 1960, of the Montevideo Treaty and the General Treaty for Central American Economic Integration, Latin America's basic problems

> . . . can be solved only if the following fundamental fact is recognized: Latin America, however great the external assistance it receives, however high the rate at which its exports expand—and they cannot do so very rapidly—will be unable to carry out its development plans, will be unable even to regain the rate of growth it achieved in the ten post-war years, unless it makes a sustained effort to establish within its own territory the capital goods industries of which it is in such urgent need today, and which it will require on a large scale during the next quarter of a century. . . . In order to produce these capital goods and develop all the intermediate goods industries required in order to launch these highly complex dynamic industries . . . Latin America needs a common market.[1]

Several factors lie at the root of these economic arguments in favor of integration: Latin America's reaction to the ever-widening difference between the levels of development and welfare in the world and the state of recurrent crises in which the region's economy finds itself; dissatisfaction—shared in increasing degree by other underdeveloped regions—with international economic relations, based on what Gunnar Myrdal calls "a false principle of equality" among the unequal; and an awareness that, in the present world of political and economic blocs, for bargaining power the weak countries of the various underdeveloped regions must depend on the possibility of unifying their

[1] *The Latin American Common Market* (Mexico City: United Nations, 59. II. 1959; G. 4), p. 1.

criteria and policies over against the industrial centers of West and East.

In terms of historical experience, the aims pursued by the advocates of Latin American economic integration and the policies they propose are hardly original. They are similar to the objectives sought by the British colonies in North America when they obtained their independence from the metropolis at the end of the eighteenth century. They also recall France's purposes in the face of Great Britain's industrial progress during the first quarter of the last century, and, not long thereafter, the establishment of the *Zollverein* in Germany in the face of the economic hegemony of England and France. The similarity between the present attempts at integrating national economies of the underdeveloped regions into larger groupings and the development, up to the mid-nineteenth century, of national states starting from small economic and political units should not come as a surprise to those who are persuaded that "we are all aware of the fact that we live in the most catastrophically revolutionary age that men have ever faced." [2]

Nor is it surprising that attempts to establish a theoretical basis for the doctrine of Latin American integration, and of other integration plans in the underdeveloped regions, should clash with the neoclassic theory of international trade that originated in the industrial centers and was extended to the field of integration in the comparatively recent past (the early 1950's). The same thing happened at the close of the eighteenth century, when the development needs of what then were the peripheries of the Atlantic world encountered the classical theory of trade that had been worked out in England. The current debates between the Marshall-Viner-Haberler and Nurkse-Myrdal-Prebisch schools, between the advocates of free trade and the proponents of inward-directed development (who transfer the "infant industry" concept from a country to a region) are not exclusively economic. Nor were economic arguments the sole basis for the no less violent controversy of a century and a half ago between the economists of industrially advanced England and the Alexander Hamilton and Friedrich List school,[3] which pleaded the case for the then underdeveloped United States and Germany.

[2] Barbara Ward, *The Rich Nations and the Poor Nations* (New York: W. W. Norton, 1962), p. 13.

[3] Sidney Dell, in his *Trade Blocs and Common Markets* (New York: Alfred A. Knopf, 1963), pp. 207–8, quotes a very interesting statement by Alexander Hamilton, which, with a few slight changes, could have originated today in Latin America. Back in 1791, Hamilton wrote: "The United States cannot exchange with Europe on equal terms; and the want of reciprocity would render them the victim

The theoretical precepts on international trade advocated by the neoclassical school and its disciples cannot be applied to situations prevailing in today's peripheries, for the simple reason that the representatives of the neoclassic school have little interest in the general problems of economic growth, nor do they take into account the nature of the underdeveloped world and of its politico-social problems.[4]

In consequence:

> In contrast to the general richness and synthesized character of much of pure theory in its comparative statics, dynamic propositions in international trade are comparatively few and bear no trace of any uniform design, each having been developed in virtual isolation. Dynamic trade theory, where it exists, has grown up in an essentially *ad hoc* fashion and has witnessed none of the interaction of analysis which usually accompanies the development of an area of knowledge and produces a common design, a unifying frame.[5]

All this would be relatively innocuous, albeit intellectually unsatisfactory, if the matter at hand had only to do with speculative exercises indulged in by economically advanced countries. However, the problem becomes much more serious when, as has occurred, these exercises form the basis of what J. K. Galbraith calls the "conventional wisdom," [6] which, in turn, determines the doctrinal positions of the industrial countries against the rest of the world and is transmitted through the imitation mechanism to the intellectual elite of the underdeveloped countries. When, in the name of these "conventional truths," the underdeveloped regions are offered a series of proposi-

---

of a system which should induce them to confine themselves to agriculture, and refrain from manufactures. A constant and increasing necessity, on their part, for the commodities of Europe, and only a partial and occasional demand for their own, in return, could not but expose them to a state of impoverishment compared with the opulence to which their political and natural advantages authorize them to aspire. . . . If Europe will not take from us the products of our soil, upon terms consistent with our interest, the natural remedy is to contract, as fast as possible, our wants of her."

[4] The proceedings of the international conference on trade theory, convoked in the autumn of 1961 in Brissago, Switzerland, are meaningful in this connection. Sir Roy Harrod, one of the editors of these proceedings, pointed out that the discussions had revealed "how radical a change in concepts is required by the essential nature of growth theory, as contrasted with statics or comparative statics." See International Economic Association, *International Trade Theory in a Developing World* (New York: St. Martin's Press, 1963), p. xiv.

[5] J. Bhagwati, "The Pure Theory of International Trade," *The Economic Journal*, LXXIV, No. 293 (March, 1964), 48.

[6] J. K. Galbraith, *The Affluent Society* (Boston: Houghton Mifflin, 1958), chap. ii.

tions concerning integration programs (which, for that matter, are no longer followed very strictly, even in the countries in which they originated), there is a grave risk that the poor regions, by accepting these precepts, would close one of the few roads remaining to them leading out of their situation of stagnation so fraught with social and political dangers.

Among the criteria that the advanced countries prescribe for the underdeveloped world's integration programs, the following are particularly worthy of note:

1. Even admitting that regional integration in the underdeveloped areas can increase the welfare of the participating countries—which, according to the neoclassic school, is by no means a certainty—the essence of integration consists of the freeing of regional trade.

2. In order for a customs union in developing countries not to have harmful effects on such nations, as well as on the world economy, a degree of common protection for the participants should be provided for, no greater than the average existing formerly at the national level. The union should also establish a firm commitment for the complete freedom of movement of all production factors.

3. Within the framework of a customs union, market forces should be left at liberty, so that they may determine the new allocation of production factors on the basis of comparative advantage.

4. Since the objective of a customs union should be a more efficient functioning of competitive forces, any action tending to limit them—e.g., industrial-specialization agreements—would foster the emergence of monopolistic situations, distort trade within the union itself, and eventually lead to welfare losses.

5. Although it might be advisable for economic policies to be coordinated within the union to some extent, with the exception of a common tariff this should not disturb the structure of existing economic relations with the rest of the world. It would be highly inadvisable, for example, to establish regional payments systems, since they would have a negative effect on free convertibility on a world-wide scale.

From a perusal of the meager literature published to date on the subject of economic integration in Latin America, it might be deduced that the position defined by these criteria has already been successfully assailed. The fact is, however, that an analysis of the effective policies and concrete attitudes adopted within and without the region regarding this matter does not support so optimistic a conclusion. In practice, the influence of the doctrines summarized above is felt at all times and in connection with integration problems of every type.

If the representatives of "conventional wisdom" were acquainted with the real world and realized that, instead of helping solve today's problems in Latin America, their position creates others that are even more serious for the future, they would readily perceive that their proposals have only an extremely tenuous bearing on the growth needs of underdeveloped areas. Instead of free trade and optimum welfare conditions, secular stagnation and the absence of free trade constitute the basic point of departure for all regional integration attempts in such areas. Hence, it is not a matter of abandoning a presumably optimum situation in favor of less advantageous alternatives, but of seeking solutions that can prevent a progressive worsening of the existing conditions.

The freeing of trade cannot be the sole objective of a customs union in an underdeveloped area. In the first place, in the light of its present low levels, trade needs more to be promoted than freed. Secondly, differences in the economic development levels within a single region in these areas are much greater than those existing within the developed sector of the world economy.[7] Consequently, unless the member countries all had comparable levels of underdevelopment, a customs union in an underdeveloped environment, centering exclusively on the freeing of regional trade, would function much after the fashion of trade between the industrial centers and the peripheries. The result would be an increase in the economic distance within this union in favor of those countries which are better endowed with resources and whose acquired advantages are superior. The fate of two customs unions in Africa—the East African Common Market (Kenya, Uganda, and Tanzania) and that of the recently dissolved Federation of Rhodesia and Nyasaland—demonstrates this truth conclusively. Or reference might be made to an even more familiar case: the economic results of the unification of Italy one hundred years ago.

If the purpose of a customs union of poor countries is to promote economic development, and if the latter is defined as diversification induced in the production structure and in industrialization, a union might very well need more protection than that available to the participants individually prior to the establishment of the union. This situation would occur in the event that union-inspired economies of scale were to permit, under a certain margin of protection, an undertaking of productive activities that would be out of the question if confined to the national framework of the member countries, e.g.,

[7] The difference between the economic-development levels reached by Bolivia and Paraguay, on the one hand, and Brazil and Argentina, on the other, is a good deal greater than that separating any pair of developed countries in the Northern Hemisphere. The same phenomenon is even more accentuated in Africa.

when the size of the new market renders feasible the transition from the assembly stage to the production of certain durable and heavy manufactures.[8] When considering a customs union for industrialization purposes between two countries whose industrial sectors do not yet exist, it is easy to refute *ad absurdum* the demand for a common external tariff equal to the average domestic duty rates in force. Obviously, a customs union in an underdeveloped area should not be forced to maintain a common level of protection *no greater* than that which each country has had previously. The common external tariff of a union will, in any case, be *less* than the national tariffs that would be needed to permit each member the separate achievement of the level of development that the establishment of a union should make possible.

As stated earlier, to leave the allocation of production factors exclusively to the free interplay of market forces would be equivalent to concentrating development on the more advanced countries among the union membership. Such a result would immediately run afoul of the prodevelopment pressures existing in the remaining union associates. Owing to the demonstration effect, the intensity of such pressures is perhaps greater in the extremely underdeveloped countries than in those which have already traveled a certain distance toward the take-off stage. From an academic point of view, it might be feasible to defend the proposition that, "A regional free-trade area [in an underdeveloped area] might increase inequality inside the region; . . . It should not, however, be assumed that an increase of inequality is necessarily bad, provided that the least favored become just a little better off; an increase of inequality may be justified if it is the best way of getting quick progress in the region as a whole." [9] However, considering the political actualities of our times, such an attitude is equivalent to asking for the impossible.[10]

[8] Sidney Dell is probably the only writer on customs unions who calls attention to the following paradox: The present structure of the protection systems in effect in the majority of countries under development would permit them, in case a union is established, to offer considerable concessions for competitive products from the area that they do not need, but allows scarcely any concession at all on goods that they do not produce and that are vital to development—simply because existing customs duties on these items are practically nil. See Dell's essay in this volume and his *Trade Blocs and Common Markets,* cited earlier in this essay.

[9] Sir Roy Harrod, in a review of Dell's book, cited above, published in *The Economic Journal,* LXXIII, No. 292 (December, 1963), 708.

[10] Bolivia's refusal to join LAFTA, and Ecuador's threats to withdraw from the association, are a case in point. Moreover, the East African Common Market is breaking up since its more underdeveloped members, Tanzania and Uganda, are convinced that almost all the advantages of the customs union established more than a quarter of a century ago have gone to Kenya. Although it cannot be demon-

If, as appears to be the case, the integration program founded exclusively on the freeing of trade and on the *laissez faire* policy within the union cannot ensure reciprocity of union benefits for all participants, such a program is doomed to failure. Extremely underdeveloped countries have had such regrettable experiences in their relations with the rest of the world, based on the false principle of equality, that it would be vain to try to induce them to enter into new agreements, this time regional ones, in which they would run the risk that inequality within the area would become even more pronounced. On the other hand, if they remain aloof from these dangers, they may find themselves condemned to perpetual inferiority and poverty. All this gives rise to the highly complicated problem of how to avoid intraregional conflicts and schisms that would undermine the objectives of economic regionalism and the intended community of interests of the underdeveloped sector of the world economy.

Those who would entrust the fate of a customs union of countries in process of development to the forces of free competition are endeavoring, quite superficially, to extend to the rest of the world doctrines based on certain historical experience accumulated in very limited fashion and under substantially different circumstances by the economically advanced countries. To reject all attempts by common agreement to distribute the new productive activities within the scope of an underdeveloped economic union, rationally and allowing for political exigencies, on the grounds that such an endeavor is harmful and conducive to monopolistic situations, would, once again, be indicative of a lack of knowledge of present-day reality.

The real choice of alternatives that an economic union in Latin America, Asia, or Africa must make, insofar as concerns the industrial activities representing the motive force behind development, lies between spontaneous monopolies and oligopolies, on the one hand, and monopolies and oligopolies controlled by union authorities, on the other. Perfect competition is an extremely rare phenomenon even in the advanced countries, and it should be recognized that it is a good deal scarcer in the rest of the world. The most effective way of controlling monopolistic tendencies that arise in the industrial and service sectors in underdeveloped zones consists of promoting the emergence of "countervailing powers," in the sense that Galbraith uses

---

strated that Kenya has developed within the union at Tanzania and Uganda's expense, there is no doubt whatsoever that the benefits received by the latter two were a great deal more modest than those accruing to the former. Consequently, pressures by Tanzania and Uganda against the customs union are getting out of hand.

this expression.[11] Expansion of the domestic market to a fairly broad region or zone, social change stimulated by the process of rapid development, and the modernization of the state itself (initially as underdeveloped as the economy and society) are the sole means of braking monopolistic tendencies, and that in varying degree. Those who maintain that specialization mechanisms established by agreement are essential to the operation of an economic union of underdeveloped countries are not necessarily attempting to promote monopolies. Their aim is, rather, to limit the waste of scarce production factors, insofar as possible, and to create conditions conducive to the progressive control of monopolies and the consequent attenuation of their negative aspects.

Given the fact that underdeveloped regions need regional devices that are much more dynamic than those emerging in the already developed world, the establishment of a customs union in the underdeveloped sphere will bring with it the creation of a series of economic-policy mechanisms that, from the standpoint of traditional theory, appear to be heterodox. Such mechanisms must seek to eliminate the numerous obstacles that originate in the present system of world trade and are opposed to the expansion of intraregional economic relations, and should likewise assure members of a fair share of the benefits derived from customs-union operations. Since association in an economic union involves partial abdication of national sovereignty, and since nationalism is one of the principal forces of action in underdeveloped countries, integration movements face a very complex problem: How can the need for multinational cooperation be reconciled with the demands of each nation's internal politics, motivated by the sometimes sound and sometimes perverse pressures of economic nationalism?

In the light of these considerations, and keeping in mind that no economic and political theory on customs unions applicable to underdeveloped regions has yet been formulated, it should be helpful to draft a brief outline of the conditions that an integration program should meet in order to avoid predestination to failure.

The foundation of the integration program must be a customs union or a common market that, by definition and from the outset, entails the commitment to coordinate the trade policy of the associate countries vis-à-vis the rest of the world. In such a union, it would appear to be necessary to free the bulk of *traditional* intraregional

[11] See J. K. Galbraith, *American Capitalism: The Concept of Countervailing Power* (Boston: Houghton Mifflin, 1956).

trade immediately and set up mechanisms for the progressive liberalization of various new product groups, taking into account the relative significance of those production sectors in terms of the common development of the area. The system of exceptions should be quite rigid, being limited to certain agricultural products for domestic consumption and to such manufacturing activities as weigh heavily in the industrial product of the member countries at the time the union is established. If necessary, by means of special prior agreements in which diverse criteria should be taken into account—among them, possibly, reciprocity—certain of the excepted items could remain outside the liberalization program, even after the customs union is fully organized.

The decision to reach the customs-union stage in progressive fashion should be accompanied by the immediate creation of a regional payments agency designed to: (1) promote transactions in area currencies; (2) eliminate the need for financial dealings through intermediate countries located outside the zone; (3) provide credit for the member countries (prudently limiting it to instances of transitory disequilibrium in their over-all balance of payments); and (4) serve as an instrument to enable the monetary authorities in the area to maintain periodical contact with each other.

In view of the differences existing at the time the union is created, with respect to both development levels and the availability of production factors, neither the freeing of trade nor the functioning of a payments mechanism can ensure equal benefits for all the member countries. Thus, the problem of reciprocity appears to be the thorniest and most difficult one of all, for it involves a concept that is political, as well as economic, and hence defies measurement. In the stages that preceded the signing of the Montevideo Treaty, ECLA advocated the introduction within the liberalization mechanisms of elements that would ensure the highest possible degree of trade equilibrium within the zone. The treaty itself contains clauses that enable the acceleration or attenuation of the rate of liberalization in the case of countries that suffer from chronic maladjustment of their commerce with the area. However, such attempts to relate reciprocity exclusively to total intraregional trade (in keeping with the original idea) or to the new interchange promoted by the association (as stipulated in the Montevideo Treaty) do not appear to have given satisfactory results, quite probably because they took into account only one aspect of the integration program. The concept of reciprocity has to be a broader one and might well comprise four essential aspects of integration: balance of payments; over-all growth; industrialization; and the relative level of development.

In this way, a completely new definition of equitable participation in a customs union would be established. This definition would have to start with the assumption that, in order to operate efficiently, an integration program should be based on an aggregate of regional and national policies that prevent the emergence of severe disequilibrium in intraregional trade; guarantee comparable long-term rates of development; and, at the same time, shorten the economic distance within the zone and assure that all members in the union will participate in the industrialization process.

Assuming that it were feasible to reconcile these objectives without centralizing economic policy decisions in a supranational agency—which, in the light of present conditions in Latin America, could scarcely be considered a realistic premise—an integration program based on a customs union would have to be equipped with a series of specific instruments that go beyond the trade and payments fields. The fairly obvious initial need would be to establish instruments to coordinate investment and industrialization policies and to offer additional support to the relatively less developed member countries. It is doubtful that these tasks can be undertaken without recourse to regional-development planning. In this regard, it is very discouraging that no one in Latin America—at the government level—is willing to face up to this integration-program requirement. This is just another of the many examples of the sort of wishful thinking so in vogue among Latin American politicians and economists: If real problems are not talked about, they will somehow disappear.

Coordination of investment and industrialization policies requires, further, the existence of a regional financial agency endowed with sufficient resources for the execution of infrastructure and productive investment projects that are multinational in scope. It implies, also, a joint policy of fiscal incentives for new productive activities carrying a high priority within the framework of regional development. This policy also calls for a common code to govern the treatment of foreign private investment. Finally, to eliminate completely the danger that the new productive activities will be concentrated in the more advanced countries in the union, additional mechanisms are essential that, by means of agreements, will enable equitable specialization in the industrial field and will compensate for the fiscal losses that the relatively less developed countries might incur during the first stages of integration, until such time as the emergence of regional industries in those nations serves to offset such losses.[12]

[12] It is true that the Conference of the Contracting Parties to the Montevideo Treaty has adopted resolutions that define and broaden the special preferential regime for the less-developed members. Nonetheless, as has occurred in the case of

In summary, to keep intraregional political tensions from detracting from its effectiveness, an integration program aimed at accelerating development will have to incorporate the following elements: a treaty for the gradual establishment of a customs union; a regional mechanism for settlements and monetary-policy coordination; a regional development bank; a system—also coordinated—to provide incentives for regional and external private investment; an instrument that promotes the above indicated aims of "industrial specialization by agreement"; and a fund to compensate those countries which are relatively less developed. In addition, the efficient functioning of all these elements presupposes that the developed sector of the world economy will coordinate its economic-aid policies toward the customs-union territory.

Advocating a program of this nature—given Latin America's present circumstances—may appear to be too ambitious if not ridiculously Utopian. Such, however, is not the case. The essays on Central American economic integration included in this volume indicate that the Isthmus' economic integration program contains almost all the mechanisms enumerated above: the customs union, which will be perfected before the end of 1966; the Clearing House and Monetary Council; the Central American Bank for Economic Integration (CABEI); and the Agreement for the Equalization of Fiscal Incentives. Since the economic distance between the five republics is relatively short and Central America does not appear to need a compensation fund for the weaker members, all that is lacking to complete the integration mechanism is the smooth functioning of specialization by agreement and the equitable distribution of new industrial activities. It was hoped that the latter role would be filled by the Central American Integration Industries Regime, but the life of this treaty, to date, has been very precarious, owing in large part to the negative attitude assumed by the United States, on the basis of doctrinal considerations not applicable to underdeveloped areas. In any event, the Central American Common Market authorities are cooperating in the field of industrial integration. They have agreed on the special treatment for productive activities, which establishes a priori uniform tariffs of a protectionist nature for a series of new regional industries, and have decided to extend the regional policy of industrialization, supported by Central American Bank financing, to consumer-goods industries, as well as to those supplying raw materials, semifinished products, and capital goods.

---

other Conference decisions, there is no automatic guarantee of enforcement—at least within any reasonable time.

How may one draw a comparison between the requirements of efficacious integration and the workings of the Latin American Free Trade Association, which was established in 1960? It should be recognized that the mechanism in LAFTA's case, although it has undeniable possibilities, is a much weaker one than that operating in Central America. To illustrate: The Montevideo Treaty does not require that the member countries establish a customs union, although it opens the way for them to do so. LAFTA does not at this time have any mechanism for the clearing of payments and for monetary coordination. Its Secretariat and Permanent Committee are extremely weak and refer even the most trivial decisions to the member governments.[13] It does not have a regional financial agency, nor does it, for the immediate future, provide for any coordination whatsoever of fiscal and investment policies. It is not equipped with a permanent mechanism that would stimulate industrial specialization by agreement or serve as the basis for arriving at an understanding regarding procedures to be followed in favor of the less-developed member countries. Almost all that LAFTA has done to date with regard to the foregoing has been to pass resolutions placing on record the intention to achieve the appropriate objectives. More important still, LAFTA, with very few exceptions, does not enjoy decisive political support within and without the region—a fact borne out by the frustrated attempt, in 1963, to convoke a LAFTA conference at the highest level for purposes of accelerating integration. Consequently, efforts are becoming increasingly limited to the freeing of trade, a task that, although favorable to integration, is becoming more difficult from one annual negotiation meeting to the next (because of the lack of the other mechanisms mentioned) and that, by itself, can hardly be expected to accomplish Latin American integration, even if the next twenty-five years are spent in the attempt.[14]

The present volume shows a surprising degree of agreement, among contributors from Latin America and elsewhere despite certain doc-

[13] This observation does not mean to minimize the technical work performed by the LAFTA Secretariat and Permanent Executive Committee and reflected in over 100 resolutions adopted up to the beginning of 1965 by the Conference of the Contracting Parties to the Treaty of Montevideo and in the documentation prepared by various permanent advisory commissions established in 1963.

[14] It is true that during the first four years the Montevideo Treaty was in effect intrazonal trade increased from $361 million to $638 million, measured in terms of exports. However, the share of these intraregional transactions taken up in new products, and especially manufactures, continues to be negligible. If the same rate of expansion continues, by 1970 intra-LAFTA trade will amount to some $1.5

trinal and procedural discrepancies, regarding what must be accomplished in order to make LAFTA an efficient integration instrument. The majority concur in recognizing the urgent need to accelerate progress in the direction of a common market—i.e., to establish a common customs tariff applicable to the rest of the world; to revise thoroughly present negotiating procedures regarding reciprocal customs concessions and discontinue product-by-product bargaining in favor of across-the-board reductions applicable to groups of products; to institute a system of regional payments clearings and settlements that will stimulate regional-trade expansion and advance duty-reduction goals and industrial agreements; to revise the bases for industrial "complementation" agreements and convert them into a mechanism for specialization, allowing for the needs of the less-developed countries; to persuade existing regional and extraregional financial agencies to lend economic aid to integration, for their participation in that activity to date has been extremely limited; and, finally, to strengthen LAFTA agencies, following the example set by the Central American Economic Council and the European Economic Community Commission.

As Dr. Raúl Prebisch's essay repeatedly emphasizes, in order to strengthen the Latin American integration program, LAFTA countries must make major political decisions in very short order. The general climate for such decisions, however, is not sufficiently propitious. Integration has the support of the most dynamic elements in the Latin American societies, but their combined weight is not impressive. Perhaps the most positive phenomenon is the ever-increasing interest shown by private sectors in the region in opportunities offered them by LAFTA; because of the saturation of domestic markets, they have been forced to seek new outlets for their industrial production. But the very fact of market saturation and of fear of competition makes the entrepreneurs behave superficially like "integrationists." What motivates them in reality—and, as yet, in insufficient measure—is the possible increase in export trade, with little regard for any other aspects of regional integration and cooperation.

At the same time, the active or passive enemies of Latin American integration are legion. Heading this group are politicians and government officials who use supernationalism as a demogogic weapon to divert social tensions that are building up in their respective countries, failing to realize that in this way they are only aggravating the critical situation over the long run. The crux of the matter, the true nucleus

billion, or 20 per cent of the global foreign trade estimated for the nine member countries in that year.

of the arguments with regard to LAFTA's future, a Mexican economic review maintains, may be summed up in a single question: "At a time of burgeoning nationalism in countries that have achieved the greater degree of development in Latin America, how can supranational solutions be implemented at short term?" [15] A clear answer to this query is not possible, for other forces are added to irresponsible nationalism. First, there is the dead weight of bureaucracy, the scourge of government apparatus at all levels—apparatus that are not even in a position to operate in accordance with a coordinated national concept (as witness the wavering policies and contradictory and eventually self-defeating actions that often characterize governments' behavior in matters pertaining to LAFTA) and, hence, are even less able to respond to the requirements of a regional approach. Then, there is the predominance, in public as well as private sectors, of positions inspired by the traditional doctrines briefly outlined at the beginning of this essay and originating in an imitation of ideas that have currency in the already industrialized countries. Finally, there is opposition on the part of vested interests of two types: medium-sized domestic industries that have enjoyed a situation of privilege under protectionist systems; and certain larger foreign industries whose operations in Latin America are based on dividing the regional market among their branches. There is no indication whatsoever that this odd coalition—made up of supernationalistic politicians, bureaucrats, entrepreneurs, and industrialists of the old school, plus certain foreign interests—plans to give up. Anyone acquainted with the background of the four LAFTA negotiations knows that interests opposed to integration have won a series of important battles. The fact that they also were defeated on not a few occasions is attributable to the growing and effective support that the integration program is receiving from a minority of politicians and technicians who have a more modern mentality, and thanks to whom the idea is beginning to make an emotional appeal to Latin American public opinion. Nevertheless, the battle is an unrelenting one, and its results should become quite apparent at a very early date.

It is true that there are those who believe in the automatism of economic integration. Such a line of reasoning, however, is much more applicable to economically advanced regions, where conditions favor a long-term economic policy having relatively clear objectives, and where the operation of efficient, democratic forces countervails the vested political and economic interests. In Latin America's case,

[15] See "El creciente nacionalismo en América Latina permitirá la planeación a nivel continental?" *El Correo Económico* (Mexico City), I, No. 13 (May 3, 1964), 1.

LAFTA has only two alternatives: to pick up speed; or to lose ground and become just another of a series of rather ineffective regional mechanisms. One will know the outcome before the present decade runs its course.

PART ONE

Theoretical Approaches

II

BELA BALASSA[1]

Toward a Theory of Economic Integration

> *Dans la hiérarchie des mots obscurs et sans beauté dont les discussions économiques encombrent notre langue, le terme d'integration occupe un bon rang.*
>
> —François Perroux

In recent years, much has been written on economic integration in its various forms, such as free-trade areas, customs unions, common markets, and so on. Little has been done, however, to devise a unified theory of economic integration that would encompass its different variants and would give a systematic treatment to its main problems. As a contribution towards this goal, in the present paper we will attempt to provide a consistent definition of the term "economic integration"; furthermore, we will discuss some conflicting views on the means and objectives of integration and the probable effects of this development.

The Concept and Forms of Economic Integration

In everyday usage, the word "integration" denotes the bringing together of parts into a whole. In the economic literature, the concept "economic integration" does not have such a clear-cut meaning. This

[1] The author is indebted to Charles P. Kindleberger and Robert Triffin for helpful comments on an earlier draft of this paper.

will become apparent if we survey some of the interpretations given by various authors.

In Myrdal's opinion, integration can be regarded as a social and economic process destroying barriers, both social and economic, between the participants of economic activities. "The economy is not integrated [writes Myrdal] unless all avenues are open to everybody and the remunerations paid for productive services are equal, regardless of racial, social and cultural differences." [2] It follows that Myrdal subsumes not only international but also national integration under this heading. Most economists, however, consider only international problems when employing the concept of economic integration, but areas of international cooperation are often covered by this term as well. Robert Triffin,[3] for example, considers the activities of the Organization for European Economic Cooperation (OEEC) and the European Payments Union (EPU) as forms of economic integration. A somewhat more restricted definition is given, along similar lines, by Franz Hartog, who defines integration as "a rather advanced type of cooperation, as distinct from the term 'harmonization,' which refers to a mutual consultation on important issues of economic policy." [4] Essentially the same interpretation is furnished by Robert Marjolin, who maintains that "any process which brings about a greater degree of unity," can rightly be called "integration." [5]

According to some authors, the existence of international economic relations should be used as a measuring rod. Hence, integration is already realized as a result of trade relations between independent economies on the world market.[6] A variant of this view is presented by Erich Schneider,[7] who contrasts the case of watertight isolation with that of total integration and regards all intermediate forms between these two extreme positions as varying degrees of economic integration. The problem of optimizing enters the definition of Jan Tinber-

[2] Gunnar Myrdal, *An International Economy* (New York: Harper & Brothers, 1956), p. 11. For a similiar definition, see Charles P. Kindleberger, "The United States and European Regional Economic Integration," *Social Science*, October, 1959, pp. 210–17.

[3] Robert Triffin, "Convertibilité monétaire et intégration économique," *Economie Appliquée*, October-December, 1956, pp. 618–58.

[4] Franz Hartog, "European Economic Integration: A Realistic Conception," *Weltwirtschaftliches Archiv*, 1953, No. 2, p. 165.

[5] Robert Marjolin, *Europe and the United States in the World Economy* (Durham, N.C.: Duke University Press, 1953), p. 41.

[6] See Jean Weiller, "Les degrés de l'intégration et les chances d'une 'zone de coopération' internationale," *Revue Economique*, March, 1958, p. 233.

[7] Erich Schneider, "Lineamenti di una teoria economica del mercato comune," *Revista Economica de Scienze Economiche e Commerciali*, February, 1957, pp. 107–8.

gen, who considers integration as "the creation of the most desirable structure of international economy, removing artificial hindrances to the optimal operation and introducing deliberately all desirable elements of coordination or unification." [8] This definition, if used consistently, would actually correspond to total integration in Erich Schneider's sense.

In view of the conflicting nature of the widely used concepts, there is need for a consistent definition that would appropriately delineate the field of economic integration. We will endeavor to provide such a definition.

The inclusion of social processes in the concept of economic integration by Charles P. Kindleberger[9] and Gunnar Myrdal points to the importance of social factors in destroying noneconomic barriers between communities, races, and social strata. Nevertheless, if the equalization of factor prices were regarded as a condition of economic integration, the scope of this definition would be unduly restricted by excluding free-trade areas, customs unions, and common markets where factor prices are not equalized. Social integration and the concomitant equalization of factor prices are necessary for total integration; yet the removal of trade barriers in a customs union is an act of economic integration even in the absence of social developments. Consequently, although social integration gains in importance as the unification of national economies proceeds, it is not necessary for the lower forms of economic integration, and it need not be included in our definition.

Objections can also be raised to the inclusion of national integration in the concept. In the present-day world, the problems relating to integration on the national and international levels differ to a considerable degree. On the national level, the barriers between economic units are mainly of a social, educational, or psychological character (the caste system, the lack of common values, the absence of risk-taking, etc.), and these obstacles may be stronger between various social strata of the same region than between regions.[10] One of the main instruments of national economic integration appears to be the creation of a strong national state.[11] The emergence of national states, however, creates artificial barriers between independent economies in

[8] Jan Tinbergen, *International Economic Integration* (Amsterdam: Elsevier, 1954), p. 95.

[9] The author is grateful to Professor Kindleberger for the opportunity to consult his memorandum "Notes on the Integration of the Free World Economy" (1953).

[10] The importance of the lack of suitable transportation facilities as an economic barrier should also be added, for it restricts economic intercourse between regions.

[11] This latter point is emphasized also by Myrdal, *op. cit.*, pp. 200–202.

the form of tariffs, of quantitative trade and exchange restrictions, of impediments to the mobility of labor, capital, and entrepreneur.[12] In addition, economic intercourse between nations is also hindered by national economic policies—fiscal, social, and monetary measures. National economic integration, then, gives rise to discrimination between economic units of independent countries and thereby contributes to disintegration on the international scene. On the other hand, international economic integration leads to the abolition of some of the negative aspects of national integration. In view of these differences, it appears advisable to restrict the use of the concept of economic integration to denote integration on the international level.

Excluding national integration from the concept, we can define economic integration as a process and a state of affairs. Regarded as a process, it encompasses various measures abolishing discrimination between economic units belonging to different national states; viewed as a state of affairs, it can be represented by the absence of various forms of discrimination between national economies.[13]

In interpreting our definition, distinction should next be made between integration and cooperation. The difference is qualitative as well as quantitative. Whereas cooperation includes various measures designed to harmonize economic policies and to lessen discrimination, the process of economic integration comprises those measures which entail the suppression of some forms of discrimination. For example, international agreements on trade policies belong to the area of international cooperation, whereas the abolition of trade restrictions is an act of economic integration. Distinguishing between cooperation and integration, we put the main characteristics of the latter—the abolition of discrimination within an area—in clearer focus, and it becomes possible to give the concept definite meaning without unnecessarily diluting it through the inclusion of diverse actions in the field of international cooperation.

Economic integration as a process, then, represents various measures leading to the suppression of discrimination between economic

[12] One should note here the similarity between the present-day integration of national economies and the development of national states from formerly independent economic and political units up to the nineteenth century, when this development required the abolition of tariff walls, of restrictions on labor movements, etc. In the present underdeveloped countries, however, these artificial obstacles play only a minor role.

[13] It should be noted that this definition is based on the implicit assumption that discrimination actually affects economic intercourse. The suppression of tariff barriers between Iceland and New Zealand, for example, will not integrate the two economies in the absence of a substantial amount of foreign trade, since without trade relations there was no effective discrimination anyway.

units of national states, and the resulting forms of economic integration can be characterized by the absence of discrimination in various areas. The meaning of the concept of economic integration in a dynamic sense is not restricted to total integration, but encompasses various forms of integration, such as a free-trade area, a customs union, a common market, and an economic union. Thus, the above definition carves out a well-distinguishable part of international economic problems as the area of economic integration; it avoids the excessive generality of the terms used by, for example, Triffin and Schneider, and it includes Tinbergen's concept as a special case.

Using the definition given above, the theory of economic integration will be concerned with the various forms of integration, the measures required for accomplishing these objectives, the economic effects of integration, and problems of optimization in an integrated area. The theory of economic integration can be regarded as a part of international economics, but it also enlarges the field of international-trade theory by considering factor movements, the coordination of economic policies, and so on, which are not discussed in traditional theory.

The various forms of economic integration represent varying degrees of integration. In a free-trade area, tariffs (and quantitative restrictions) between the participating countries are abolished, but each country retains its own tariffs against nonmembers. The establishment of a customs union involves, besides the suppression of discrimination in the field of commodity movements within the union, the creation of a common tariff wall against nonmember countries. A higher form of economic integration is attained in a common market, where not only trade restrictions but also restrictions on factor movements are abolished. An economic union, as distinct from a common market, combines the removal of restrictions on commodity and factor movements with a degree of harmonization of economic, monetary, fiscal, social, and countercyclical policies. Finally, total economic integration presupposes the unification of economic, fiscal, and other policies and requires the setting up of a supranational authority whose decisions are binding for the member states.[14]

Location Theory and Economic Integration

As it is well known, the traditional theory of international trade neglected the spatial element; and, in the Ricardo-Mill-Marshall-

[14] The reader is reminded here of the need for social integration to accomplish total integration. Some degree of social integration is also necessary to induce labor movements.

Haberler theory, trade takes place between countries that are regarded as having no spatial dimensions. During the 1930's, Ohlin proposed the incorporation of international trade theory in a general location theory,[15] but he has not accomplished this task, mainly because his treatment of regions does not differ materially from that accorded to countries in traditional trade theory. Further efforts towards the creation of a general location theory have been made by Lösch,[16] Isard,[17] and Lefeber.[18] Isard conceives the general theory of location and space economy as "embracing the total spatial array of economic activities, with attention paid to the geographical distribution of inputs and outputs and the geographical variations in prices and costs." [19]

International trade theory, then, can be regarded as a special case of general location theory. "One proceeds from the latter to the former by assuming a given locational structure of economic activities, by erecting appropriate barriers within the world economy to correspond to the boundaries of nations." [20] Tariffs and other trade restrictions appear as additional costs of the transfer of goods from one country to another. Or, as Bastiat expressed it a century ago, "Un droit de douane, c'est un anti-chemin de fer." Putting it in a slightly different form, we may distinguish between geographic and tariff protection of industries, where the former is a result of natural, and the latter of artificial, barriers. Lösch has given ingenious expression to the role of location in trade, emphasizing the continuously decreasing impact of any market on productive activity as we move away from the center.[21] If we assume the existence of a small number of industrial centers, the area of attraction of any center can be visualized as a hexagon, when artificial barriers distort this configuration. Thus, international trade between Germany and France, for example, cannot be conceived as trade between two homogeneous areas, because, economically, two border towns of these countries will have more com-

[15] Bertil Ohlin, *Interregional and International Trade* (Cambridge, Mass.: Harvard University Press, 1933), p. vii.

[16] August Lösch, *The Economics of Location* (New Haven: Yale University Press, 1954).

[17] Walter Isard, *Location and Space Economy* (New York: The Technology Press and John Wiley & Sons, Inc., 1956).

[18] For a recent treatment of the theoretical problems involved, see Louis Lefeber, *Allocation in Space-Production, Transport and Industrial Location* (Amsterdam: North Holland, 1958).

[19] Walter Isard, "The General Theory of Location and Space Economy," *Quarterly Journal of Economics*, November, 1959, p. 505.

[20] *Ibid.*

[21] Isard, *Location and Space Economy*, p. 57.

mon characteristics than have a French border town and Paris.[22]

To repeat, modern location theorists regard international-trade theory as a part of general location theory when tariffs appear as an additional element of the cost of transfer of inputs and outputs. The theory of economic integration, then, could also be regarded as a special case of location theory, since it would be designed to examine the effects of the abolishment of trade barriers between the participating countries on location and on production specialization.[23] Such a view, however, appears to be unduly narrow. It may sound paradoxical, but the findings of modern location theory can be better applied to international trade and to problems of economic integration in the setting of the period before World War I than in our times. Before 1913, government policies other than commercial policy had only a slight effect on industrial location. Under these conditions, tariff barriers could have been regarded simply as additional elements in the cost of transfer. Since then, however, the augmented scope of government intervention and increased uncertainty in international trade relations, resulting from the intensification of nationalistic tendencies, have acquired importance. As Nurkse rightly expressed: "National frontiers as such are basically irrelevant to economic analysis; it is only government policies that make them relevant." [24] Consequently, location theory, which disregards the impact of monetary and fiscal policies on economic activity and attempts to reduce all elements of discrimination to differences in transfer costs, will supply only part of the answer. The theory of economic integration cannot restrict itself to the locational aspects of the abolition of trade barriers, but must also examine the impact of government policies on economic activity inside of the union; it must consider the need for the coordination of these policies and the impact of the removal of the uncertainty existing in economic intercourse between independent national economies.

[22] Lösch, "A New Theory of International Trade," *International Economic Papers*, VI, 50–65.

[23] For such a conception of the theory of economic integration, see A. Predöhl, "Weltwirtschaft in räumlicher Perspektive," *Economia Internazionale*, November, 1950, pp. 1044–65.

[24] Ragnar Nurkse, "Domestic and International Equilibrium," in S. E. Harris (ed.), *The New Economics* (New York: Alfred A. Knopf, 1952), p. 265.

The "Absolutist" Versus the "Relativist" Approach

Since the publication of Jacob Viner's *The Customs Union Issue*,[25] various arguments have been raised against the formation of regional unions. First, it has been contended that instead of removing trade barriers between a limited number of countries, we should move directly to world-wide free trade.[26] Second, it has been argued that the establishment of regional unions may lead more to trade diversion (reduction in trade between the union and the outside world) than to trade creation (increase in trade among participating countries).[27] Third, the argument has been advanced that regional unions would impede trade liberalization on a larger scale by creating sheltered high-cost areas with protectionist tendencies.[28]

With respect to the first argument, it can be stated that both the holders of the "absolutist" view and most protagonists of the "relativist" position would agree on the desirability of the world-wide removal of tariff barriers as a final objective. If factor endowments, including skills, are given, and there is little government interference in economic life, then, with certain qualifications, an efficient allocation of resources is reached under world-wide free trade. Efficient resource allocation, however, does not necessarily correspond to the optimal exploitation of growth potentialities, since changes in resources endowments will significantly alter comparative cost-relationships, especially in the case of large differences in income levels between countries. Dynamic considerations may warrant the temporary application of protectionist measures, and the inefficiencies of protectionism would be reduced as the size of the protected area increases. This reasoning can be applied, for example, to the integration projects of the Latin American countries where economic development is the main issue.

The argument for universal free trade is also based on a limited degree of state intervention in economic affairs. Given the present scope of governmental economic policies, an optimal allocation of resources would not come about in a regime of free trade, since divergences in monetary, fiscal, and, partly, social policies would distort competitive cost relationships. Thus, a certain degree of harmoniza-

25 Jacob Viner, *The Customs Union Issue* (New York: Carnegie Endowment for International Peace, 1950).

26 *Ibid.*, p. 139; and Gottfried Haberler, "Defects in the Concept of Regionalism to Solve Trading Problems," *Indian Journal of Economics*, July, 1957, pp. 25–30.

27 Viner, *op. cit.*, pp. 52–53; Haberler, *op. cit.*

28 Viner, *op. cit.*, p. 139; and Wilhelm Röpke, "Gemeinsamer Markt und Freihandelszone," *Ordo*, XVIII, No. 10, 51.

tion in economic policies becomes necessary. This, however, is not feasible for the world as a whole, not only because world-wide machinery would be cumbersome and inefficient, but also because coordination of economic policies amounts to abandonment of sovereignty in favor of a world organization to an extent that is unlikely to be undertaken—at least in the near future. On the other hand, more far-reaching results can be attained within a smaller group of countries. A union of adjacent countries might possess the sentiment of solidarity a larger group could not muster. The mutual benefits derived from a regional solution can also be more easily appraised. Finally, it is likely that governments will have less difficulty resisting special interests when the advantages of economic integration are more directly seen in other sectors.

These considerations indicate the desirability of economic integration within a regional framework. The expedience of such a proposal has been criticized, however, by referring to the possible trade-diverting effects of a union. The extent of trade creation and trade diversion cannot be determined a priori. In the case of adjacent countries, the author believes that trade creation is likely to outweigh trade diversion. To argue in reverse, no one would insist that the continental United States should be broken up into forty-eight sovereign states, creating the same tariff barriers between the states as the United States has around herself in order to avoid the diversion of trade.[29] In addition, even if the immediate effect of the union was, on balance, trade-diverting, increased income in the union and other dynamic factors could benefit the world in the long run.[30]

It is not to be denied that a union might lead to autarky if protectionist tendencies predominate. Protectionist interest for example, may see the possibility of creating an autarkic block in an integrated area, while autarky would not have been possible in smaller national units. It is often noted that, whereas the Soviet Union's economy is largely self-sufficient, foreign trade is absolutely essential for Switzerland or Sweden. Integration in Western Europe, however, has developed in a different direction. In the case of the European Payments

[29] For an interesting mental exercise along these lines, see "Los Estados Unidos 'desunidos,'" appendix to J. L. Sampedro, "Principales efectos de la unidad económica europea," in *Estudios sobre la Unidad Económica de Europa* (Madrid, 1957), pp. 691–705.

[30] In regard to the European Common Market, Gottfried Haberler notes that the "income effect" may outweigh the "substitution effect." See "Die wirtschaftliche Integration Europas," in *Wirtschaftsfragen der freien Welt* (Erhard-Festschrift) (Frankfurt, 1959), p. 525. See also my review of Erdman and Rogge, *Die Europäische Wirtschaftsgemeinschaft und die Drittländer*, in *Kyklos*, XIV, Fasc. 1 (1961), 114–16.

Union, the pessimistic anticipation of some economists has been disproved by the fact that the exports of its member countries to the dollar area increased considerably more than trade among the participating countries themselves.[31] A considerable expansion of foreign trade has taken place, too, in the Benelux countries and the European Coal and Steel Community. In general, a union will not become a sheltered high-cost area as long as the beneficial effects of the removal of trade barriers between the participating countries are not counteracted by raising tariffs toward third countries or by restricting competition within the area. Competition between the firms of member countries will not fail to reduce costs, and the freeing of factor movements in a common market will also contribute to this result.

Economic Integration in Developing Countries

The above arguments suggest that the absolutist view unduly neglected the favorable possibilities of regional integration. This conclusion has special force in the case of developing economies. This becomes clear if we consider that, whereas the absolutist approach concerns itself with the reallocation of existing resources after the formation of a union, in less-developed areas integration is designed to serve the development of these resources. In the language of welfare economics, the objective function of the traditional theory of customs unions exemplified in the absolutist approach is the attainment of static efficiency, while the objective function relevant for developing economies is the maximization of the rate of economic growth.

If the purpose of integration in developing areas is the acceleration of economic growth, the categories of trade creation and trade diversion will have only limited relevance here. In such a situation, the question is not how the reallocation of given resources will affect trade flows after integration; but, rather, the possibilities of expanding trade after the transformation of economic structures need to be investigated. A consideration of the present trade pattern among developing economies can serve to clarify this issue.

It has been argued that the possibilities of specialization in an integrated area are indicated by the degree of economic intercourse among the prospective member countries. According to this proposition, the higher the proportion of trade conducted among the member countries prior to the formation of the union, the greater will be the

[31] See Robert Triffin, *Europe and the Money Muddle* (New Haven: Yale University Press, 1958), p. 265.

expansion of intra-area trade and, thus, the increase in welfare.[32] This test would indicate the desirability of the European Common Market where 36 per cent of the pre-union trade of the member countries was with one another, but it would show the prospects for integration in less-developed regions in an unfavorable light, given that intra-area trade in Latin America and Africa does not reach 10 per cent of total trade, and, excluding entrepôt trade, the corresponding proportion is less than 15 per cent in Asia. In fact, it has been argued that the small amount of intraregional trade in Latin America provides evidence of the inherent limitations of the reallocation of productive activity in a Latin American union.[33]

Yet the low degree of economic intercourse in less-developed areas can hardly be used as an argument against their integration. Rather, the differences observed in regard to intra-area trade in Western Europe and in underdeveloped regions reflect differences in the level of their economic development. While far-reaching specialization has evolved among the highly industrialized economies of Western Europe, the scope of exchange is limited in low-income countries that specialize in primary commodities. These countries often produce, and export, the same commodities, and the bulk of their imports consists of manufactured goods purchased from industrial economies.

Similar considerations apply to the issue of complementarity versus competitiveness and to the size of the union, which, according to the traditional theory, would determine the welfare effects of a customs union. An evaluation of the desirability of customs unions on this basis assumes unchanged economic structure, but this assumption has little relevance for present-day less-developed countries. The conclusion follows that the traditional theory of customs unions has only limited applicability to the integration of developing economies and that an appropriate theory should be devised to deal with this problem.

Such a theory should examine the interrelationship of integration and the transformation of economic structure in the process of economic growth with a consideration of large-scale economies that can be obtained in an enlarged market. Undoubtedly, much painstaking research and empirical investigation is necessary further to reduce the area of ignorance on the economics of integration in developing countries.

32 See, for example, R. G. Lipsey, "The Theory of Customs Unions: A General Survey," *The Economic Journal*, LXX (September, 1960), p. 508.

33 See, for example, C. P. Kindleberger's testimony before Congress, in *Foreign Economic Policy*, Hearings before the Subcommittee on Foreign Economic Policy of the Joint Economic Committee (84th Cong., 1st sess.), p. 521.

III

STAFFAN BURENSTAM LINDER[1]

Customs Unions and Economic Development

There is a well-defined general customs-union theory that derives, in turn, from a traditionally accepted theory of international trade. To discuss customs unions and economic development should, therefore, amount to nothing more than routine use of conventional tools. But the idea underlying this paper is that, in reality, the analytical problem is a great deal more complex because the traditional theory of international trade cannot be readily applied to trade problems of underdeveloped countries. If this premise is accepted, the possibility of a universal theory of customs unions and economic development is automatically ruled out.

Our task is thus twofold: to outline an alternative theory of trade in a development process; and to derive from it a customs-union theory.

The Role of Foreign Trade in a Development Process

Trade with highly industrialized countries. Trade with advanced countries is strategically important because it enables the importation of various goods that cannot be produced at home, but are necessary for the maintenance and expansion of production. We shall term these products of crucial importance in the development process

[1] Research in connection with the preparation of this paper was made possible through the generous financial sponsorship of the Swedish Bank Research Institute.

"input imports" and shall divide them into two main classes: "maintenance imports" and "expansion imports."

Maintenance imports consist of replacement capital goods and raw materials needed to keep the productive capacity intact and enable full employment of existing domestic production factors. If maintenance imports cannot be obtained in sufficient quantities, production will lag behind installed capacity.

Expansion imports comprise various types of capital goods that will ensure that additional domestically generated factors of production (i.e., savings and expanded labor force) are channeled to the productive process rather than being dissipated. If the primary aim is to avoid underemployment of existing domestic factors, expansion imports represent an import need above and beyond maintenance imports.

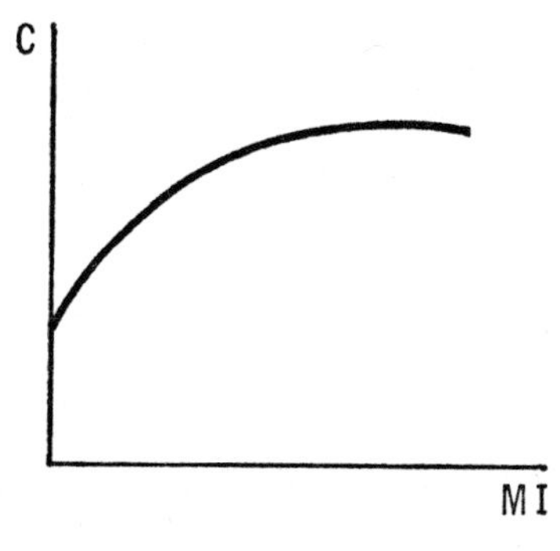

FIGURE 1

Two simple diagrams will illustrate these relationships. In Figure 1, an existing domestic capacity (C) is measured on the vertical axis, in terms of labor, capital, and natural resources. On the horizontal axis, we measure maintenance imports (MI). Even with no maintenance imports, it is likely that some domestic factors could be employed. Thus, the curve drawn in the diagram has a positive intercept with the vertical axis. As the quantity of MI expands, the use of capacity increases and reaches its maximum when the maintenance imports are sufficient to keep all domestic resources fully employed.

In Figure 2, we measure the rate of growth (r) on the vertical axis and the total amount of input imports (II) on the horizontal axis. We assume that the country brings in a sufficient amount of input imports to keep existing capacity fully utilized before using imports to expand capacity. Under this assumption, the curve drawn in the dia-

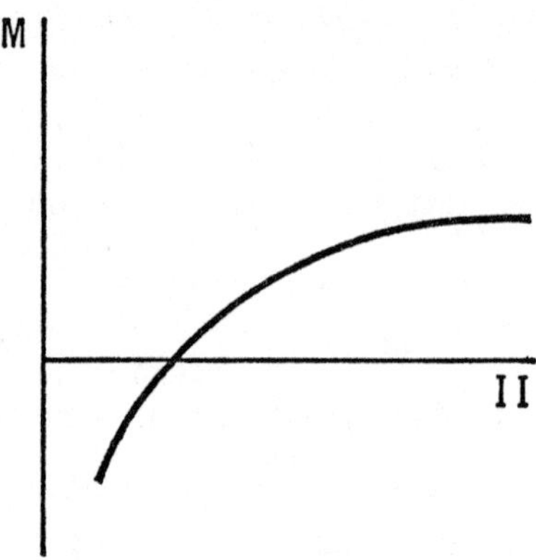

FIGURE 2

gram to relate the two magnitudes intersects the horizontal axis, thereby indicating that there will be a zero rate of growth when input imports must all be devoted to keeping existing factors employed. The relationship between the two figures should be noted: The curve in Figure 1 reaches a maximum where the curve in Figure 2 intersects the horizontal axis. The input imports to the left of this intersection thus represent maintenance imports. If there are fewer maintenance imports than indicated by the intersection, there will be a negative rate of growth (depicted by the negative values appearing to the left of the intersection). If input imports exceed the amount necessary to keep existing factors in use, there will be a positive rate of growth. This is so because additions to the labor force can be absorbed and because savings are stimulated by the presence of input imports with which domestically generated capital can be combined. Imports to the right of the intersection with the horizontal axis qualify as expansion imports. The function reaches its maximum when expansion imports are of such magnitude that all domestic factors that can be generated within the period have been employed. This maximum, of course, may be below the minimum rate of growth that would be socially acceptable. If, for instance, the domestic savings potential is low, a very modest amount of expansion imports per period will suffice to obviate a frustration of that potential. If the savings potential increases, more expansion imports are needed. Under such a circumstance, the curve in Figure 2 would level off farther to the right on the horizontal axis.

The next step in the development of our theory of trade between underdeveloped and advanced industrial countries is the recognition of the limited capacity of underdeveloped countries to export to developed countries. The past difficulties encountered by underdeveloped countries when attempting to expand their exports to advanced countries are well known, and all export forecasts indicate that no change can be expected. For a clearer understanding of the broad implications of this problem, it should be useful to explain in some detail why it is difficult for an underdeveloped country to expand its exports. In this portion of our exposition, we shall distinguish between raw-material exports and exports of manufactures.

The chief and long-recognized obstacle to raw-material exports is the low price- and income-elasticity of demand for such commodities. For all practical purposes, it may be considered that underdeveloped countries have exhausted the possibilities of stepping up their export trade in raw materials, at least in the sense that the factors that will determine their future foreign-exchange earnings from this source are largely beyond their control.

In the case of manufactures, the obstacles in the path of expanding exports stem not so much from the demand situation abroad as from the supply situation at home. It is extremely difficult for an underdeveloped country to produce goods that can be marketed successfully in advanced countries. Manufactures from underdeveloped countries suffer from too many shortcomings as to quality, design, degree of standardization, compliance with contracted delivery dates, etc., to be acceptable to discriminating buyers in high-income countries. Only the least complicated consumer goods, such as textiles, which are in demand in underdeveloped as well as advanced countries, may expect to find a worthwhile market in advanced countries.[2]

It is important to observe that these export difficulties are structural, in the sense that they would persist even if the country were to pursue ideal expenditure policies, i.e., eschew inflationary practices that would hamper exports. This observation is appropriate by way of underlining the peculiar difficulties of underdeveloped countries. On the other hand, it should not be allowed to obscure the fact that many such countries compound their difficulties through inept fiscal and monetary policies.

[2] The author has elsewhere attempted an explanation of the pattern of trade that differs from the factor-proportions theory (*An Essay on Trade and Transformation* [New York: John Wiley & Sons, 1961], pp. 82–124). According to the factor-proportions theory, the underdeveloped countries would have a comparative advantage in all relatively labor-intensive manufactures and would, therefore, experience no particular difficulties in exporting such products to the advanced countries. The implications of this factor-proportions theory differ, indeed, from what we observe in reality.

If a minimum amount of input imports is needed to realize the growth potential of the economy, and if a virtual ceiling exists on exports, it is evident that *the minimum amount of imports may exceed the maximum amount of exports*. This is the deplorable situation in which a large number of underdeveloped countries seem to find themselves. Under these circumstances, an underdeveloped country faces what we shall refer to as a "foreign-exchange gap," i.e., a deficit in its balance-of-payments program. This program deficit may be reflected in an actual deficit if the country can find the means of financing it, for instance, by permitting a drain on foreign-exchange reserves. Or, it will result in a lower quantity of input imports than would be compatible with full use of the growth potential of the economy. The greater the proportion of noninput items in the country's importation pattern, the more pressing its foreign-exchange problem.

The principal theoretical implications of these observations are as follows: The role of trade in a development process is more important than indicated by conventional trade theory, which regards commerce as the vehicle by which exports provide the means of paying for imports that, at margin, would cost more to produce at home than did the exports. The traditional balance-of-payments mechanism is not operative, for even if it were politically feasible to take appropriate measures as regards expenditures, the simultaneous attainment of internal and external balance would not necessarily follow; hence, the basic postulate in the pure theory of trade to the effect that external and internal balance can always be achieved through optimum expenditure policies is invalid. In short, the commercial-policy conclusions derived from the classical theory of international trade are not applicable to underdeveloped countries.

Trade among underdeveloped countries. Disregarding for the moment the important fact that there are extreme differences in the level of development from one underdeveloped country to another, the relationships that led to a reformulation of the theory of trade between developed and underdeveloped countries are not present in trade among underdeveloped countries. In the first place, there is no reason why a genuine foreign-exchange gap should arise among underdeveloped countries. With appropriate expenditure policies, it should be possible to achieve balance-of-payments equilibrium among underdeveloped countries without impairing their internal balance. This means that the conventional theory of international trade is applicable to commerce among underdeveloped countries. In other words, trade among underdeveloped countries is a means of ensuring that existing and future productive resources are allocated in the most efficient way. Although often overlooked in the welter of critical comment on trade theory as applied to the relationships between developed and underdeveloped countries, factor allocation is the kernel of conventional trade theory, and its importance should be stressed in the present context. Intensive trade among underdeveloped countries should also stimulate economic development by enabling constructive competition and optimum-size production units. Through trade, the wasteful duplication of small inefficient monopolies can be avoided. As regards trade among underdeveloped countries, then, the commercial-policy conclusions drawn from the conventional theory of trade should be directly applicable. The only complication is that, to the extent development plans, rather than price levels, exert a decisive influence on the pattern of growth, an international confrontation of development plans becomes requisite.

The Basic Problem

We now have two distinct sets of commercial-policy conclusions for individual underdeveloped countries, the first relating to trade with advanced nations and the second relating to trade with others in the underdeveloped group. With respect to trade with advanced countries, we have observed that the conventional theory of commercial policy cannot be applied. An alternative commercial policy would, among other things, call for techniques for the conservation of foreign-exchange resources to finance input imports. This is of great importance for our theory of customs unions and development. It is essential to save foreign exchange for input imports in order to try to make possible full capacity use and avoid dissipation of the gradual additions to domestic resources. In consequence, a strong case can be made for the control of certain imports (noninput imports), which might be termed "luxury imports," to tie in with a much-ridiculed case posed by the conventional commercial-policy theory. According to that theory, the restriction of luxury imports is not defensible because appropriate expenditure policies induce coexisting external and internal equilibrium, in which the composition of imports is determined by the pattern of comparative advantages. If the country has a comparative disadvantage in the production of the luxuries for which there is a demand, so the argument runs, these luxuries should be imported rather than produced more expensively at home.

Free trade with other underdeveloped countries would be desirable, provided we disregard in this initial analysis the complications deriving from the marked differences in levels of development. Here the idea behind free trade would be to reap the traditional benefits of commerce as envisioned by the conventional theory of international trade.

The question, then, is whether these two different sets of commercial policies can be implemented at the same time.

The Solution

Having posed the problem in this way, we find ourselves, in effect, involved in a theory of customs unions and economic development. This is so because we reply to the above question in the affirmative: The two sets of commercial policy conclusions can, indeed, be simultaneously applied—through the formation of customs unions between certain underdeveloped countries or, ideally, through the formation of one huge customs union embracing all underdeveloped countries. The purpose of a customs union, after all, is precisely to make it possible to pursue free trade among one group of countries, and at the same time, to retain whatever restrictions are deemed essential against some other group.

But apart from furnishing a formal opportunity for retaining restrictions on imports from one set of countries, a customs union also serves to make such controls efficient. If an underdeveloped country tries in isolation to curb noninput imports from an advanced country, the restrictions might constitute nothing more than a pious gesture. The money spent formerly on the noninput imports will be spent on some other goods after the controls have been instituted. It is very difficult to absorb this purchasing power through harsh fiscal policies without stifling the development effort in other ways. It is also unlikely that the money would be saved voluntarily; and if it is spent on goods smuggled into the country, the foreign-exchange situation would be no better than before. If the controls are to be efficient, the money must be spent on import substitutes; moreover, the resources that go into the production of these substitutes must not be diverted from the production of export goods. The possibilities of providing acceptable import substitutes if an underdeveloped country acts in isolation are likely to be considerably fewer than if it acts in concert with other underdeveloped countries within a customs union.

Consequently, a customs union of underdeveloped countries has the following strategic attraction: It enables an underdeveloped country to maintain restrictions on noninput imports from industrial countries while enjoying the advantages of free trade with other underdeveloped countries. In this way, the efficacy of a greater number of restrictions on noninput imports is heightened, and those controls that would be effective even in isolation are rendered less expensive.

Comparison with Traditional Customs-Union Theory

As we have seen, once the role of trade in general in a development process has been clarified, the implications with respect to the customs union as a device for furthering economic development become evident. In this connection, customs unions have been demonstrated to have great advantages.

In order to shed further light on our theory of customs unions and economic development, it should be helpful to contrast our approach with the conventional customs-union theory.

Traditionally, customs unions are said to be beneficial to the extent that they lead to trade creation rather than trade diversion. Trade creation occurs when the elimination of customs duties between members in the union leads to the extinction of inefficient producers who could survive only behind tariff walls. When such tariff walls are eliminated, there will be a new trade flow into the country; there will also be a new outflow of commodities produced by those industries which, in the country in question, have proved to be more efficient than their competitors in other member nations. Trade diversion, on the other hand, is what happens when goods formerly imported from countries outside the union are brought in from a member country in response to the new element of discrimination. Since the new source of imports is more expensive, trade diversion is detrimental. Trade creation leads to an improved allocation of existing resources, whereas trade diversion leads to an inferior allocation of existing resources.

Customs unions, realized or attempted, have often been judged on the basis of these criteria.[3] The assessment has usually resulted in somewhat negative conclusions as to the merits of forming customs unions among underdeveloped countries. The customary supposition is that there will be almost no trade creation, but fairly extensive trade diversion. However, since we have rejected the application of this customs-union theory to underdeveloped countries, we obviously must consider such judgments erroneous.

We shall state our objection more specifically, in the language of the neoclassical theory: To the extent that it consists of diverting the importation of noninput goods away from advanced industrial countries, trade diversion is almost the very essence of the customs union postulated. It enables the concentration of scarce foreign exchange on input imports, thereby enhancing capacity use and growth. The point at issue is not whether the new producer is more or less efficient than the former one. The question is, rather, whether it is not more advan-

[3] See, for example, R. L. Allen, "Integration in Less-Developed Areas," *Kyklos*, XIV, Fasc. 3 (1961), 315–36.

tageous to buy a commodity from a new producer than to waste foreign exchange on importation from an advanced country. It is not enough to compare the efficiency of two alternative producers. We must broaden our comparison to take into account the side effects of using one or the other. The producer who in a partial analysis is shown to be the less efficient of the two proves to be the most economic under a more general analysis.

It should, however, be observed that, to the extent that the customs union does not embrace all underdeveloped countries, there might be trade diversion away from an underdeveloped country outside the union to another inside the union. Such trade diversion would be harmful. This conclusion is entirely in line with our application of the conventional theory to trade relationships among underdeveloped countries.

The fact that we can apply the conventional trade theory to intra-union trade also implies that trade creation is considered to be beneficial among the underdeveloped member countries. If the underdeveloped countries have tried to develop on their own intra-union trade over a long period and have used extensive controls to keep out unessential imports, there should be ample opportunity for trade creation. Only if the "do-it-yourself" approach in commercial policy had proved so difficult that the development effort had been significantly held back would there be little room for trade creation. In this case, there would be few domestic resources to reallocate, owing to the negligible rate of growth. Even at that, it would be foolish to concentrate solely on trade creation through reallocation of existing resources. The scope of the neoclassical theory must necessarily be extended to include its own growth implications. The formation of the customs union should be looked upon as an attempt to make future additions to productive resources as extensive and as efficiently allocated as possible.

The customs union composed of underdeveloped nations is formed to ensure that future resources are employed in such way that there is trade diversion—but trade diversion in a specific direction, i.e., from an advanced country to the most efficient producer of a given commodity among the union membership. Thus, participation by an underdeveloped country in a customs union would not involve an attempt to divert trade from an advanced country to itself, unless, of course, it happened to qualify as the most efficient producer in the underdeveloped group.

When we consider future additions of resources and their best use, the elements of trade creation and trade diversion fuse into a single concept of "efficient trade diversion." This form of trade diversion is intended to enable a livelier trade in input imports from the industrial countries, with a view to eventually eliminating differences in development. Once this is accomplished, there will be no further need for the special trade arrangements we have discussed here. In conclusion, a customs union of underdeveloped countries, unless it be so badly implemented as to be unworthy of the name, has a greater number of strictly economic arguments in its favor than does its counterpart among industrial countries.

IV

HIROSHI KITAMURA[1]

Economic Theory and the Economic Integration of Underdeveloped Regions

The movement toward regional economic grouping or integration in the present-day world is not limited to the industrially advanced areas, but also encompasses, perhaps more forcefully, the underdeveloped regions on the periphery. The analytical tools at our disposal for considering the economic effects of regional integration schemes, however, are usually those which belong to the traditional theory of customs union, concentrating on welfare gains or losses arising from the changed pattern of trade. Beyond the static welfare effects of trade creation and trade diversion, some attention has been paid to gains from economies of scale and from changes in the market structure. However, the dynamic effects of regional economic integration on more basic problems of economic growth, such as the pattern of investment and technical progress, have largely been left out of the account.

Even for an industrially developed area such as Europe, there is

[1] The present paper is a revised version of the author's article "Economic Theory and Regional Economic Integration in Asia," published in *The Pakistan Development Review*, II, No. 2 (Summer, 1962), which was primarily addressed to the problem of regional economic integration in Asia. It is considered that the main arguments can be applied to the underdeveloped and developing regions in general. The author is indebted to the editor of *The Pakistan Development Review* for kind permission to use the published material.

The author is chief of the Economic Development Branch, United Nations Economic Corporation for Asia and the Far East (ECAFE), Bangkok, Thailand;

some doubt as to whether the most significant aspects of the integration problem can be adequately dealt with along the lines of this basically static analysis; yet it must be admitted that, insofar as the main problem is that of trade expansion, with few or, at most, marginal changes in the economic structure involved, the traditional theory of international trade provides a useful point of departure for analysis. The problem for underdeveloped and developing regions, however, presents itself in a different light. Here, it is not the change in gains from foreign trade as such, but the need for accelerated economic development, that provides the fundamental motive, as well as the criterion, for regional economic integration. As the economic growth of countries in these regions necessarily involves rapid and far-reaching structural changes in the pattern of production and trade, an analysis of the welfare implications of a shift in the existing trade pattern may be less important than an analysis of the impacts on investment and technical progress over time.

The present paper primarily attempts to examine the relevance of economic theory to the problem of regional economic integration among underdeveloped countries. The analysis of the main economic effects of such an integration will be followed by some observations on the methods of integration applicable to underdeveloped regions.

The Concept of Economic Integration

The discussions in this paper are focused on the concept of integration as the goal of rational economic policy, as distinct from the rather elusive concept of cooperation. It may be useful at the outset to make clear the idea underlying the choice of concept. Cooperation between independent nation-states may include a wide range of actions relating to technically well-defined fields, such as patent laws or communications; some of these cooperative actions may be of economic importance, but must be relegated to secondary place in a discussion of economic policy. Some international consultations in matters relating to economic policy, such as agreements on trade policy at a forum of the General Agreement on Tariffs and Trade (GATT) or at International Monetary Fund (IMF) consultations, are examples of international economic cooperation that are not included in the concept of integration. They do not contain elements pointing to the creation of a new and desirable institutional framework. On the other hand, when its objective is institutional, cooperation can be a stage in

---

however, the views expressed in the present paper do not necessarily reflect those of the ECAFE.

the process of integration. The trade consultations carried out under the aegis of the OEEC were clearly a case in point. Insofar as integration is considered a process, some forms of international cooperation can be regarded as a lower stage of integration.

Because the concept of economic integration has been chosen as the frame of reference in this paper, the start is made from the institutional goal that can be defined with Jan Tinbergen as "the creation of the most desirable structure of international economy, removing artificial hindrances to the optimal operation, and introducing deliberately all desirable elements of coordination and unification." [2] It follows that the problem of economic integration is part of a more general problem, namely, that of how to formulate and implement the optimum economic policy. Although the concept of integration itself implies the desirability of a certain degree of unification—and there is a school of thought which maintains that integration means an equal opportunity for all parts—the approach suggested here can be somewhat selective and flexible. A full unification is not advocated for all cases.

It is sometimes suggested that economic integration would pass through three different stages—namely, cooperation, coordination, and full integration—one leading progressively to the other in accordance with the extent to which national sovereignty is surrendered. It is also implied that a higher form of integration should be a more efficient one from the point of view of policy. So far as the process of economic integration is concerned, however, the surrender of national sovereignty is only one of the means to achieve the goal and may not be as important as other means.

The relative importance to be given to the removal of barriers, especially to movements of commodities and factors of production, may also differ from case to case. This relativist approach is in conflict with the dogmatic point of view of economic liberalism. According to the latter, economic integration is identified with the successive steps of liberalization of trade as well as factor movements, and the need for harmonization or coordination of economic policy as a whole will emerge only after a full liberalization of commodity and factor movements has been achieved in the form of a common market. In other words, the coordination of policy is something that characterizes only the higher forms of integration, namely, economic union or total economic integration.

In the present-day economy, however, where the extent of government intervention in economic life for various policy objectives has

[2] Jan Tinbergen, *International Economic Integration* (Amsterdam: Elsevier, 1954), p. 95.

been considerably increased, the purely negative action of trade liberalization may not go far in achieving the desirable degree of integration unless it is accompanied by complementary measures of a more positive nature. It is probable that the attempt to coordinate and harmonize national economic policies will be an important instrument even in the earlier stages of the integration process. In certain circumstances, in fact, integration may be accomplished to a considerable extent without lifting the existing trade barriers; in that case, trade liberalization will follow to give effect to the harmonization of national economic policies. This consideration is particularly relevant to the issue of economic integration insofar as it arises in the context of underdeveloped areas.

Economic integration is, thus, a process in which an attempt is made to create a desirable institutional framework for the optimization of economic policy as a whole. Many forms of international cooperation will be excluded from the discussion here either because they do not aim at the institutional goal or because they are not related to the central problems of economic policy. On the other hand, the concept of economic integration is broad and flexible enough to cover an extremely varied range of cooperative actions. For instance, integration can start with some decisions limited to a partial field of economic activity. Then we have integration by sector, as exemplified by a commodity common market in the form of the European Coal and Steel Community. As a result of the close interdependence that exists between various sectors of the economy, disequilibriums will emerge, which inevitably will bring home to the countries concerned the need for, and the benefit to be expected from, a closer integration in a wider field.

To start from the goal of economic integration is not to say that the regulations of current trade transactions are not important for the process of integration. The expediting of current trade relations undoubtedly contributes to the strengthening of mutual understanding and confidence, which, in turn, creates conditions favorable for further steps toward economic integration. Once a form of international integration is established, there will always be an inherent tendency to move into a higher form of integration. Suppose that a free-trade area is created. Since the tariff rates of individual countries vis-à-vis the outside world are maintained at different levels, the need to control re-exports from one member country to others will inevitably move the scheme in the direction of a customs union. Once a common tariff is established, the need to liberalize factor movements will suggest itself, in order to secure the most efficient allocation of resources within the framework of a common market. At this advanced stage, however, a certain degree of coordination of fiscal, monetary, and wage policies will be a necessary ingredient of the integration policy and point to the establishment of an economic union.

It can be argued, therefore, that it does not greatly matter at what point and in what field of economic activity an integration movement is initiated. This is also the basic reason why our frame of reference has been deliberately chosen in flexible and relativist terms.

In the present-day world economy, an integration move is undertaken predominantly in some kind of regional framework, rather than on a global basis. This is not due merely to a historical accident. The experience gained from the world's postwar attempt to establish a new and stable economic framework, following the far-reaching disintegration that took place during the 1930's and the war period, clearly indicated that the road to a multilateral and free world-wide system of trade and payments is long and hazardous. The factors that were responsible for the historical disintegration are still operative in many respects; the degree of state intervention in the economic life of nations has enormously increased, and the need for state planning for accelerated economic growth has been added, thus making the existing dislocations and disequilibriums in the world economy more strongly felt. In these circumstances, all attempts at world economic integration involve continuous consultation among governments and the reconciliation of divergent interests and points of view. It is clear that such cooperation can be much more easily organized in depth among countries with similar historical backgrounds and economic interests; that is, it can be more easily accomplished at a regional than at a universal level.

Nor is the tendency toward such a regional approach purely transitional. It is partly based on the fact that recent technological changes have broadened the scope of economies of scale, involving the need for forming a large and stable market. The economic policies of individual nation-states must also take cognizance both of the bargaining power that tends to increase proportionally with the size of the economic bloc and of the recent developments in political thinking that tend to make the concept of a nation-state appear as something belonging to a bygone age. It seems that economic integration on a regional scale, rather than on a global scale, has become one of the major goals of economic policy in our time. Indeed, it can be said that "regional arrangements are no longer a matter of choice. They are imposed by the requirements of technology, science, and economics" [3] in the contemporary world.

[3] *Foreign Economic Policy for the Twentieth Century* (Report of the Rockefeller Brothers Fund, Special Studies Project Report III [New York, 1958]), p. 30.

CRITERIA FOR EVALUATION

The issue of economic integration at a regional level involves a choice among alternative long-run institutional arrangements in the relations of one country with others, both within the same region and outside the region. The pertinent question is what institutional framework of international relations is most conducive to accelerating the economic growth of each country as well as of the region as a whole. The particular way, however, in which the problem is formulated poses a series of questions that must be clarified in advance.

First of all, the objective function to be optimized is economic growth, or rate of growth. Now, the choice of the growth function will depend upon the nature of the problems at hand. In our context of trade and development, the accepted view will be that economic growth is a function of real capital formation in which the effective supply of capital and investment goods plays a cardinal role, provided that a sufficient capacity to absorb capital exists in the domestic economy. Insofar as most of these capital and investment goods are imported from abroad, as is the case with a typical underdeveloped country of today, the rate of real capital formation is conditioned by the import capacity and by the possibility of substituting capital goods for consumer goods in total imports. The import capacity, in turn, is either based on the country's export earnings or created by foreign-capital inflow. Given the capital flow and the composition of imports, it can be said that the country's growth potentials will be exploited to the optimal extent if the country's export base can be expanded to the maximum without disrupting production for domestic demand. Or, in general, an optimum rate of economic growth will be achieved when the supply of foreign exchange for imports of capital goods is maximized. To the extent that savings can be incorporated in capital goods domestically produced, it will be necessary to take into account the complementary structure of real capital; but the country's capacity to import will still remain the basic determinant for the degree to which its growth potentialities are actually realized.

However, the influence of the choice made among alternative economic environments will not be confined to its effects on export earnings and capacity to import. The magnitude and direction of productive investment will also be directly affected by the change in the size of potential markets implied in the making of this choice. The expansion of potential markets may, for example, bring about increased opportunities for profitable activity of foreign and domestic investors. It is true that investment is not so sensitive to a given inducement in a typical underdeveloped economy as in an industrially advanced one, but these effects of the market demand on investment activity should not be neglected altogether. In the long run, the changed nature of investment will have a greater influence on the future pattern of output than the shift in the present trade pattern.

If a given choice of institutional framework of economic policy should help the country concerned toward achievement of a balance-of-payments equilibrium, this beneficial effect could be considered a side condition for optimizing the rate of economic growth. However, the present gap in the balance of payments in underdeveloped countries is, in general, a reflection not simply of monetary and price imbalances but, more fundamentally, of the real forces creating an increasing gap between the import requirements and the stagnant capacity to import. Moreover, the imbalance is of a structural nature, in the sense that underemployment and underutilization of domestic resources are combined with external deficits—as contrasted with the external imbalances in economically advanced countries, which usually result from full employment and domestic inflation. The price and market mechanism cannot, therefore, smoothly work out an optimum solution. The existing disequilibrium not only makes it impossible for a country to achieve the desirable rate of growth on a balanced basis, but also calls for an increasing degree of exchange controls and trade restrictions, which further distort the pattern of trade and production and the equilibrium prices. These restrictive measures are usually motivated by the need to secure imports of essential goods, mainly of capital and investment goods from the developed countries outside the region. The main burden of adjustment being thus placed on imports of nonessential goods or of goods that can be produced with relative ease at home, the restrictions tend to discriminate against other similarly situated underdeveloped countries in the same region.

This consideration is of particular importance for any discussion of regional economic integration in the underdeveloped areas at the present time. We do not start with an over-all equilibrium and universal free trade, for the present international environment does not seem to allow a typical underdeveloped country to grow satisfactorily under the unrestricted play of action and interaction of the market forces. On the contrary, the tendency will inevitably be toward a further distortion of the price structure and the patterns of production and trade. With respect to production, the country will be forced increasingly into making direct investment in production for the domestic market, at whatever cost, as substitution for imports. For the analysis of our present problem, this severely limits the relevance of the traditional economic theory, which is based on the static assumptions of equilibrium and perfect competition. It will not make much sense to discuss the consequences of regional economic integration in the underdeveloped regions in the light of a hypothetical situation of a balanced and free trade. Rather, the consequences of integration must be considered against not only the alternative of the existing disequilibrium but the alternative of what is likely to emerge in the absence of such an integration if the present trends towards international and domestic disequilibriums should be permitted to persist.

If we admit the existence of disequilibriums and still want to remain in the realm of a static equilibrium theory, it is appropriate to characterize the problem of regional economic integration as a case of "second-best optimum" solution. Now, the general theory of second best tells us that, "given that one of the Paretian optimum conditions cannot be fulfilled, then an optimum situation can be achieved only by departing from all the other Paretian conditions." [4] To attempt to test the consequences of a regional economic integration against the optimum criteria of free trade is not very meaningful. Even a limited move toward the ideal of free trade does not necessarily represent an approach in the direction of the second-best optimum. Insofar as the choice is between two nonoptimum situations, there is no a priori principle on which to decide which one is preferable. This conclusion, although logically correct, may appear too restrictive at a level that is a little removed from purely a priori reasonings. Especially where deviations from the optimum conditions in a definite direction are implied, it must be possible for a theory, when reinterpreted in a dynamic context, to say something about the order of preference.

This is the case with our problem of regional economic integration. The distortion in the trade pattern of a typical underdeveloped country tends to be at the expense of specialization among neighboring countries of the same region. If a reversal of this tendency should prove helpful in optimizing the country's or the region's rate of economic growth through maximizing the supply of foreign exchange for capital goods, then it would appear that there is presumption in favor of an institutional arrangement such as regional integration. In this dynamic context, a certain element of irreversibility is introduced into the system of interdependence among economic variables, and this is the reason why a theoretical solution can escape, in some way, from the purely negative character of the static theory as applied to the second-best optimum.

[4] R. G. Lipsey and Kelvin Lancaster, "The General Theory of Second Best," *The Review of Economic Studies*, XXIV, No. 63 (1956–57), 11.

Gains from Regional Economic Integration

Insofar as the rate of economic growth is chosen as the final criterion for evaluation of gains, it may be well to note at the outset that the process of economic growth possesses multiple dimensions and that it is of a cumulative nature. The process cannot be decisively remodeled by once-for-all measures, such as changes in international institutional arrangements. Economic growth also necessitates, and is accompanied by, a continuous change in the structure of production and trade; and the latter is a process of quite a different dimension from, for example, a removal of trade barriers that can be effected at one stroke. An attempt at regional economic integration is, therefore, most unlikely to change immediately the basic determinants of economic growth. But it may, in the long run, create certain conditions of accelerated growth by eliminating some bottlenecks limiting economic expansion. And I would like to maintain that, since the international environment to be chosen is not of a transitional character, this log-run effect may be quite important.

Regional economic integration implies a broadening of the regional market and a reduction in the country's or the region's dependence on trade with the outside world, at least in relative terms, that is, as compared with the situation likely to prevail in the absence of integration. Where the tendency in the import-substitution policy has been toward discrimination against imports from within the region, this tendency will be reversed so as to increase the volume of imports from, and of exports to, the regional markets. As a consequence, not only the pattern and volume of trade, but the total volume and pattern of investment, will change.

The main link between trade and development here comes into play. In the case of underdeveloped countries, which rely mainly on industrially advanced countries outside the region for the supply of capital goods, the reduction of their dependence on trade with the outside world is likely to take place in the field of consumer goods and other commodities that can be produced in underdeveloped areas with relative ease. Because of the broadened market in the region, these commodities can now be imported in a greater quantity from other countries in the region, instead of from the outside world. Through this intercountry substitution, the availability of the foreign exchange required for imports of essential development goods from the outside world is increased. Therefore, assuming that the bulk of real capital goods originate from countries outside the region, the supply of real capital goods and the magnitude of investment can be considerably increased by regional economic integration.

Such an increase in the capacity to import capital goods from the outside world could, of course, be achieved also through intercommodity substitution in imports. If a typical underdeveloped country is to grow on the basis of a rather slow growth of export earnings, and if there is no broadened regional market, the import substitution policy will have to be aimed at the maximum degree of self-sufficiency, at whatever cost, in commodities whose imports can be replaced by any means. Such a policy will result in a reduction in the ratio of foreign trade to the country's domestic expenditure, entailing a sacrifice of the gains from specialization. However, the creation of a broadened regional market can permit a country to achieve a desirable rate of economic growth without foregoing possible gains from specialization.

The establishment of a more rational pattern of trade and production is, therefore, the most important justification for regional economic integration. There seems little doubt that a pattern of production based on greater specialization within the region will be more economical than one directed toward maximum self-sufficiency on the basis of narrow national markets. If such a pattern of production and investment maximizes the supply of capital goods without disrupting production for domestic demand, as is the case with a typical underdeveloped country, it is at the same time most conducive to economic growth from the dynamic point of view. From the standpoint of a static theory, it is true that regional economic integration will not establish the all-round optimum relations between prices of domestic and internationally traded goods, but the situation can be legitimately called the second-best solution, insofar as the relative price and production patterns, even in a limited sphere, are shifted toward optimum conditions through intraregional specialization.

There is thus room for presumption that economic gains will be secured if there is a net expansion of trade, the tendency toward declining over-all ratio of foreign trade to national expenditure being more than offset by the increase in intraregional trade. The question for the development policy is only how to direct the increased flow of resources into investment by increasing and maximizing the supply of capital goods. From this dynamic point of view, therefore, intercommodity substitution must be considered together with the intercountry substitution with which the theory of customs union is mainly concerned. In certain cases, the goal of maximization of the supply of foreign exchange for capital-goods imports from the outside world may come into conflict with the expansion of intraregional trade. In such cases, it is clear from the point of view of development policy that the objective of trade creation within the region, part of which may be trade diversion in the terminology of theory of customs union, should not be pushed forward beyond the optimum limit.

In general, it is easy to exaggerate the advantage of free trade and, for that matter, of international division of labor and specialization. Foreign trade is, in most cases, marginal to the total circular flow of goods in the economy; and a change in institutional barriers to trade, such as tariffs and quantitative restrictions, affects only a small part of the trade flow. However, some part of the goods secured through trade channels may be qualitatively very important, and the trade policy designed under a given development strategy will have to be highly selective. This selectiveness is important not only with respect to substitution of commodities but also with respect to intercountry substitution. That is why the problem of regional economic integration becomes an important issue in trade policy for economic development.

The static theory of customs union does not seem to give adequate answers to this vital problem. Its analysis is usually confined to welfare gains and losses arising from varying degrees of specialization as a result of shifts in the existing trade patterns. Some attention has been paid to gains connected with economies of scale and changes in terms of trade, but the effects of a customs union on the level of aggregate economic activity or on the rate of economic growth have hardly been touched upon. Although some important insights into the mechanism of intercountry substitution have been gained, the relevance of such a theory to the problem of regional economic integration seems to be severely limited.

This limitation applies also to the main realm of the theory, the analysis of welfare gains from specialization. As is natural in a static analysis, the main pillar of the traditional theory is the distinction between the trade-creating and trade-diverting effects of a customs union. It was originally considered that trade creation was beneficial to the welfare of a country and the world, whereas trade diversion would bring about a loss to world welfare. However, it has been established, in the course of further development of the theory, that this simple distinction is an inadequate criterion for judging the effects of a customs union. If the effects on consumption are considered in addition to the production effects, it is no longer correct to say that trade diversion is bad in all cases.[5] Even when a regional integration has only trade-diverting effects, that is, when higher-cost sources of supply are substituted for the lowest-cost sources of supply, a country,

[5] See R. G. Lipsey, "The Theory of Customs Union: Trade Diversion and Welfare," *Economica* (New Series), February, 1957, p. 41.

as well as the world as a whole, may gain from such a market arrangement.

In the case of a typical underdeveloped country, it is safe to assume that a regional economic integration will always result in a primary net expansion of trade. The secondary effects are, of course, much more complex. As a consequence of reduced demand for products of the outside world, the terms of trade are likely to turn in favor of the underdeveloped country concerned, as compared with what the terms had been under the preintegration conditions of tariff protection. The extent of this favorable trend will depend on the bargaining power of the country and the region as a whole, which will tend to be strengthened vis-à-vis the outside world by the creation of a regional market. Moreover, such an expansion of trade will not fail to exert considerable influence on the process of income creation, the gains with respect to which will go far beyond the realm of purely static trade gains. The income effects, so far as trade with the outside world is concerned, will clearly tend to increase considerably the scope for beneficial exchange of goods with third countries, and this secondary trade expansion may very well more than offset the possible initial reduction of this particular type of trade. After all, the main objective of the integration move is the optimization of the supply of foreign exchange for capital-goods imports from the outside world, and there are fairly good grounds for assurance that the over-all volume of trade will somewhat be increased, although its composition will be changed.

One might be inclined to say that a regional economic integration of underdeveloped areas will, in the long run, result only in the creation of trade, and that there will be no over-all trade diversion.[6] I prefer to stick to the original meaning of the concept and to argue that there certainly is and must be a trade-diverting effect. This is one of the essential characteristics of regional economic integration. After all, what sense is there in conceiving of a regional economic integration without a degree of discrimination against the third countries? Discrimination belongs to the nature of all tariffs and quantitative restrictions prevailing in the world economy of today. To be effective in countering the prevailing discrimination, regional integration must also partake of a discriminatory character, and, especially in underdeveloped regions, the margin of preference must be extensive enough to promote economic growth through creating a broadened regional

[6] This is the position taken, for example, by Professor Raymond F. Mikesell in his paper "The Theory of Common Markets As Applied to Regional Arrangements Among Developing Countries," Roy Harrod and D. C. Hague (eds.), *International Trade Theory in a Developing World* (London: Macmillan and Co., 1963) pp. 205–29.

market. In the light of these considerations, trade diversion appears as an essential ingredient of the integration policy, as a positive, rather than negative, factor in the evaluation of regional economic integration.

There have been some attempts to appraise in quantitative terms the static welfare gains from a shift of the existing trade pattern. Such a shift will certainly involve a reallocation of productive resources and consumption, but the calculation has invariably shown that the economic gains from a greater degree of specialization, conceived in static terms, will not be very considerable. Such a conclusion seems inevitable, so long as welfare gains are identified with the differences between marginal social costs of imported goods and their domestically produced substitutes, which are reflected in the changes in tariffs. Even where the change in the volume of trade is considerable, the tariff changes to be chosen as the base of welfare calculation will tend to minimize gains. However, the main part of the effects of a change in the institutional market arrangement may be absorbed by interfirm and intersector reallocation of resources within the same country, rather than be reflected in a change in trade. Even in the short run, the process of such a reallocation may affect very significantly the level of productivity. Over a longer period, the productivity effects of a regional economic integration will be felt more strongly through a change in the nature, direction, and volume of investment.

There is reason to assume that the immediate effects of regional economic integration on the efficiency of an underdeveloped country's economic organization will be negligible. However, a change in economic environment in the direction of the broadening of regional markets will, in the long run, affect investment, particularly in those fields where considerable economies of scale remain to be exploited. These productivity gains are additional to the dynamic benefits to be derived from the increased volume of productive investment made possible by the increased supply of capital goods through imports. The effects of a regional economic integration may, therefore, be the greatest on certain types of industries yet to be created or greatly to be expanded in the region. The productive process in such industries is usually characterized by a high degree of capital intensity, a long gestation period, and large economies of scale; and the products of these industries are faced with a demand which is highly growth-elastic. In other words, a broadened regional market may open up quite a new dimension in the prospects of industrialization both to individual underdeveloped countries and to the underdeveloped regions as a whole.

Viewed in this dynamic perspective of industrialization, the impact of an economic integration in the underdeveloped regions appears to be more important in some respects, and less important in others, than it is in the industrially developed regions. Less important are the effects on the market structure through an increased competition, which is less likely to be found in an integrated underdeveloped area than, for example, in Europe, where great emphasis is laid on the productive effects of a vigorous competition. The limitations operating on the supply side in the underdeveloped countries may make it impossible for them to exploit immediately the potential economies of scale to the fullest extent. Paradoxically enough, it is precisely this last factor that provides a point of departure for a powerful argument for economic integration as a means of industrialization.

It is well known that the limited factor supply and productive capacity in the underdeveloped countries form a real obstacle to the practical implementation of the policy prescription of balanced growth. The possibility of simultaneous expansion of all interrelated industries from which potential external economies may originate is restricted by the quantities of productive factors and the feasible amount of investment. The limited size of the market is only one of the relevant aspects, and it tends to be overemphasized in the doctrine of balanced growth. Supply limitations would permit the exploitation of economies of scale only if the available resources were used in a concentrated way, that is, if a limited number of industries were developed without regard to interindustrial external economies. This unbalanced pattern of development would, however, involve disadvantages in the form of discrepancies between supply and demand. It is clear that there are certain advantages to be derived from balanced growth, and others from unbalanced growth, and that each of these growth patterns has its own drawbacks. Now, economic integration may create the conditions under which the benefits of unbalanced growth can more easily be combined with those of balanced growth.[7]

The essential point is that, within the framework of an enlarged regional market, particular industries can be permitted or encouraged to advance ahead of the rest of the economy, because they can be assured of effective support in the markets of partner countries. The economies of scale and the stimulating effect on technological progress inherent in concentrated growth can be fully appropriated. More importantly, however, large external economies can be exploited through interdependence of industries in production and consumption, in this case through interdependence with the industries newly established in partner countries on the basis of some kind of agreed

[7] See Paul Streeten, *Economic Integration: Aspects and Problems* (Leyden: A. W. Sythoff, 1961), Preface. See also Bela Balassa, *The Theory of Economic Integration* (Homewood, Ill.: Richard D. Irwin, 1961), p. 155.

specialization. From this point of view, integration means not only an enlargement of the market but also the creation of a mutually supporting, complementary industrial structure within a regional framework. Thus, "growing points" can be created in an integrated area in a coordinated manner, and rapidly growing industries or sectors will provide both opportunities and incentives for the development of the lagging industries or sectors.

This kind of dynamic interpretation of the growth process provides a firmer basis for the integration argument for the underdeveloped and developing regions than the trade gains from an enlarged market provide. In these regions, in view of the limited size of national markets (in terms of income) and the smaller scale of average plants, the scope for the exploitation of economies of scale proper through economic integration is considerably greater than in the industrially advanced regions. Interindustrial relationships have still to be established in many countries of these regions, but it is precisely this fact that makes quite large the advantages to be derived from nonmarket external economies and interindustry transmission of technical progress. The need for increased investment as a precondition for accelerated economic growth is, however, likely to give a peculiar shape to the process of integration in the underdeveloped regions. The role of development planning and the importance of coordinated creation of social and economic overhead capital will inevitably have a bearing on the forms and methods of economic integration in these areas.

Forms and Methods of Regional Economic Integration

Our analysis of the economic gains to be expected from regional economic integration for the underdeveloped countries seems to provide at least one important pointer for a practical approach to the problem: It should not be through a removal of trade barriers only, or primarily through such a measure, that economic integration of an underdeveloped region is organized. Apart from the insignificant nature of trade gains, the existing pattern of production and trade in these regions is not such that the mere lifting of mutual trade barriers would considerably increase the trade volume. The reallocational effects of trade liberalization may be important in industrially developed regions such as Western Europe, but, in the underdeveloped areas, the price and market mechanism is not expected to work efficiently enough to effect a radical change in allocation of resources in a more rational direction. The pattern of resource utilization is also subjected in these regions to a greater degree of government intervention than elsewhere. In many countries, planning is the main instrument in the development policy, and the objective of accelerating economic growth can be realized only within the framework of planning, to which trade liberalization must be clearly subordinated.

A mutual agreement among the countries to lower the hindrances to intraregional trade, on a preferential basis, may constitute an important step and means for the realization of regional economic integration. But, in all probability, the beneficial effects of a free-trade area or a common market in the underdeveloped regions will be somewhat limited. The basic reason is that the structural changes of the country's economy necessary for achieving an accelerated rate of growth would not be brought about automatically by liberalization of trade. To achieve the principal goal, mutual cooperation among the countries will, rather, have to be extended to the sphere of production, with a view to changing the composition and magnitude of investment. This means that the purely negative action of removing existing trade barriers is not enough. Something more positive is required.

I suspect that the type of cooperative action that is urgently required in these regions is what is usually called coordination or harmonization of economic policies. Even in the context of an industrially advanced region, it is often argued, with respect to agricultural products, that it does not make sense to make trade free without taking measures aimed at readjustments of production. In this particular field of production, some action to coordinate and harmonize national production programs is, today, virtually accepted as a prerequisite to the removal of trade restrictions. The same applies with a greater justification to the economies of underdeveloped regions in general, where the state intervention is needed to counter distortion arising from structural disequilibriums. In these circumstances, there is weighty reason to assume that an optimal allocation of resources would not automatically come about under a regime of free trade; hence, the need for a certain degree of harmonization of economic policies relating to allocation of resources. But, on the other hand, it should be clearly recognized that such coordination can pave the way to expansion of trade. The market can be expanded, not by liberalizing, but by organizing.

Such an organization of regional markets will inevitably be on a basis of regional preference. For the problem of a regional market has, today, become a pressing issue of trade policy exactly because an integrated world economy has patently failed to come into being since the disintegration of the 1930's and the war period. Inasmuch as the expansion of government controls over the economic life of nations has increased the scope and the need for negotiated, rather than spontaneous, policy harmonization among politically independent countries, it has become clear that such a harmonization cannot be negotiated on a world-wide scale. Not only would a world-wide machinery be cumbersome and inefficient, but the political preconditions for the necessary adjustments in the exercise of national sovereignty are still lacking. There are also several reasons to suggest that greater potentialities exist for a more intimate form of coordination and harmonization of policy, through regional negotiations among highly interdependent countries that are well prepared for coordinated action by a common geographical and historical background and a relatively homogeneous stage of economic development.

The last point mentioned, namely, cooperation and integration among countries at a relatively homogeneous stage of economic development, may deserve a little further exploration. According to the classical pattern of exchange between manufactured goods, on the one hand, and foodstuffs and raw materials, on the other, it should have been more advantageous to organize cooperation among countries at different stages of economic development and with heterogeneous factor endowments. Why, then, does the unmistakable trend of the present-day world economy point to an increasing cooperation and integration among economies at a more or less similar stage of economic development? It is a fact that trade has recently tended to increase relatively among industrially advanced countries, while declining between industrialized countries and primary-producing underdeveloped countries. This remarkable trend may probably be connected with a certain change in the determinants of the trade pattern; now, it is perhaps differences in technology, rather than differences in natural endowments, that increasingly determine the patterns of specialization. Or, to put it differently, technical superiority, partly based on the advantage of economies of scale, is playing an increasingly important part in determining relative cost differences among nations and is increasingly taking the place of the classical principle of factor endowments.

The last statement applies particularly to the comparative cost differences with regard to manufactured goods. For other categories of goods, the conditions of relative factor endowments still remain the most important factor determining the location of production. But for manufactured goods, which are favored by historical shifts in world demand, there is a large element of historical accident in decision as to where a particular type of production is to be located, especially where there is only a slight intercountry difference in relative endowments of capital and labor. Here we have a new principle of international division of labor, which is to an increasing degree replacing the classical principle of factor proportions (Heckscher-Ohlin theorem) in the present-day world economy.

Regional economic integration, in our context, is a case of trade cooperation among countries at a more or less similar stage of economic development. As the countries are also at a comparable stage of capital accumulation, there cannot be much difference in factor endowments, so far as the relationship between capital and labor is concerned. It is clear, therefore, that the new principle of international specialization is one that should appropriately be applied to our case. One of the characteristics of this principle is lack of stability in the pattern of division of labor. Since competition is based on a variable relationship of technology that can easily be changed, with or without changes in factor combinations, it involves a large risk of rendering the established pattern of specialization extremely unstable. Some degree of mutual agreement is required, therefore, in order to derive economic benefits from specialization. On the other hand, the main basis of technical superiority is economies of scale, rather than advantages of location. Such economies can be realized more or less anywhere, provided the market is broad enough to absorb the increased products. Therefore, agreed specialization is not only a necessary, but also a feasible, proposition. It should not be too difficult so to locate joint industrial ventures as to satisfy the demand of all the countries concerned.[8] Thus, the principle of agreed specialization will be an important and legitimate ingredient in any scheme of regional economic integration among underdeveloped countries.

The task of negotiated, rather than spontaneous, coordination and harmonization of economic policies will be enormously facilitated by the fact that almost all underdeveloped countries have adopted the planning approach to the problem of economic development. Where there are already development plans incorporating more or less long-term policy directives, it is easier than it would otherwise be for countries to confront one another with their plans and to bring about some mutual adjustments when certain inconsistencies are found. The only thing required is that each government should be prepared to submit its programs to common scrutiny by a group of its fellow governments, with a view to undertaking coordinated actions in the mutual interest of all the countries concerned. To illustrate how such a coordination can be worked out in practice, two examples from recent history are briefly examined below.

The first example is related to the recent movements toward coor-

[8] A similar optimism about the prospects of agreed specialization is expressed in Tibor Scitovsky, *Economic Theory and Western European Integration* (London: Allen and Unwin, 1958), p. 51.

dinated economic planning in the Eastern European bloc, where the idea of national planning had been predominant from the beginning.[9] The early history of unsuccessful operation during the initial period of the existence of the Council for Mutual Economic Assistance (COMECON) seems clearly to confirm our view that regional cooperation limited to trade would not go very far if the spheres of production and investment were neglected. The original assumption was that the import requirements and export possibilities generated by independently drawn-up national economic plans would somehow balance out in intrabloc trade conducted under long-term agreements. This assumption did not prove justified. Since 1956 and 1957, therefore, the attention of COMECON was increasingly directed to the working out, by a series of technical committees, of concerted production and investment programs in a considerable number of key industries, with emphasis on metals, chemical power, and fuel. However, the task of "balancing" the sectoral programs in a mutually consistent system of national development plans tied together by a network of long-term trade agreements did not prove to be easy to accomplish at one stroke. To avoid the difficulties of multinational "coordination of many details," resort has increasingly been made to bilateral negotiations and agreements between pairs of members, especially with a view to working out specialized and mutually dovetailed production programs in various key industries.

For most of the East European countries, the objective of rapid industrialization on an inadequate resource base, fragmented by political barriers, was posing an almost insoluble problem, and the only feasible solution was found in an attempt at regional integration based on the principle of "socialist division of labor." The lines of action now contemplated are to promote intraregional cooperation in attacking the perennial basic-materials and energy bottlenecks and to organize industrial specialization along the most economical lines, on the basis of mutual agreement, possibly introducing some measure of intraregional mobility of capital through joint-investment projects. One of the outstanding examples is the development of Poland's coal mining with the help of East German and Czech equipment credits. However, the correction of the distorted and uneconomic industrial structure, created in the past by uncoordinated planning, may prove to be more difficult. During the Seven-Year Plan period, 1958–65, the

[9] The basis for the following brief evaluation is mainly derived from Oleg Hoeffding's instructive paper, "Recent Efforts Towards Coordinated Economic Planning in the Soviet Bloc" (Santa Monica, Calif.: The RAND Corporation, 1959).

trade volume in the COMECON area was planned to increase by more than 60 per cent, while the rate of industrial output expansion was expected to be of the order of 70–80 per cent. Whether the development results in an increased integration of the bloc or not, this is a clear indication that the expansion of intraregional trade is an objective secondary to the major goal of accelerated economic growth.

The second example refers to the experience of the OEEC in its early period, which is more instructive for the underdeveloped regions than are its later operations. The OEEC started as a permanent mechanism to formulate and give effect to a joint recovery program of postwar Europe. New techniques of international cooperation were developed to ensure that the plans and policies of individual countries were compared and subjected to very close mutual scrutiny, that inconsistencies were removed as far as possible, and that conflicting targets harmonized into a "common planning" of Western Europe. In the process of examining the different national programs, certain inconsistencies emerge, especially in the field of trade objectives. It is important to note that, as an OEEC report says, "the 'confrontation' of plans served to pinpoint the main problems and alert the different national authorities so that they could cooperate in their solution." [10] The continued process of policy coordination resulted in the Recovery Program, 1948–52/53, and in the 25 per cent Expansion Program, 1951–56.

There is no doubt that these coordinated programs considerably helped individual countries, as well as the European region as a whole, in quickly overcoming the postwar crisis and in embarking upon the process of accelerated economic growth. Under the regime of planned recovery, even the Western European countries had to resort to major efforts toward coordination and harmonization of development and recovery policies. To some observers, the essence of these operations was, according to the original intention, nothing but "a discriminatory common planning," although the OEEC mechanism was never used to plan for Europe.[11] The experience of OEEC in this period deserves, therefore, a close study by all who are concerned with the problem of economic integration among the underdeveloped countries that have, in general, adopted the planned approach to economic development. In Western Europe, during this

[10] OEEC, A *Decade of Cooperation, Achievements and Perspectives,* Ninth Report (Paris: OEEC, 1958), p. 32.

[11] Thomas Balogh, "Liberalization or Constructive Organization, or: The Hair of the Dog that Bit," *Bulletin of the Oxford University Institute of Statistics,* XIX, No. 1 (February, 1957), 39.

period, there was in the 1949 "plan of action" a serious attempt at coordination of investment, with a view to ensuring that investment projects should be developed rationally, avoiding inconsistencies and excess capacity in particular lines. Although OEEC itself did not coordinate investment programs, the mutual scrutiny of programs improved the basis on which investment decisions were taken and helped to stimulate a rational allocation of resources.

The success of harmonization of economic policies in Western Europe can be seen in the rapid progress that has since been made in the direction of liberalization of trade and payments and other integration moves, such as the Benelux Union, the European Coal and Steel Community and the European Economic Community (EEC). Policy coordination has paved the way to freeing trade and payments within the regional framework. But in somewhat different circumstances, if the start is to be made with an attempt at regional trade liberalization, the movement to a higher form of integration will make inevitable the introduction of some measure of policy coordination and harmonization. From the general point of view of economic integration, it does not make much difference where the beginning is made. The experience in Western Europe, however, indicates that, under the conditions of disequilibriums, measures of policy coordination have to claim precedence over those of trade liberalization. In the present-day underdeveloped areas, this is all the more true, as the existing structure of production and trade does not permit a considerable trade expansion to take place simply as a result of removals of trade hindrances; and the main task of policy is rather to create deliberately new lines of trade.

One of the essential elements of the formulation of optimum economic policies on a regional basis is to make use of the most advanced techniques of economic analysis and economic theory. In order to estimate the future export possibilities to a given region, for instance, we need to estimate the prospective development of national income of a number of countries within the region, together with the prospective movement of demand for particular products. This operation is a simple application of economic projection models. Such a long-term projection may serve as a basis for regional policy recommendations, assisting the national economic policy-makers in bringing their programs and policies into line with those of neighboring countries. Should we call the totality of such regional economic projections a regional plan, as Jan Tinbergen proposes?[12] We are here concerned

[12] Tinbergen, "A Note on Planning in the ECAFE Region," a paper submitted to the first session of the Conference of Asian Economic Planners, New Delhi, September-October, 1961.

not so much with the terminology as the substance. Even in Western Europe today, much of forward-looking economic policy is formulated in terms of planning and projections. In our case, too, regional economic integration is, in essence, a matter of regional planning.

PART TWO

Latin American Free Trade Association

V

MIGUEL S. WIONCZEK

A History of the Montevideo Treaty

Provisions of the Montevideo Treaty

Signed by seven countries (Argentina, Brazil, Chile, Mexico, Paraguay, Peru, and Uruguay) in February, 1960, and subsequently joined by Colombia and Ecuador, the Montevideo Treaty establishing the Latin American Free Trade Association (LAFTA) is, despite its relative brevity, a rather far-reaching legal instrument. It not only embodies provisions for gradual trade liberalization within the area but also establishes a basic, albeit sketchy, structure of a regional economic-integration program.

The treaty's sixty-five articles, grouped under twelve chapters, are followed by a number of explicative protocols and two resolutions (on credits and payments problems and on Bolivia's adherence to LAFTA). Applicable to substantially all the reciprocal trade among the signatories, it provides for gradual elimination—within no more than twelve years from the effective date of the treaty (June 1, 1961)—of all "duties, charges and restrictions as may be applied to imports of goods originating in the territory of any Contracting Party." [1] For purposes of the treaty, "duties and charges" mean customs duties and any other charges of equivalent effect—whether fiscal, monetary, or exchange—that are levied on imports.

The trade liberalization will be achieved through negotiations aimed

[1] All the quotations follow the text of the treaty published in *Multilateral Economic Cooperation in Latin America,* I: *Texts and Documents* (New York: United Nations, 1962; 62. II G. 3), pp. 57–69.

at establishing: (a) national schedules, specifying annual concessions that each country is to grant to the others; and (b) a common schedule, listing the products on which the contracting parties collectively agree to eliminate completely, within a period of not more than twelve years, duties, charges, and other restrictions in connection with commerce within the free-trade area.

Each contracting party is committed to granting annually to other members of LAFTA reductions in duties and charges equivalent to 8 per cent of the weighted average applicable to third countries. The common schedule shall constitute, in terms of the aggregate value of the trade among the member countries, 25 per cent of such trade after the first three years; 50 per cent after six years; 75 per cent after nine years; and "substantially all of such trade" at the end of the twelve-year period. Concessions granted on products that appear only in the national schedules may be withdrawn by negotiation among the contracting parties in return for adequate compensation; however, the inclusion of the products in the common schedule is final and irrevocable.

The method of weighted averages in reducing tariffs aims at endowing the contracting parties with a certain freedom of action in subsequent negotiations, thus assuring a gradual adaptation of the national productive structure to the trade-liberalization program. Thus, any country that wants to protect one of its domestic industries, for a certain transitory period, may grant relatively limited concessions to products of the competitive industries within the area, provided that more substantial concessions will be extended to other products in such a way as to reach the required annual average.

The purpose of the negotiations, Article 10 of the treaty declares, shall be "to expand and diversify trade and to promote the progressive complementarity of the economies of the countries of the area." For that reason, the percentages referred to, with respect to the gradual expansion of the national and common schedules, "shall be calculated on the basis of the average annual value of trade during the three years preceding the year in which each negotiation is effected."

The concept of "reciprocity of concessions" was drastically revised during a series of negotiations prior to the signature of the treaty and does not provide for the balancing of trade of each member country with the rest of the free-trade area. As expressed in Article 13, "the reciprocity . . . refers to the expected growth in the flow of trade between each Contracting Party and the others as a whole, in the products included in the liberalization program and those which may subsequently be added." If, as a result of the concessions granted, significant and persistent disadvantages are created in respect to trade within the area, the member countries will, says the treaty somewhat vaguely, "consider steps to remedy these disadvantages with a view to the adoption of suitable, nonrestrictive measures designed to promote trade at the highest possible levels."

To reduce the possibility of a recurrence of situations in which the trade liberalization would bring "significant and persistent disadvantages" to a member country, "the Contracting Parties shall make every effort—in keeping with the liberalization objectives of the present Treaty—to reconcile their import and export regimes, as well as the treatment they accord to capital goods and services from outside the Area."

The treaty establishes safeguards for two specific situations: (a) in the event that imports of products from the area under the liberalization program "have, or are liable to have, serious repercussions on specific productive activities of vital importance to the national economy"; and (b) in case of a seriously unfavorable over-all balance-of-payments situation. In the first case, the contracting parties may authorize a given country to impose on a temporary basis "non-discriminatory restrictions upon imports included in the liberalization program which originate in the Area." In the second situation, the contracting parties may likewise, and also on a temporary basis, authorize a member country to extend to intraregional trade its measures aimed at correcting a balance-of-payments disequilibrium. Should any such measures remain in effect for more than one year, the LAFTA Conference will immediately initiate negotiations with a view to eliminating the restrictions adopted.

Escape clauses do not apply to the common-schedule goods in the following sense: Although temporary import restrictions can be applied to these products as well, under the specific circumstances described earlier, they are not subject to subsequent renegotiation by a country invoking an escape clause. In other words, no member country can restrict for more than a year its import trade of goods fully liberalized within the area. On the other hand, concessions on products contained in the national schedules may be renegotiated on the basis of adequate compensation, if the result of the concessions is that specific national productive activities are seriously affected by imports of these products.

Following closely the ideas expressed earlier by the ECLA Working Group on the Latin American Common Market, the Montevideo Treaty envisages exceptions in respect to agriculture and a special regime for the less-developed member countries. At present, Ecuador and Paraguay are the only signatories that fall into this category.

With respect to agriculture, the treaty states that the member countries "shall seek to coordinate their agricultural development and agricultural commodity trade policies, with a view to securing the most efficient utilization of their natural resources, raising the standard of living of the rural population, and guaranteeing normal supplies to consumers, without disorganizing the regular productive activities of each Contracting Party." During the period provided for the establishment of the free-trade area, however, the member countries may limit their imports of agricultural commodities to the amount required to meet the deficit in internal production, giving priority "under normal competitive conditions" to products originating in the area and attempting to expand such intraregional commercial exchange.

In order to facilitate economic growth of the less-developed member countries, the treaty offers them: (a) unilateral concessions on the part of any of the other LAFTA members, to be granted "in order to encourage the introduction or expansion of specific productive activities"; (b) implementation of the trade-liberalization program "under more favorable conditions, specially agreed upon"; (c) special nondiscriminatory measures aimed at the protection of domestic industries in the less-developed countries, whether for balance-of-payments reasons or for the purpose of lending transitory encouragement to economic development; and (d) collective arrangements for financial and technical assistance to be extended by LAFTA countries as a whole or by any group of them.

Chapter 3 of the treaty, which contains certain provisions for "expansion of trade and economic complementarity," represents a conscious attempt to create the necessary conditions for a broader regional economic integration in future. It is here that a commitment is made for facilitating "the increasing integration and complementarity" of the economies of the contracting parties through their making "every effort . . . to reconcile their import and export regimes, as well as the treatment they accord to capital, goods, and services from outside the Area."

Furthermore, Article 16 envisages "progressively closer coordination of the corresponding industrialization policies" through agreements "among representatives of the economic sectors concerned." It also recommends negotiation of "mutual agreements on complementarity by industrial sectors." Participation in these agreements must be open to all the contracting parties, but subsequent concessions would not have to be extended automatically to nonparticipating member countries.

Finally, the Montevideo Treaty establishes two organs of the association, a Conference of the Contracting Parties and a Permanent

Executive Committee. Consisting of representatives of the member countries, each of which has one vote, the conference meets at least once a year to adopt decisions on all major matters. The initial agreement provided for conference decisions to be valid during the first two years of LAFTA's existence if affirmative votes were cast by at least two-thirds of the contracting parties and no negative vote was cast by any of the remaining parties; this agreement was subsequently extended for an indefinite period. Thus, in effect, each LAFTA member has a veto power on all substantive questions.[2]

The executive committee is the permanent organ of the association responsible for supervising the implementation of the provisions of the present treaty. It consists of representatives of each member country and a Secretariat headed by an executive secretary and staffed by technical and administrative personnel. ECLA and the Inter-American Economic and Social Council (IA-ECOSOC) of the Organization of American States (OAS) act as technical advisers to the association.

Even a casual student of the treaty must notice a certain disproportion between the provisions of the central part dealing with the establishment of the free-trade area and the broader aims, as defined in the Preamble and in Chapter 3 on "expansion of trade and economic complementarity."

What the treaty establishes in its main operative section, if viewed in static terms, is a fairly modest mechanism calling for a very slow and gradual expansion of intraregional trade with the emphasis on existing trade (limited before the creation of LAFTA to relatively few basic commodities, such as foodstuffs and certain industrial raw materials). Even in this respect, the scope of the treaty is closely circumscribed by a special regime for agriculture, escape clauses, and a possibility of renegotiating the composition of the national schedules in the light of the subsequent experience of the member countries.

On the other hand, the free-trade area is clearly meant to be a major vehicle for regional economic cooperation and integration. This is not only the intent of its sponsors and authors but the interpretation of the majority of Latin American economists as well. The Preamble of the Montevideo Treaty unmistakably links trade expansion among the seven initial signatories and future adherents to LAFTA with the

[2] A paper by the U.N. Economic Commission for Africa (ECA), published in December, 1960, recalled that the OEEC operated successfully for many years on the basis of the unanimity principle and expressed the opinion that "given a basic will in all countries to make the Treaty work, there is no reason why the same principle would not prove satisfactory in the context of Latin America." See *The Significance of Recent Common Market Developments in Latin America* (Addis Ababa, 1960; E/CN. 14/64), p. 69.

basic objective of the whole region: acceleration of economic growth. It declares, *inter alia*, that the participating countries are:

> Persuaded that the expansion of present national markets, through gradual elimination of barriers to intraregional trade, is a prerequisite if the Latin American countries are to accelerate their economic development process in such a way as to ensure a higher level of living for their peoples,
>
> Aware that economic development should be attained through the maximum utilization of available production factors and the more effective coordination of the development programs of the different production sectors in accordance with norms which take due account of the interests of each and all and which make proper compensation, by means of appropriate measures, for the special situation of countries which are at a relatively less advanced stage of economic development. . . .
>
> Determined to persevere in their efforts to establish, gradually and progressively, a Latin American common market and, hence, to continue collaborating with the Latin American Governments as a whole in the work already initiated for this purpose, and
>
> Motivated by the desire to pool their efforts to achieve the progressive complementarity and integration of their national economies on the basis of effective reciprocity of benefits. . . .

Furthermore, as mentioned above, the text of the treaty itself contains very broadly defined provisions for "increasing integration and complementarity" within the area, by reconciling import and export regimes and the treatment accorded to capital, goods, and services from outside the zone, and by industrial complementarity agreements in particular industrial sectors.

Clearly, the Montevideo Treaty, in spirit if not in letter, aims at establishing something potentially larger than a free-trade zone but, at the same time, much less ambitious than a common market. On the other hand, it leaves open, presumably for future negotiation, not only all the basic measures needed to implement regional integration objectives but also certain important issues that are of critical importance to the adequate functioning of a free-trade zone in a region characterized by a very uneven and still incipient over-all economic development. The LAFTA agreement, for example, deals only parenthetically (in one of the annexed resolutions) with the key problem of an intraregional payments system, without which it will be difficult to expand the flow even of existing trade. The treaty is also fairly nebulous with respect to practical measures that would assure the full advantage of participation for countries "at a relatively less advanced stage of economic development."

Previous Quest for Regional Solutions

For the purpose of clarifying this dichotomy of the Treaty, it is necessary to review developments that led to its birth. Economic trends in the underdeveloped parts of the world economy in the post-Korean period, the growing realization of dangers involved in economic stagnation of Latin America, and various futile attempts to forestall this stagnation influenced the final shape of LAFTA no less than did political developments in the outside world and the orthodox approach to the problem of growth on the part of international financial organizations.

Together with Asia and Africa, the southern part of the Western Hemisphere has been facing serious difficulties since the beginning of the 1950's. This occurred after fifteen years of a relatively rapid economic expansion in the region, sparked by the outbreak of World War II and stimulated by the prolonged boom in international commodity markets, which tapered off with the cessation of hostilities in Korea. During the period 1940–55, major Latin American countries (Argentina, Brazil, Chile, Mexico, and, to some extent, Colombia) registered an impressive progress in diversifying and industrializing their economies, notwithstanding the lack of well-thought-out development policies. But the industrial growth in that period followed the pattern of that in Europe and the United States in the nineteenth century, being concentrated mainly on consumer-good industries, which involve relatively modest investment outlays and are easily adaptable to the limited size of individual national markets.[3]

By the beginning of the 1950's, when all the major Latin American countries had completed this first stage of industrialization, they were ready to enter the next one—that of building up a broader industrial base including the manufacture of certain capital goods. Dependent as it was, however, upon increase in the level of investments and imports and upon the availability of sizable markets, such a development was seriously hampered by the fact that the import capacity could expand no further. On the other hand, pressures for continued industrialization were growing, not only because of the "demonstration effect" of the living standards in the fully developed Western economies, but also because of the population explosion, which was a concomitant of the improved health conditions in the area.[4] Although

[3] The size of effective domestic markets varies considerably within the region, covering about 80 per cent of the population in the southernmost republics; perhaps 30–40 per cent in Brazil and Mexico; and much less in the least-developed parts of Latin America: the Caribbean region, Central America, Venezuela, Peru, etc.

[4] The rate of demographic growth in Latin America (2.7 per cent) is the highest

smaller Latin American republics, for very many reasons, did not translate the decade and a half of extremely satisfactory export proceeds into any tangible internal economic growth (and, in that respect, the distance between more- and less-advanced countries increased in Latin America in modern times), they also became deeply affected by the double impact of the population explosion and the "revolution of rising expectations." [5]

The position of the whole region was further aggravated, on the one hand, by the refusal of many of the governments concerned to stop improvising domestic economic policies and to introduce certain basic structural reforms and a more rational allocation of resources; and, on the other, by the insistence of the United States and international organizations upon orthodox economic and financial policies, which under completely different circumstances were responsible in part for the West European postwar recovery. Under these rather depressing conditions, the concept of Latin American economic cooperation was born.

The crystallization of the idea within the ECLA group was preceded by years of work by its economists on adapting the economic-development theory to particular Latin American conditions, numerous studies on interregional trade, and persistent efforts towards integrating a group of five Central American republics.[6] But, until 1956, no one in the region, not even the ECLA group itself, had any clear notion of the need for a Latin American regional economic integration, a common market, or a free-trade zone; although ECLA, through its annual *Economic Studies* and related papers issued since the beginning of the 1950's, had continuously been offering pessimistic views on the future of the region's economy, in the light of external trends, and had occasionally been making well-documented calls for international economic cooperation, i.e., for increased U.S. aid to Latin America.[7] At that time, concrete problems preoccupying Latin

---

in the world, and it is estimated that the region's population will double within the next quarter-century.

[5] For a detailed analysis of the primitive export economies, see Jonathan V. Levin, *The Export Economies: Their Pattern of Development in Historical Perspective* (Cambridge, Mass.: Harvard University Press, 1960), pp. xvi, 347.

[6] Theoretical contributions of the ECLA group to the understanding of the Latin American development process, which started with the setting up of this regional U.N. body in 1948, were dismissed for about a decade by economists and governments of the advanced countries as useless exercises of doubtful scholarly value. ECLA work on Latin American trade within the region and with the rest of the world started in 1952, and the Central American economic integration program was initiated in 1951.

[7] See particularly, ECLA, *International Cooperation in Latin American Develop-*

American experts were those of terms of trade, external aid, and the traditional flow of goods within the region. Since the only commercial exchange worth mentioning, with the exception of the Venezuelan oil trade, was that among the four southernmost countries (Argentina, Brazil, Chile, and Uruguay), the early efforts under ECLA auspices were directed to the solution of the trade problems within the southern zone of Latin America and were not truly regional arrangements.[8]

A concept of regional cooperation based on trade preferences as a *means* toward the acceleration of Latin American economic growth appears for the first time in studies elaborated in 1956–57 for the ECLA Trade Committee, which was created in 1956 and whose initial function was to analyze and help resolve problems related to commercial policy, payments, maritime transport, and the like, primarily of the countries already participating actively in intraregional trade.[9] Even at the Inter-American Economic Conference, held at Buenos Aires in the fall of 1957, when, for the first time, the idea of regional economic cooperation was fully discussed, concepts were far from clarified; and the debate covered proposals on a common market, a free-trade zone, subregional trade grouping, hemispheric integrations, etc. However, aware of the continuous deterioration in the external and internal economic position of Latin America, of the absence of any coherent and promising policy toward the region on the part of the industrial countries, and of the signature, in March, 1957, of the Treaty of Rome, participants in the Buenos Aires gathering voted a resolution stressing "the convenience of establishing gradually and progressively, in a multilateral and competitive manner, a Latin American common market" and recommending that ECLA work out, with the participation of the Organization of American States, specific proposals on the structure and modalities of such a regional agreement.

Within a year of the first meeting of the ECLA Working Group on the Latin American Common Market (Santiago, February, 1958), fundamental principles and basic recommendations of an arrangement covering the whole of the subcontinent were ready for presentation to the ECLA conference at Panama City (May, 1959). Certain

ment Policy (New York: United Nations, 1954; 54. II. G. 2), submitted to the Inter-American Meeting of Ministers of Finance and Economy, held in Petrópolis, Brazil, in late 1954.

8 As a matter of fact, one of these pioneer ECLA studies, published under the title *Study of the Prospects of Inter-Latin American Trade* (New York: United Nations, 1954), carried the subtitle *Southern Zone of the Region.*

9 For details, see Víctor L. Urquidi, *Free Trade and Economic Integration in Latin America* (Berkeley and Los Angeles: University of California Press, 1962), pp. 52 ff.

features of these proposals found their way into the Montevideo Treaty signed nine months later.

An ECLA-Sponsored Common-Market Plan

The general principles to be followed by a Latin American common market should have included the following, according to the ECLA Working Group proposals made in 1959:

1. Membership in the regional market must be open to all Latin American countries.
2. The ultimate aim of the regional market should be the inclusion of all goods produced within the area; this does not mean, however, that the regional market must become effective immediately for all such goods.
3. The less-advanced countries should be accorded special treatment to enable them, through progressive industrialization and the over-all strengthening of their economies, to share fully in the benefits of the regional market.
4. It will be desirable eventually to establish a single customs tariff vis-à-vis the rest of the world.
5. The specialization in industries and other activities, which is one of the objectives of the arrangements, must be the outcome of the free interplay of economic forces.
6. In the interest of greater efficiency, the regional market must have a special system of multilateral payments conducive to maximum inter-Latin American trade reciprocity.
7. Member countries must have the right to impose temporary import restrictions.
8. Participating countries must also have the right to restrict imports of agricultural commodities.
9. Rules of competition should be established to prevent the export trade of a member country from prejudicing the activities of other participants in the regional market.
10. The regional market must be provided with an effective system of credit and technical assistance.
11. An advisory body constituted by the member governments should be set up, as well as a system of arbitration.
12. During the formation of the regional market it would be highly desirable to enlist the active cooperation of Latin American free enterprise.

These basic principles served as guides during the subsequent elaboration of concrete proposals for presentation at the ECLA Trade

Committee conference at Panama City in May, 1959.[10] They provided for the establishment of a free-trade zone, which was to be transformed progressively into a customs union. The Working Group recommended that the reduction of tariffs and other restrictions in intraregional trade be implemented in two stages. During the first stage, to last ten years, a substantial reduction (but not the complete elimination) of restrictions on trade among the participants would take place, with the scope of the reduction depending upon the commodity category. During the second stage, the reduction of tariffs and other trade restrictions within the area would be completed and the common market would be established, according to procedures agreed upon by negotiations to be undertaken before the end of the first stage.

The draft proposed, furthermore, a division of commodities entering intraregional trade into three major groups: (1) primary products; (2) capital goods and other manufactures, the demand for which is growing rapidly; and (3) manufactured consumer goods. During the first stage, tariffs and other restrictions on trade in the first category of goods would be completely eliminated, with certain exceptions of agricultural commodities. Tariffs and other restrictions on goods of the second category would be reduced as much as possible to stimulate intraregional exchange of the products of the so-called dynamic industries. In regard to the last group, trade liberalization would be implemented slowly to provide for internal adjustment in the field of existing industrial activities. Agricultural commodities would be subject to a special regime, in consideration of the relative backwardness of this sector and the need for domestic protection, for some time, of the primitive agricultural subsistence sector, which would otherwise become the first victim of the more efficient producers in certain countries in the area.[11]

10 All pertinent documents can be found in *The Latin American Common Market* (New York: United Nations, 1959; 59. II. G. 4).

11 Commenting on the complicated mechanism proposed by the ECLA Working Group with respect to the distinction to be made between different commodity groups, a U.N. Economic Commission for Africa study, *The Significance of Recent Common Market Developments in Latin America*, stated: "The danger was foreseen that if the establishment of a common market were based too closely upon the models provided in Europe too much attention might be concentrated on competition between Latin American industries and too little upon the expansion of industry in the area as a whole. Any common market set up in an underdeveloped region such as Latin America should, it was felt, be concerned first and foremost with the encouragement of economic development, and only secondarily with promoting competition between existing industries. It was for these reasons that the ECLA Working Group considered that a slower process of transition to free trade should be envisaged for the products of such industries."

Taking into consideration the different degrees of development achieved by the Latin American republics and fearful that the complete dismantling of trade restrictions within the regional market would expose the least-developed countries to dangerous competition from the more-advanced members and foster the transfer of resources to the richer republics, the regime that the ECLA Working Group proposed for relatively less developed countries provided for classification of all participants into three groups, according to their respective margins of import substitution and export potential. Within this framework, the liberalization targets for the less-developed countries would be implemented more slowly than in the case of the more advanced participants; furthermore, special concessions were to be extended to the poorer countries in the form of additional facilities with respect to their intrazonal exports of manufactures as well as primary commodities.

For the purpose of assuring reciprocal-trade benefits to all participants, it was suggested that these benefits be measured by actual trade flows. Whenever a member country achieved an increase in its exports to the area without a corresponding increase in its purchases, whereby its benefits would be greater than its concessions, it would have to speed up its liberalization measures. A country finding itself in an opposite situation and facing balance-of-payments difficulties as a result of trade concessions granted to the regional group would have a right to slow down, temporarily, the implementation of its liberalization commitments.

The ECLA Working Group proposal also stressed the necessity to organize a payments and credit regime to facilitate the multilateral liquidation of transactions between member countries; to foster specific subregional complementarity and specialization agreements by countries "linked by geographical proximity or common economic interests," not to be automatically extended to the other members; to coordinate trade policy with third countries; and to define at an early date criteria to be followed for determination of the origin of goods.

After a thorough discussion of the report, the Trade Committee asked the ECLA Secretariat to set up a group of governmental experts, appointed by the interested member countries, for the purpose of preparing a draft agreement for a Latin American common market. This was to be submitted at an early date to the various governments for approval and eventual adherence. The matter, however, took an unexpected course in view of the parallel preparations of a plan for a subregional free-trade zone, by a group of southernmost countries (Argentina, Brazil, Chile, and Uruguay). The expert body proposed by the ECLA Trade Committee has never met, and the rest of the year 1959 was taken up by intense diplomatic negotiations all over Latin America aimed at reconciling longer-term objectives of the Working Group with concrete short-term measures envisaged by the four southern republics. The Montevideo Treaty was the final result of these activities. Although much more modest and simpler than the structure proposed by ECLA, the treaty incorporated some ECLA provisions and followed closely the main objectives of a regional integration program.

The doctrinal and theoretical justification of all these efforts is contained in a brief study prepared for the Panama City conference by the ECLA Secretariat.[12] It presents the case for Latin American integration through trade liberalization in the following way:

During the period 1945–55, Latin America underwent a process of rapid economic development, which, despite an increasing rate of demographic growth, enabled the region as a whole to maintain product growth per capita at 2.7 per cent annually. The satisfactory economic expansion was possible largely because the purchasing power of exports increased at a similarly high rate. This important factor was helped by the import-substitution process through industrialization, and a considerable inflow of foreign capital enabled the steady increase in the volume of investment required by the rapid rate of economic growth in the region.

Available data suggest that the favorable combination of external factors outlined above is unlikely to be repeated in the forthcoming decades. Conversely, it can be asserted that Latin America has entered upon a new stage of economic development, in which "it will encounter international conditions resembling those it had to face after the world depression rather than those which prevailed in the postwar years." [13] As a consequence, independently of prospects for external financing in the form of economic aid and private-capital inflow, the region must speed up the import-substitution process considerably, if it wants to develop at a rate similar to that registered in the first postwar decade.

It is difficult to believe—continued the ECLA experts—that this substitution process could be achieved with the fragmentation of the Latin American economy into twenty individual national markets. Larger countries need to substitute many capital-goods exports, but their production, involving high investment and economies of scale, is not feasible without access to broader markets. Smaller republics, in

[12] "Influence of the Common Market on Latin American Economic Development," in *The Latin American Common Market* (New York: United Nations, 1959; No. 59. II. G. 4), pp. 51–89.

[13] *Ibid.*, p. 53.

many cases, cannot even enter the first stage of industrialization without unduly high protection. Thus, the integration of individual markets is a prerequisite to the maintenance of the postwar rate of growth or the region's economy, with two other conditions of paramount importance—the liberalization of terms under which international financing is granted to the less-developed areas and the diversification of Latin American trade with the rest of the world.

The intraregional trade in the 1950's was found to be of marginal importance to almost all the republics, but its potentialities were considered very great. According to the ECLA projections, based on realistic assumptions regarding extraregional exports during the period 1960–75, as well as on the behavior of the import coefficients, external resources available to Latin America by 1975 from its exports to the outside world would be able to cover only slightly more than one-half of the total import needs. Consequently, there was room for a tenfold increase in the volume of inter-Latin American trade—at 1955 prices—from some $750 million a year in recent years to about $8.3 billion in 1975. This would mean that Latin America itself would supply almost half its own import requirements in that year. In some industrial commodity groups, the percentage would be even higher.

Fulfillment of these quantitative objectives would depend to a great extent on trade liberalization within the area. This, in turn, was considered urgent because pilot studies on the relationship between prospects for inter-Latin American trade and economic development strongly suggested that, if a common market were established, development would be more rapid than if the market were not organized, "not only in Latin America as a whole, but in each of the individual countries of the region." [14] The program to be implemented would have to take into consideration, of course, the different degrees of productivity characterizing countries at various stages of development and accept certain reasonable disparities in the individual rates of growth.

The Project of Southern Latin American Free-Trade Zone

Representing more than half of the intraregional commercial exchange in the postwar period, trade among the four southern republics (Argentina, Brazil, Chile, and Uruguay) has a long tradition. Although recently certain manufactures have figured in it in limited volume, in the 1950's trade still tended to be concentrated on basic commodities, such as wheat, meat, sugar, fats, and fruits. Argentina and Brazil appeared in this market as suppliers, whereas the other two

[14] *Ibid.*

countries, Chile and Uruguay, had recourse to the two larger neighbors in order to obtain the foodstuffs that their own domestic production supplied either in insufficient quantities or not at all. Because the policies of the respective governments aimed at attaining self-sufficiency in agricultural products, the prospects for steady expansion of this type of exchange have never been too bright; nevertheless, zonal trade played an important role as a source of supply to compensate for domestic deficits. For the same reason, it fluctuated widely from year to year.

For a long time, the trade among the four neighboring countries had been governed by a series of bilateral compensation agreements, involving the selective use of exchange and trade controls. Difficulties encountered in bilateral settlements, which led to the decline of trade in the mid-1950's, and the gradual simplification of cumbersome systems of controls on trade and payments, made it advisable to seek a revision of existing arrangements, expecially since all four republics were anxious to continue their trade contacts in view of serious balance-of-payments deficits with the outside world. After having achieved some uniformity in the bilateral payments arrangements through ECLA's technical assistance, they sought a more permanent solution. The formula chosen was that of a free-trade zone. Since Brazil, Chile, and Uruguay had joined GATT in the early postwar period, it was thought necessary to follow GATT rules in that respect. The decision to set up a limited regional trade arrangement was taken at an ECLA-sponsored expert meeting, in August, 1958; and in the spring of the following year, a few weeks before the ECLA conference in Panama City, which was to consider its Working Group's recommendations concerning a Latin American Common Market, the four republics finished drawing up a detailed draft of their treaty.

This document, submitted for information at the Panama Conference, stressed the urgency to expand trade among the sponsoring republics and expressed the hope that the proposed arrangement would represent a contribution to the subsequent broader regional trade integration. It indicated the willingness of the authors to negotiate a regional common-market agreement as soon as details were worked out and, in the meantime, invited other countries to join the proposed free-trade zone to be established within a ten-year period. The draft envisaged trade liberalization by means of annual 8 per cent tariff reductions for the interzonal exchange of goods, so that after the first three years, 25 per cent of this trade would be totally freed; 50 per cent after six years; 75 per cent after nine years; and not less than 80 per cent at the end of the period. It provided also for standardization of export and import regimes with respect to third countries and the

Latin America: Projection of Sources of Supply of Selected Products, 1975

Commodity	Unit	Total Demand	Source of Supply		Intraregional Supplies as Percentage of Total
			Intraregional	Extraregional	
Machinery and equipment	millions of dollars	9.122	5.435	3.687	60
Passenger cars		1.790	1.308	482	73
Steel and semimanufactured steel products	thousands of tons	37.600	32.300	5.300	86
Copper and semimanufactured copper products	thousands of tons	540	443	97	82
Petroleum and derivatives	millions of dollars	201	193	8	96
Chemicals and chemical products	millions of dollars	8.155	7.265	890	89
Paper and paperboard	millions of dollars	1.545	1.331	214	86
Cotton yarn and textiles	thousands of tons	1.655	1.655	...	100
Staple agricultural commodities	millions of dollars	13.500	13.280	220	98

Source: ECLA, "Influence of the Common Market on Latin American Economic Development," in *The Latin American Common Market* (New York: United Nations, 1959; 59. II. G. 4), p. 59.

application of the most-favored-nation clause to all members of the zone. Escape clauses permitted member countries to impose quantitative restrictions on products whose domestic production was of major importance for the national economy or subject to special governmental support measures. Although no specific and additional concessions were offered to the less-developed countries, the draft foresaw the possibility of temporary arrangements to aid them in fostering certain productive activities. Payments within the zone were to be subject to the multilateral settlements system elaborated at the end of 1958 by a meeting of experts from Latin American central banks.

The simultaneous appearance of two concrete, but competitive, proposals forced upon ECLA and the Latin American governments the necessity to define speedily their respective positions and the course to be followed. The debates at the Panama City ECLA meeting made it clear that the southern project had one basic advantage, which represented also a direct threat to the ECLA-sponsored plans. The southern free-trade zone would have been established *before* the common market. Would the latter be able to absorb a more limited subregional arrangement in time? Should the remaining republics establish a similar subregional arrangement in the northern part of Latin America and try to merge it with the southern group later on? Would not a temporary division of the region into two separate groupings create conditions conducive to a permanent split, similar to that taking place in Western Europe, but much more dangerous? Was there any way to reconcile the two projects? These were the questions facing the ECLA Secretariat and leading Latin American economists and policy-makers during the summer of 1959.

The fact that the southern project left adherence to the free-trade zone open to other Latin American republics seemed to offer the way out. In the next stage, the four-country project was extended somewhat by inviting Bolivia, Paraguay, and Peru, neighbors of the original group, to take part in the negotiations. Even then, however, the composition of the expanded group strongly suggested a subregional arrangement. Willing to prove that this was not the case, the southernmost republics asked Mexico and Venezuela to send observers to a formal diplomatic conference, convoked in September, 1959, at Montevideo, for the purpose of preparing a final draft of a free-trade zone treaty. Both countries accepted willingly; and Mexico's President, Adolfo López Mateos, declared during his South American tour, in the closing weeks of 1959, that his country would accede to participation in the free-trade zone together with its original sponsors. By that time, the treaty draft had been expanded by inclusion of various important features of the plan that originated with the ECLA Working

Group on the Latin American Common Market. It embodied detailed provisions on the treatment to be granted to the less-advanced countries, its reciprocity and escape clauses had been somewhat clarified and redefined, and the chapter on expansion of trade and economic complementarity was considerably strengthened. The final draft of the treaty, however, followed with very few changes the main operative parts of the southern project governing the mechanism of the free-trade zone, the timing of trade liberalization, and similar decisive points. Because of the vehement opposition of the International Monetary Fund, the solution of the payments problem was left in abeyance.

The negotiators agreed that adherence to the treaty would be open to all republics in the region and that, on the expiration of the twelve-year term, the member countries would "initiate the necessary collective negotiations with a view to fulfilling more effectively the purposes of the Treaty and, if desirable, to adapting it to a new stage of economic integration." Thus, the final formula accepted by all seven sponsors has all the characteristics of a compromise. Some say that its most important virtue consists of avoiding a political and economic split in Latin America on the occasion of the first serious attempt to create conditions for long-term regional economic cooperation.

GATT and the International Monetary Fund: Opposite Attitudes

The attitude of the General Agreement on Tariffs and Trade toward Latin American integration efforts and that of the International Monetary Fund were, until the fall of 1963, diametrically opposed. The former, on many occasions, demonstrated an understanding of the objectives of the program and a willingness to cooperate, whereas the latter took a position of doctrinal and vehement insistence on the "sacred rules" of international trade and finance.[15]

Four out of the seven original participants in LAFTA had long been GATT members, and Argentina had been considering such a step since 1958. This explains why care was taken during the negotiations of the Montevideo Treaty to approximate it, as far as possible,

[15] "The conditions imposed on the underdeveloped countries by the IMF, seen through the eyes of the outside observer, have run too much in the tradition of the banker and too little in the tradition of the entrepreneur. They have too easily subordinated the objectives of growth to those of stability. There are times, of course, when stability of some sort is a prerequisite to growth. But there are times, too, when growth is the instrument through which balance is eventually achieved," wrote a Harvard scholar, Raymond Vernon, in "A Trade Policy for the 1960's," *Foreign Affairs*, XXXIX, No. 3 (April, 1961), 466.

to GATT rules concerning regional trade arrangements. It was officially known that, for one principal reason, the GATT Secretariat had not been ready to give favorable consideration to projects that emanated in 1958–59 from the ECLA Working Group: These proposals were envisaging a two-stage approach to the trade-liberalization program and provided a detailed definition of the mechanism for the implementation of the first ten-year stage only. GATT argued that this might result in the establishment of a preferential system, without any assurance that this arrangement would eventually become a free-trade zone. GATT's objections to the early versions of the project drafted by the four southern countries were less fundamental in nature; and subsequent contacts and discussions between the Latin American members of the organization and the GATT Secretariat were most amicable, since GATT was doing its utmost to make allowances for the region's special difficulties in the field of trade and economic growth.

GATT was kept informed at all times regarding the progress of regional negotiations, and an early draft of the treaty, providing for a free-trade zone, was submitted for information by Brazil, Chile, Peru, and Uruguay at the fifteenth session of the contracting parties of GATT, held in Tokyo in the fall of 1959. In 1960, in response to the official presentation of the Montevideo Treaty to GATT, the latter's Secretariat prepared a long questionnaire to be completed by LAFTA members. Upon its return, a GATT working group was set up for the purpose of analyzing the relative compatibility between the two legal instruments. Following precedents established in the case of the Treaty of Rome and the Stockholm Convention, the working group recommended that note be taken of the Latin American arrangement and of the willingness of its participants to follow GATT rules governing free-trade zones and customs unions; however, final judgment as to whether the treaty was fully compatible with Article 24 of GATT was to be held in abeyance, subject to further study. This ruling, GATT declared, "should not prevent the signatories of the Montevideo Treaty from proceeding with the implementation of the Treaty after its ratification."

That this ruling should not be construed as reflecting a hostile or indifferent attitude toward LAFTA was confirmed, in very clear terms, by the then Assistant Secretary of GATT, Jean Royer, at the ECLA conference held in Santiago in May, 1961. Royer declared that:

> We are gratified at the entry into effect of the Montevideo Treaty, which responds to the twofold endeavor to found Latin America's eco-

nomic development on a broader base without affecting its trade with the industrial countries. Thanks to close cooperation between the ECLA and GATT secretariats, it has been possible to eliminate the numerous obstacles that had arisen, remedy situations that at times were too strict, and facilitate recognition by the contracting parties to the General Agreement, of the treaty signatories' right to execute the Latin American integration project, while simultaneously maintaining the benefits of the most-favored-nation clause for their exports. The contracting parties are particularly grateful to the Montevideo Treaty signatories for their efforts to adapt their association to GATT rules with regard to the establishment of free-trade zones. GATT is not motivated by a doctrinaire spirit when stating its conviction that the association has taken on the form of a free-trade zone and not that of a preferential agreement. . . .[16]

Efforts to stimulate interregional trade through multilateral handling of payments predate the crystallization of the idea of Latin American economic integration. In late 1956, the ECLA Trade Committee recommended that monetary authorities in the region seek a way to establish gradually a multilateral payments system that would take the place of existing bilateral agreements and facilitate commercial transactions between the nonconvertible-currency republics of the south and the northern republics belonging to the dollar zone. A standard bilateral agreement, worked out by a group of eight South American central banks in the middle of 1957 under ECLA auspices, and adopted by Argentina, Bolivia, Chile, and Uruguay, subsequently brought some measure of uniformity into the payments situation in the region, but was considered by all the parties concerned only as a preliminary and interim solution.

At the end of 1958, another central-bank conference was held, in Rio de Janeiro, to study ECLA proposals for a multilateral settlements system, and, eventually, for the establishment of a Latin American payments union. The success of any action in the field of regional economic cooperation, declared the ECLA paper submitted to that meeting,[17] "will depend largely on effective collaboration in two interdependent and, for the purpose at issue, indivisible fields: payments and trade policy." In view of the absence of convertibility in most of Latin America, plus the general shortage of hard currencies

[16] Translated from the Spanish text distributed by ECLA Secretariat at the third conference of the ECLA Trade Committee on May 8, 1961. *Documento informativo*, No. 3, p. 3.

[17] ECLA Trade Committee, *Payments in Inter-Latin American Trade*, mimeographed paper submitted to the second session of the Central Banks Working Group, Rio de Janeiro, November 14–December 4, 1958, p. 3.

and wide fluctuations in intraregional transactions, ECLA supported the early creation of a mechanism for the multilateral compensation of bilateral balances in the area, to be ultimately replaced by a payments union. The first-stage agreement would provide for the compensation of outstanding balances originating from bilateral trade transactions, under a system similar to that which was put into effect in Western Europe, between 1947 and 1950, to prepare the way for the European Payments Union. The Latin American payments union proper was to have been established after the interim arrangement had been in operation for a few years, provided that trade between members under the stimulus of increasing liberalization had become substantially free from restrictions and discrimination.

ECLA insisted that it was not premature to conduct a preliminary examination of the feasibility of completely multilateral regional operations, in view of emerging plans for the formation of a regional market: "If . . . the regional market is to be open to all Latin American countries, one *sine qua non* of its operation will be the existence of a multilateral payments regime under which the participants would incur no exchange risks. Hence, while still allowing prudent advances to be made towards the establishment of a common market, an analysis of the essential aspects of the multilateral payments regime proper will help to clarify certain problems which must gradually be solved before the regional market is established." [18]

Concrete proposals for setting up a regional system for multilateral settlements of bilateral trade balances (along the lines of that still operating today, under the management of the U.N. Economic Commission for Europe, and covering bilateral transactions between Western and Eastern European countries) were submitted in the name of a group of the republics to the ECLA Trade Committee conference at Panama City, with the understanding that such an arrangement would be followed by the creation of a payments union in some more distant future. The plan was rejected *in toto* by the IMF representatives, who considered it completely superfluous and unacceptable, in view of the recent progress in the area towards convertibility and liberalization of trade and payments. The five main objections raised by IMF were as follows:

1. Latin American bilateral trade was much smaller than that which took place in Europe immediately after the end of the war.

2. The danger that the suspension of bilateral trade would lead to large-scale unemployment, as was the case in postwar Europe, did not exist in the case of Latin America.

3. Multilateral settlements were even less necessary in view of the

[18] *Ibid.*, p. 11.

recent return to convertibility in Argentina, Bolivia, Chile, Colombia, Paraguay, and Peru.

4. Bilateral payments agreements in force in the region could be easily substituted by direct arrangements between central banks and other financial agencies.

5. Establishment of a payments union would easily result in the perpetuation of bilateralism "even though that might not be the intention of its authors."

IMF's negative attitude to any solution of payments problems in the region other than settlement in freely convertible currencies became even more vehement at the next meeting of the central banks, in February, 1960, when a final attempt was made by the sponsoring countries and ECLA to incorporate measures providing for the solution of regional payments problems into the free-trade-zone treaty. All but one of the participants in that conference,[19] which was held in Montevideo, were willing to support the revised and expanded ECLA proposals; but IMF stood fast in defense of its position that the proposed Latin American free-trade area must be accompanied not by a region-wide compensation system, with automatic or semi-automatic credits, but by a system of settlements in freely convertible currencies.[20] IMF was perfectly aware of its strength in dealing with the sponsors of the integration program, as the majority were in the midst of stabilization programs, sponsored and financed by the Fund. Under these circumstances, any "rebellion" against IMF conditions was clearly impossible. The issue was shelved by agreeing on the formula that the problems involved required further study. No studies were initiated afterward, however, notwithstanding the fact that, in the meantime, the Montevideo Treaty had been signed and ratified and was to become effective as of June 1, 1961. There was actually no need for them, since IMF's position continued without the slightest change, as witnessed by the following brief reference to LAFTA made by the IMF representative at the ECLA conference held in May, 1961, at Santiago: "With respect to the payments difficulties which the regional markets may create, I am convinced that as long as the countries persevere in their stabilization efforts and in the defense of the convertibility and stability of their currencies, the Fund will give

[19] Peru, a country with trade surpluses with the rest of Latin America until 1962.

[20] In their search for compromise, ECLA experts proposed as an alternative an arrangement, defined as an a posteriori system of credits, providing for settlement of current operations in dollars and for the deposit in the payments agency, at certain intervals, of a part of the trade surpluses of creditor nations. These funds, in turn, would be placed at the disposal of the debtor countries in the form of loans.

sympathetic consideration to the possibilities of financial aid aimed at eliminating these difficulties." [21]

It was not until October, 1963, at the seventh meeting of Technicians of the Central Banks of the American Continent, in Rio de Janeiro, that IMF changed its attitude. During the plenary session of that conference, F. A. G. Keesing, an IMF official, declared on behalf of the Fund that it was willing to study the possibility of establishing a regional payments mechanism, provided that the system was a voluntary one from the standpoint of both participation and radius of operations, and with the further condition that automatic credits be eschewed.[22]

It is fairly easy to refute the IMF line of reasoning, presented at the Panama meeting in 1959 and defended during the following years:

1. A comparison of the magnitude of bilateral trade in Europe in the late 1940's with current inter-Latin American trade made little sense, if one assumed that the purpose of a regional free-trade zone was to stimulate such trade to the utmost.

2. Mentioning the absence of the danger of unemployment in the event of the suspension of bilateral trade in the area must have been based on the curious belief that Latin American economies function on the basis of full use of their resources.

3. It was assumed, erroneously, that convertibility achieved in past years in certain Latin American countries was the same, in substance, as convertibility of the dollar or the Deutsche Mark.

4. The direct arrangements proposed were based on the availability of large foreign-exchange reserves in individual countries and only slight fluctuations in intraregional trade, both of which assumptions were readily contradicted by IMF statistics themselves.

5. If the establishment of a payments union would lead to the perpetuation of bilateralism, then the EPU was an unfortunate and retrogressive incident in Europe's progress toward freedom of trade and convertibility.

These and other counterarguments were used by Latin American experts and outside observers as well.[23] The paper of the U.N. Eco-

[21] Translation from the Spanish text of a speech made at the third session of the ECLA Trade Committee in Santiago on May 9, 1961, by the IMF representative, Jorge del Canto. *Documento informativo*, No. 14, p. 3.

[22] See "Declaración del F.M.I. en la Reunión de Río de Janeiro," reproduced in CEMLA, *Problemas de pagos en América Latina* (Mexico City, 1964), pp. 203–6.

[23] See Sidney S. Dell, *Problemas de un mercado común en América Latina* (Mexico City: CEMLA, 1959), especially chap. vi, "Sistemas de pagos—Problemas generales," pp. 133–52; and U.N. Economic Commission for Africa, *op. cit.*, pp. 75–82.

nomic Commission for Africa (ECA) pointed out, for example, that the need for incorporation of a multilateral payments system into the free-trade-zone project in Latin America stemmed from one extremely important fact, which the IMF has never been able to deny: the persistent shortage of hard currencies in the entire region. The over-all liquidity position of Latin America continued to weaken throughout the 1950's, measured both in terms of the relative participation of the twenty republics in world gold and foreign-exchange reserves and in terms of the relationship between reserves and imports.[24]

The improvement in that respect, in the late 1950's, for which IMF took full credit, was of a purely statistical nature, since it failed to take into account the tremendous increase in the external debt of the major Latin American countries, a phenomenon that, in the long run, completely nullified the moderate improvement in the reserve position of certain of the republics. The "dollar glut," which took the place of the "dollar shortage" in the industrial part of the world economy at the beginning of the present decade, did not, unfortunately, become any major headache for Latin Americans. Quite the contrary, the region is worse off today with respect to the availability of hard currencies than it has been at any other time in the postwar period. Were this not the case, there would be no point in the U.S. Government's organizing and expanding emergency aid programs to Latin America or, indeed, in the proud assertion of the Fund itself to the effect that its financial assistance to the region was growing. If Latin America were not continuously facing balance-of-payments crises of varying intensity, there would be no reason for individual republics to condition their return to convertibility to acceptance by the Fund of measures in the field of exchange and trade restrictions, which, in many cases, rendered the convertibility announcements quite meaningless.[25]

The U.N. Economic Commission for Africa study previously cited leaves no doubt with respect to the impact of IMF attitudes on the future of the Latin American integration program:

> If the Latin American countries all had very large reserves of gold and foreign exchange, they could, perhaps, afford to face the prospect of temporary balance-of-payments deficits arising from liberalization of imports without undue concern. For their gold and foreign exchange would provide them with the margin of time needed for corrective measures deal-

[24] For details, see *Aspectos monetarios de las economías latinoamericanas, 1959* (Mexico City: CEMLA, 1960), pp. 86–89.

[25] Every conceivable rationalization has been applied to these measures, so that the IMF Articles of Agreement appeared to be fulfilled to the letter.

ing with the basic causes of such deficits to take effect. . . . It therefore appears that for many countries in Latin America, the reduction of trade restrictions may be incompatible with full payments in convertible currencies. If they are to pay wholly in dollars for their imports from other countries in the area, they may find themselves compelled to maintain restrictions on trade with one another not less severe than the restrictions which they employ in trade with the rest of the world. In other words, given the existing foreign-exchange position in Latin America, the conduct of intra-regional payments on the basis of complete settlement in gold and dollars would defeat the whole purpose of a common market by making the liberalization of trade impossible, or at least very difficult [p. 76].

However, it would be a mistake to assume that the lack of progress in solving the Latin American payments problem was attributable exclusively to the attitude of the International Monetary Fund. Actually, various factors were involved. In the first place, since the Montevideo Treaty was the outcome of attempts to find a common denominator among the very divergent positions of the contracting parties, the treaty itself did not offer any concrete recommendations regarding action that member-country governments should take in the monetary and financial field. Moreover, proposed solutions to regional payments problems—for many years the target of IMF attacks—were drawn up prior to the signing of the Montevideo Treaty and proceeded on the assumption that the regional agreement would be much more ambitious than the one eventually embodied in the treaty. Finally, the attention of most of the monetary authorities in the area was then, and continues to be, taken up with major and pressing short-term problems.

It is quite possible that these factors provide a better explanation of the lack of progress in the field of monetary and financial cooperation within LAFTA than does the rather oversimplified argument that the stumbling block in the path of a solution to the payments problem is basically "the desire to refrain from following a line that might be interpreted as indicative of disagreement with international commitments concerning monetary policy." [26] This, however, does not mean that the International Monetary Fund's position has not had a negative effect on the possibilities for monetary and financial cooperation among LAFTA members during the initial years of operation of the Montevideo Treaty.

[26] See *Realizaciones y perspectivas en el proceso de mercado regional* (Mar del Plata: CEPAL, April 18, 1963; E/CN. 12/668), p. 86.

The United States and Latin American Integration Efforts

In contrast to the wholehearted support extended since the inception of the Marshall Plan to the concept of European economic cooperation and the active assistance given later to the European Economic Community, the U.S. attitude toward Latin American integration efforts during the years preceding the advent of the Kennedy Administration was ambivalent, to say the least.

> To date [one of the Democratic leaders in the U.S. Senate, Mike Mansfield, wrote a few weeks before the signature of the Montevideo Treaty] the Administration has taken the view that a common market in this hemisphere is a Latin American affair. While the idea has not been discouraged, little has been done to encourage it. . . . The present concern of Latin America with the common market concept affords the U.S. one more opportunity to end the downward spiral in inter-American relations. What is needed is a policy initiative which is at once dynamic, understanding and creative. Unless we act promptly in displaying that initiative we shall leave the impression, as we have done so often in the last few years, that we are little concerned with Latin America's interests unless we are prodded and shocked. Should that impression once again take hold in connection with the American common market concept, any subsequent positive action on our part will be stripped of much of its value.[27]

It is true that, at various inter-American meetings held between 1958 and 1960, the United States joined the Latin American countries in passing a number of resolutions expressing support, in general terms, of the idea of regional trade cooperation. But these resolutions and declarations always spoke of the advisability of establishing regional *common markets* and not the Latin American common market as proposed by ECLA. An excerpt from the final official communiqué from the Inter-American Conference of Foreign Ministers, held at Washington, D.C., in September, 1958, gives an example of a formula then acceptable to the United States. It declared that:

> It would be well for the governments directly concerned and the international organizations directly interested, chiefly the Organization of American States, the Economic Commission for Latin America and the Organization of Central American States, to expedite their studies and concrete measures directed towards the establishment of *regional markets in Central and South America*.[28]

[27] Senator Mike Mansfield, "Common Market for Latin America," *The New Leader*, January 25, 1960, p. 9.

[28] Quoted from the full text published in *The New York Times*, September 25, 1958, p. 7 (italics added). The approach, consisting of putting the Central Ameri-

Although Harold M. Randall, the U.S. delegate to the ECLA conference in Panama in 1959, declared that "we are not trying to decide whether the Latin American countries prefer one or more common markets," and "any alternative can be beneficial so long as the market or markets are established on a competitive basis," the impression prevailed for a long time all over Latin America that, since it was doing nothing to encourage Latin American integration on a truly regional scale and, as a rule, used the term "common markets," the United States was not interested, until very recently, in anything exceeding loosely linked subregional trade groupings in the area.

Official U.S. documents and the writings of leading U.S. experts in hemispheric affairs abound in circumstantial evidence that, until the middle of 1960, the United States looked upon integration efforts with a mixture of ideological disapproval and deep distrust. This attitude had some roots in the basic clash of interests ably described in a paper prepared for the U.S. Senate Committee on Foreign Relations by a private research institution, the National Planning Association (NPA), and released in Washington in the summer of 1960. The study referred, in the following terms, to the general framework of U.S.–Latin American economic relations in the postwar period:

> The intensity of their [Latin America's] desire for development, diversification, and higher standards of living, in the face of changing market conditions abroad and instability in terms of trade, has created issues involving fundamental principles of trade and finance which do not have the same historical significance and the same practical implications for underdeveloped countries that they have for industrialized countries. . . .
>
> The basic issues between the United States and the countries of Latin America which began to project themselves during the early period of postwar readjustment to peacetime hopes and plans centered in the field of economic and financial policy. These precluded agreements on economic principles at Bogotá in 1948 and again at Buenos Aires in 1957 and consistently erected obstacles toward finding solutions to the economic problems of the hemisphere.[29]

---

can Common Market and LAFTA on the same level and discussing their respective advantages and disadvantages in comparative terms, still persists in the United States. It gives origin to a feeling of frustration among the LAFTA supporters who make a clear distinction between the regional character of the free-trade area and the subregional objectives of the Central American scheme. It is generally assumed in Latin America that, with the progress of LAFTA, Central American republics will one day join it as a group.

[29] U.S. Senate, *United States–Latin American Relations* (Washington, D.C.: Government Printing Office, 1960), p. 525. A compilation of studies prepared under the direction of the Sub-Committee on American Republic Affairs of the Committee on Foreign Relations of the U.S. Senate.

The lack of interest was also closely related to U.S. attitudes toward ECLA, which, for many years, was looked upon by many in the United States as an intruder into hemispheric affairs, a defender of dangerous statist tendencies, and a competitor of the Organization of American States.[30] During the conservative Republican Administration in Washington, proposals coming from, or sponsored by, ECLA were considered, by virtue of that very fact, a continuous incitement to Latin American countries to "gang up" against the United States in order to force economic and other concessions, which the latter was not willing to grant to the republics separately. These attitudes were further strengthened by the thinly disguised fear of influential U.S. foreign-trade interests that expansion of intraregional trade in Latin America would be detrimental to U.S. exporters. The absence of interest in Latin American economic-development problems among U.S. economists and political scientists did not help to dispel this fear.[31]

Thus, the statement to the effect that "U.S. policy toward the formation of Latin American regional markets has been favorable provided the proposals meet certain standards," calls for a detailed definition and analysis of such conditions.[32] They were presented in Washington in February, 1959, by U.S. representatives in a working group of the Committee of Twenty-one, an *ad hoc* organ of the Organization of American States, in the following general terms:

1. Regional market arrangements should aim at trade creation and increased productivity through broadening opportunities for competitive trade and should not simply be trade-diverting. This means that the arrangements should provide for trade liberalization in all commodities—not just those in which members are competitive with nonmembers—and that duties and other restrictions applied by members of a regional market to nonmembers should not be higher or more restrictive after the formation of the market than before.

2. The arrangement should provide a definite schedule for the gradual elimination of virtually all barriers to intraregional trade, and this process should be completed within a reasonable period of time. The U.S. Government does not favor an arrangement that provides simply for regional preferences, with little more than a vague hope of eventually creating a free-trading regime.

[30] *Ibid.*, pp. 525–35. This section deals with U.S. policies in international organizations concerned with Latin America.

[31] This writer is not aware of any serious U.S. article or discussion of Latin American economic-integration problems before the middle of 1960, the date on which the Council on Foreign Relations set up a study group to analyze the Montevideo Treaty.

[32] *United States–Latin American Relations*, p. 467.

3. The arrangement should be in accordance with the principles of GATT (Article 24) for the creation of a free-trade area or customs union, and should be submitted to GATT for approval. This is believed to be important, not only because the GATT rules are in accordance with U.S. views with respect to regional trading arrangements, but also because agreements of this kind must be reconciled with the General Agreement, in order that the effectiveness of GATT and the orderly system of world trade established under it may be preserved. If the Latin American countries were to set up their own arrangements without GATT's blessing, it is feared that the whole GATT machinery might break down as a consequence of a proliferation of special regional preference systems all over the world. Latin American members of GATT include Brazil, Chile, Cuba, Dominican Republic, Haiti, Nicaragua, Peru, and Uruguay. It is believed that inclusion of the regional trade organization in GATT would also facilitate negotiations for a gradual reduction of barriers with nonmembers on a reciprocal basis. This is in accordance with the principle that regional arrangements should represent a step in the direction of world-wide trade liberalization.

4. Regional trade arrangements should aim at increasing the degree of competition within the area. This means not only that all, or virtually all, commodities should be freed from restrictions on interregional trade but that exclusive monopolistic privileges should not be given to particular industries and that there should be no control agreements preventing competition. It is believed not only that intraregional competition will increase productivity and investment within the area but that these conditions will also help to induce private foreign investment.

5. Regional arrangements should provide for free trade in commodities as well as for the free flow of labor and capital in response to economic forces. Labor and capital should be free to move to places where they will be most productive. In this way, it will be possible to achieve the maximum benefits from economic integration.

6. Any regional market arrangement should provide for the financing of trade with convertible currencies. Neither bilateral payments agreements nor a restrictive regional payments regime, which involves discrimination against nonmembers, is justified.

The statement summarized above and representing the only detailed and specific definitions of the U.S. position until the birth of the Alliance for Progress, embodied all the "fundamental principles of trade and finance" applied, albeit only in theory, to relations among economically advanced countries. It did not contain a trace of willingness to consider the special problems facing the underdeveloped part of the world. As a result, in many instances, it raised nonexisting issues or proposed solutions for real issues, which could not be enforced because of the nature of the development process in Latin America.

At the beginning of the statement, emphasis was put on "trade creation" rather than "trade diversion," as though Latin America with its lopsided and underdeveloped production structure could really afford to consider such an alternative. It is extremely difficult to envisage any trade diversion in the case of Latin American economic integration. Given the idle resources (land, raw materials, and labor) in all LAFTA member countries, the expansion of intraregional trade could hardly have a negative effect on the area's capability for exporting its traditional primary goods to the rest of the world. Progressive industrialization should, at the same time, offer the area the possibility of creating new exports, not only to other members of the Montevideo Treaty, but to the industrial sector of the world economy. Consequently, the over-all import capacity of the group would increase in the long run, and the presence of suppressed demand of tremendous magnitude, within the area, would make it possible to go on expanding the over-all import trade. Thus, the issue of trade creation versus trade diversion would appear to be completely spurious within the frame of reference of a trade arrangement involving a group of underdeveloped countries in Latin America.

For the purpose of trade creation and increasing productivity through broadening opportunities for competitive trade, arrangements should be made for trade liberalization in *all* commodities, according to the U.S. position. In the first place, not even the European Common Market fulfills this condition; and, in the second, both the very low mobility of resources and the scarcity of capital and technology characteristic of the less-developed countries preclude the acceptance of such a condition. Following this advice would play havoc with the industrial structures, always precarious, that were created before the establishment of the regional trade grouping. Furthermore, no democratic government in Latin America or elsewhere could embark on such an operation without risking a political crisis at the very least, or, in less favorable circumstances, overthrow by force.

The next assertion—that if a regional trade arrangement was not completely in accordance with the principles of GATT, "the whole machinery might break down as a consequence of a proliferation of special regional preference systems all over the world"—may be answered easily with two counterarguments: (1) It might well be that GATT itself needed overhauling, if regional trade groupings of countries engaged in a development effort did not fit into it. (2) Since the regional trade arrangements should, in the long run, bring about an expansion of world trade and welfare, they should not be considered as negatively affecting "the orderly system of world trade," unless this last expression was to be construed as meaning the preservation of the present division between industrial-goods exporters and primary-goods producers.

As far as increasing the degree of competition within the area is concerned, one would assume and hope that this would be the case in any regional trade arrangement involving the less-developed countries. The sheer increase in the size of the over-all market would make possible the functioning of more than one optimum-size plant in a number of industries. The limited size of individual markets in Latin America is in itself very conducive to monopolistic practices. On the other hand, there is little proof, at least in this part of the world, that increase in competition is a factor that induces private foreign investment. Monopolistic tendencies seem to characterize any large dynamic enterprise, whatever the nationality of its owners or executives.

No regional arrangement in Latin America could possibly provide for the free flow of labor and capital, now or in the foreseeable future, "in response to economic forces." All the Latin American republics are presently labor-surplus areas, in terms of open or disguised unemployment, and the population explosion is the region's most serious worry. A free movement of capital within the area would clearly lead to concentration of industrial growth in the more-advanced zones, which are better endowed from the standpoint of infrastructure, thus accentuating intraregional differences in development levels. On the contrary, the scarcity of capital resources and the needs of the least-developed Latin American republics make it necessary to devise special mechanisms for directing new capital resources of domestic and external origin into certain activities and areas.

Finally, the U.S. position that "neither bilateral payments agreements nor a restrictive regional payments regime, which involves discrimination against non-members, is justified," amounted in practice to rejection of payments and credit arrangements of any type. It was divorced from Latin American reality and represented a very serious obstacle to all present integration programs.

The conditioning of the U.S. support for Latin American *common markets* upon the fulfillment of specific standards was accompanied occasionally by private proposals asking for a "hemispheric common market" including the United States and even Canada. The lack of response and interest in Latin America to these ideas, as expressed by Nelson Rockefeller among others, was often taken as another proof that Latin American projects were, at least in political terms, aiming at weakening U.S. links with the rest of the continent.[33]

Sometime during the year 1960, under the impact of the Cuban events and growing signs of anti-American feeling in other parts of Latin America, the United States started reappraising its postwar economic policy toward the region. Within that over-all reappraisal, which became evident in the months preceding the inauguration of the Kennedy Administration, U.S. scholars made some initial effort to analyze the doctrinal premises of integration plans for the purpose of finding out why Latin Americans attach so much importance to these programs and tend to reject summarily the standards set by the United States.

In some instances, these scattered U.S. voices showed a willingness to admit that, contrary to general belief, Latin America and other underdeveloped regions press for regional economic integration, not for the purpose of "ganging up" against the United States or because of immaturity or a perverse compulsion to violate the sacred rules of free trade, but because of necessity.

> All of the underdeveloped nations [wrote one of the late President Kennedy's first advisers on Latin American problems] are rightly preoccupied with economic development as one of their major objectives. All want to diversify their economies, to improve agricultural productivity and to industrialize. . . . It can be predicted with some assurance that most or all of these countries will seek to promote industrialization through protection of domestic industry from foreign competition. . . . In these circumstances the realistic question is whether such protection

[33] The National Planning Association paper previously quoted approved of Western Hemisphere integration proposals, declaring that, in the framework of the Cold War, "the nations of the Western Hemisphere may find themselves becoming more and more dependent on one another as sources of supply and as markets." In consequence, "acceptance of the goal of increasing Western Hemisphere integration by the United States, Canada and the Latin American states would do much to increase hemisphere morale and to improve hemisphere relations in the short term as well as to foster progress toward the long-range objective." *United States–Latin American Relations*, pp. 429–30.

The NPA position started losing supporters in the United States in the early 1960's, as suggested by Lincoln Gordon of Harvard University in his article "Economic Regionalism Reconsidered," *World Politics*, January, 1961, pp. 231–53: "[The proposal for a Western Hemisphere common market or a free-trade area] is neither desirable nor feasible. It would cut across the developmental aspirations of the industrializing nations of Latin America, nations whose governments differ in many economic policies but agree on the importance of protecting their infant industries from being throttled at birth by massive American competition. The very proposal would raise charges of a new form of economic imperialism from the 'Yankee colossus of the north.' "

> will be based on the very small markets of the individual sovereign units, leading inevitably to inefficient small-scale production and the frustration of many developmental opportunities, or whether it will be on a regional basis with some promise of adequate market size and investment scale, and even some hope for competitive pressures within the regional areas. These are the most pressing reasons for fostering deliberately a form of 'developmental regionalism.' . . . Desirable as they might be, it is unlikely that many underdeveloped countries will be prepared to join full-fledged customs unions or free trade areas. . . . A practicable policy of developmental regionalism will have to devise more limited forms of integration.[34]

By the spring of 1961, this new attitude spread to the more progressive U.S. business circles, as witnessed by the following statement by the Committee for Economic Development (CED): "The United States should encourage the movements toward economic integration in Latin America. . . . Many of the Latin Americans do not subscribe to the General Agreement on Tariffs and Trade and we should not expect their regional arrangements to conform to the provisions of the GATT governing free trade areas and customs unions." [35]

From that moment, the following propositions related to Latin American integration efforts started meeting with a slowly growing acceptance in U.S. intellectual circles:

1. The purpose of trade regionalism in less-developed regions is to foster economic growth.

2. Individual national markets are insufficient to support many types of modern industry or to encourage the degree of specialization necessary for increased output.

3. Recent trends in trade between primary-product countries and industrial countries would not appear to guarantee to the underdeveloped countries, at least in the immediate future, sufficient external revenue to finance individual industrialization efforts, even when such an endeavor is otherwise feasible.

4. Neither can external financial aid in the form of credits and grants under present international programs be expected to fill the gap and provide resources for the development of these regions.

5. Common effort aimed at expanding present, and creating new, regional trade can have an important development effect and contribute to world welfare, since integration would diminish the discrimination resulting from trade barriers and the domestic economic policies

[34] Gordon, *op. cit.*, p. 248.

[35] *Cooperation for Progress in Latin America: A Statement on National Policy by the Research and Policy Committee of the Committee for Economic Development* (New York: Committee for Economic Development, 1961), p. 35.

of the countries participating in such regional trade groupings.

6. Present GATT rules were set up for the advanced countries. As far as customs unions and free-trade areas are concerned, they might possibly work also in the case of groupings of the extremely underdeveloped nations on the opposite end of the scale; however, they cannot be followed by the semideveloped regions.

7. In the case of groupings like LAFTA, the "infant economy" argument cannot be lightly dismissed; consequently, there is need for a very gradual dismantling of individual protection policies, accompanied by the system of exemptions, escape clauses, etc.

8. The advanced countries, especially the United States, should help regional trade groupings achieve their growth objectives, instead of insisting on their acceptance of standards and rules pertaining to relations among the industrial centers of the world.[36]

This slow change, which a U.S. scholar described as a shift from an absolutist to a relativist approach to world trade problems,[37] was, for the first time, more tangibly in evidence during the preparations for the conference at Punta del Este.[38] OAS members unanimously agreed to include regional economic integration on the meeting's agenda. In this connection, two U.S. experts, Bert Hoselitz of the University of Chicago and Raymond F. Mikesell of the University of Oregon, participated, although in an unofficial capacity, in the elaboration of a technical document submitted for the delegates' consideration.[39]

It is in this document that all the members of the OAS Working Group jointly declared:

> The steps thus far initiated toward integration [of Latin American economies] are evidence of a desire to avoid, on an international scale, the

[36] "One can say of these regional trade arrangements only that they offer an opportunity for the speed-up of growth, but not an assurance that the speed-up will occur. If in their development they offer wider markets, more opportunities for specialization, more diversified sources of credit and a multiplication in sources of supply, the growth objective will be closer at hand. The influence of the United States should be used to ensure that the arrangements work in that direction." Raymond Vernon, *op. cit.*, p. 467.

[37] Bela Balassa's essay published in this volume, p. 21.

[38] The fact that the U.S. Delegation at the ECLA Trade Committee conference at Santiago, Chile, in May, 1961, did not make any positive contribution to the long debate on problems related to the implementation of the Montevideo Treaty was regarded in Latin America at that time as a reflection of the lack of an officially redefined position.

[39] Pan American Union, Special Meeting of the Inter-American Economic and Social Council, at the Ministerial Level, *Latin American Economic Integration* (Topic 2 of the Agenda) (Washington, D.C., 1961), pp. 2–3.

> waste of scarce resources and to use and pool these resources more effectively. This means realizing the advantages of an international division of labor and of large-scale production in Latin America, and, at the same time, creating more favorable conditions for increasing trade with the rest of the world. . . .
>
> The lack of dynamism and the discouraging fluctuations of the foreign markets for primary products, together with Latin America's growing and legitimate ambition to develop as a social consciousness develops and becomes stronger, are elements contributing to the desire for integration. Integration offers hope of filling the gap, real or threatened, left by the weakness of traditional markets and of establishing the conditions necessary for sustained growth.

The document arrived at the conclusion that, once orthodox fears regarding the diversion of trade, the subversion of the "orderly system of international commerce," etc., were eliminated, or at any rate attenuated, trade groupings on the order of LAFTA "should be considered a dynamic factor in the economic development of the countries directly involved and of the region as a whole."

This thesis was the point of departure for a series of concrete recommendations, among which the following merit special mention:

1. The trade-liberalization process within the free-trade zone should be stepped up through the use of the two mechanisms established in the Montevideo Treaty, namely, the sector-by-sector agreements and the ordinary product-by-product negotiations.
2. National development plans should be coordinated so as to determine the degree to which they are susceptible of complementary functioning and to measure compliance with over-all goals in given production sectors.
3. When applying external financial resources, consideration should be given to investment needs relating to the economic-integration program. Specifically, these resources should be used for the purchase of capital goods produced in Latin America, and appropriate authorities should study the possibility of establishing regional mechanisms "to encourage, via medium- and long-term external credits, Latin American capital goods exports in intraregional trade and outside the area as well."
4. Special credit grants (perhaps by the International Monetary Fund) to cover intraregional balances resulting from trade liberalization in the zone would serve as a stimulus to the freeing of commercial interchange in Latin America.

No less important and meaningful is the fact that the above document proposed an economic cooperation agreement between LAFTA and the Central American Common Market, "based on special advantages in favor of signatories to the General Treaty for Central American Economic Integration, taken as a group, by reason of their relatively lower level of economic development, and in line with the provisions of the Treaty of Montevideo." Thus, at long last, the authors of the Latin American Free Trade Association found acceptance of their idea that that agency should represent the principal instrument of Latin American economic integration.

There is some evidence that the willingness of U.S. experts who participated in the preparations for the Punta del Este conference to accept and support Latin America's line of reasoning in favor of the integration program tailored to regional needs was not entirely shared by official circles in the United States as late as a few scant weeks before the Punta del Este gathering. It is known, for example, that the draft agreement for the establishment of the Alliance for Progress, drawn up by the U.S. government and distributed among OAS members in the middle of July, 1961, made no reference whatsoever to regional economic integration; even though it did represent very substantial progress in comparison with earlier U.S. government positions on basic development problems in Latin America.[40]

Nevertheless, in his major address at the Punta del Este conference, the U. S. Secretary of the Treasury, Douglas Dillon, made it clear that the United States would support regional integration. His statement reads as follows: "Ratification of the Montevideo Treaty enabling the establishment of the Latin American Free Trade Association constitutes another important step on the road toward a Latin American common market. Let us hope that the members will be able to rapidly increase the list of products subject to free interchange so that they may obtain all the fruits of integration."

During the subsequent discussions, the U.S. delegation raised no objection to the inclusion in the final text of the "Declaration to the Peoples of America" of a paragraph committing the signatories to "accelerate the integration of Latin America in pursuit of the same objective of strengthening the economic and social development of the continent—a process already begun with the General Treaty for Central American Economic Integration and, in other countries, by means of the Latin American Free Trade Association." [41]

[40] A brief résumé of this document appeared in *The New York Times*, July 15, 1961; subsequently, the complete text was published by the Colombian press.

[41] Organization of American States, *Alliance for Progress: Official Documents Emanating from the Special Meeting of the Inter-American Economic and Social*

The delegation sent by the United States also cooperated in drawing up Title 3 of the Punta del Este Charter, which recognizes that the two treaties are efficacious instruments for accelerating Latin America's economic development process. The same portion of the charter urges the establishment of adequate ties between LAFTA and the Central American Common Market and recommends further that: special attention be given to the application of external resources to investment in multinational projects that help strengthen the integration process; part of these resources be channeled through financial institutions devoted to integration; negotiations be undertaken with IMF and other sources to persuade them to supply the means needed in solving transitory balance-of-payments problems, which may arise in countries belonging to economic-integration systems; and steps be taken to coordinate transport and communications facilities that will accelerate the integration process.

Finally, thus, toward the end of the summer of 1961—more than a year after the Montevideo Treaty had been signed—the attitude of the United States toward Latin American economic integration appears to have been clarified and defined.

The purpose sought by this brief history of the origins of the Montevideo Treaty, the negotiations that preceded the signing of that document in 1960, and the attitudes adopted outside the region in respect to economic-integration ideas in Latin America is to place the Latin American Free Trade Association in its proper perspective. For reasons beyond the control of LAFTA's founders, plus others that reflect the lack of experience and timidity of Latin American political leaders, the legal instrument designed to accomplish integration is quite weak if statically considered. From the point of view of potentialities, however, it is sufficiently ambitious.

By 1964, four years after the Montevideo Treaty was signed, the contracting parties had unquestionably fulfilled the minimum program for trade liberalization drawn up for the period. At the same time, it should be recognized that they continue to refuse to adopt the dynamic spirit of the proponents of integration, who, as yet, represent a minority in Latin America's political and economic picture.

Paradoxical, perhaps, but nonetheless true, is the fact that the idea of integration, conceived by the minds of the region's intellectual elite among economists and technicians, has gained more ardent supporters among the complex of dynamic elements in the private sectors of

---

Council at the Ministerial Level Held in Punta del Este, Uruguay, from August 5 to 17, 1961 (Washington, D.C.: Pan American Union, 1961), p. 4.

the different republics than among the politicians.[42] The inability of the politicians, with a few meritorious exceptions, fully to comprehend Latin America's great problems and to give thought to their solution contrasts with the positive role played by European statesmen during the process of mapping out and building the European Economic Community. It also contrasts with the growing acceptance by the world's industrial centers of the need for Latin American economic integration. If the integration program does not soon pick up speed and breadth, but instead degenerates into a preferential trade zone of very limited scope, the blame can hardly be placed on the existence of unfavorable circumstances or the action of external forces.

[42] See "Integration in Latin America," *Bank of London and South America Quarterly Review*, IV, No. 1 (January, 1964), 1–15.

VI

SIDNEY S. DELL

The Early Years of LAFTA's Experiences

The Treaty of Montevideo was signed in February, 1960, and has been in force since June, 1961. What conclusions may be drawn from the first years of experience under the treaty?

Observers tend to evaluate that experience largely in terms of their own expectations. On the one hand, there are those who compare the Montevideo Treaty with the Treaty of Rome, usually to the detriment of the former. On the other, there are those who have realized all along that the Treaty of Montevideo was the beginning of a process, not the end, and that that process would have to go on for many years before sure foundations could be laid for a common market in Latin America.

Recent figures on trends in trade among the Latin American countries are moderately encouraging. It appears that the steady decline in regional trade since 1957–58 was reversed in 1962, as may be seen from the figures below.

At the same time, the situation reflected in these data gives no grounds for complacency. It is true that mutual trade concessions by the member countries of the Latin American Free Trade Association have already opened up certain important new channels of trade among Latin American countries, notably between Mexico and the rest of the region. But there have been counterbalancing disappointments. It was certainly very discouraging, for example, to read, in early 1962, that there had been a sharp drop in trade between Argentina and Chile just after the first round of mutual tariff negotiations among the member countries of LAFTA had come to a conclusion.

This decline was not due, of course, to the LAFTA negotiations, but rather to an increase in tariffs imposed by Argentina, for the protection of its growing steel plant in San Nicolás, against imports from Chile—to which Chile retaliated with an increase in the duty on Argentine meat and butter. These developments in no way undermine the basic argument for closer trading relations between Latin American countries; on the contrary, they tend to reinforce it, by giving a practical demonstration of how inadequate cooperation leads to an actual decline in trade.

INTRA-LATIN AMERICAN EXPORTS

(*In Millions of Dollars*)

Year	*Amount*
1957	760
1958	760
1959	720
1960	690
1961	580
1962	660
1963	730
1964	980

Source: United Nations, *Monthly Bulletin of Statistics.*

It is, nevertheless, interesting to inquire why trade among Latin American countries should not have responded more significantly to the lowering of obstacles to such trade since mid-1961. Why did not Latin America begin to experience the same sort of intra-area trade boom that has been characteristic of the European Common Market since the signature of the Treaty of Rome?

First of all, it is still early to judge the impact of the first rounds of LAFTA tariff negotiations. It obviously takes time for the necessary regulations to be promulgated by national authorities and for businessmen to respond to them by placing a larger volume of orders across national frontiers. Moreover, even if there had been time for the new order volume to build up, an additional period would have to elapse before the correspondingly greater deliveries would be reflected in foreign-trade statistics.

There are, however, more important reasons why the Latin American experience has not paralleled that of the European Common Market thus far. In the first place, the Treaty of Rome was signed under the most favorable conditions possible, i.e., during a period of very rapid growth in Western Europe. Even prior to the signature of that treaty, industrial production in the member countries had been rising at an annual rate of 8–10 per cent a year, and the volume of their trade with one another had been growing even faster. Although production and trade have continued to rise very rapidly in the Common Market nations, there is no assurance that this has been due, to any very great extent, to the Treaty of Rome.

Very different is the climate in which the Treaty of Montevideo has had to operate. Indeed, the objective of economic integration in Latin America gained widespread acceptance precisely because the existing rate of development, both in production and in foreign trade, was so unsatisfactory. The Montevideo Treaty was not superimposed on a situation of growth and prosperity, but of slowdown and stagnation. In Western Europe, the rate of growth has declined somewhat since the Treaty of Rome was signed, but has still remained high enough for people to be satisfied with business prospects and to feel that the treaty, on the whole, has brought success. In Latin America, the fact that the Treaty of Montevideo has not suddenly produced a radical change in the region's economic outlook has led to disappointment and dismay on the part of many, although a moment's reflection should have made it clear that, under no circumstances, could the treaty have done any such thing.

But there is a second reason for the greater success of Western Europe than of Latin America thus far. For Western Europe, the lowering of the internal barriers to trade meant returning to a position that had previously prevailed. The barriers to trade among Western European countries that resulted from the great depression and World War II were an unnatural element in the regional economy, and the trade liberalization program that was begun early in the postwar period therefore represented a return to something that might be called normalcy. In any case, the channels of trade were all there, ready-made; transport facilities were available, and the necessary commercial contacts and relations could easily be resumed. In Latin America, on the other hand, it is a matter of creating something that never before existed. It is a question of setting up entirely new channels of trade, entirely new commercial contacts, and entirely new sources of supply and market outlets. In many cases, it even involves an attempt to provide transport facilities between points that have never had such facilities. To imagine that all this could have changed since June, 1961, is to have a completely distorted view of the problem of economic development in Latin America.

It must also be conceded, however, that the cuts in tariffs and lowering of other trade barriers in Western Europe were much more meaningful, even in the early stages, than the corresponding developments in Latin America. The Western European countries were much more drastic in their implementation of the Treaty of Rome's liberalization program than the Latin American countries have, to date, been in acting on the principles enunciated in Montevideo. At first glance, this may seem a misstatement of fact, since the average percentage of tariff reduction achieved during the first two rounds of negotiations within LAFTA has been much higher than the minimum required by the Treaty of Montevideo, namely, 8 per cent per annum. It seems clear, however, that a goodly number of the concessions made up to now have been more apparent than real, for, in many cases, the reductions are from legal rates that have never been applied in practice or, in any event, were not being applied at the time the Treaty of Montevideo was signed. For the time being, therefore, it is rather difficult to assess how much genuine lowering of trade barriers has taken place.

An additional element of uncertainty arises from the fact that the Treaty of Montevideo is so worded as to make it unnecessary for countries to free anything but their "existing trade." For example, where countries maintain import restrictions that are so stringent as to preclude all trade with their neighbors in the products concerned, the liberalization formula provided by the Treaty of Montevideo does not actually require any relaxation. Despite this, it seems that important concessions have been made, even on products not traditionally traded within Latin America; and it is, in fact, this development that has made it possible for Mexico to begin exporting to the rest of Latin America, whereas, previously, her trade with other countries in the region was practically nonexistent. There is, nevertheless, still considerable doubt as to how far this process of including new products in intraregional trade will go in practice. In this respect, the Montevideo Treaty program differs considerably from that of the Treaty of Rome, since the latter implies the removal of all restrictions on trade, i.e., not only in traditional products, but in all goods produced anywhere in the Common Market area.

The reluctance of the member countries of LAFTA to adopt a more adventurous policy in the lowering of tariffs and other trade barriers against their neighbors results largely from fears of damaging competition and of imbalance in intraregional trade and payments. With respect to the first point, the fact that Latin America already has a significant amount of industry has both positive and negative implications for the creation of a common market. On the one hand, it means that there already exists an industrial foundation on which to build a much larger and more comprehensive industrial structure. On the other hand, the industrial development of Latin America, thus far, has proceeded within the limitations of existing national markets. Each of the domestic industries is comfortably oriented towards its own national market potential and usually fears the consequences of competition from more efficient rivals (actual or potential) in neighboring countries even more than it is tempted by the prospects of the larger market opportunities inherent in the creation of a region-wide common market.

Although the protectionist tendencies of inefficient local industries must not be allowed to defeat the whole purpose of economic integration in Latin America, it is also important to distinguish between the problem facing Latin America and that confronting the European Common Market. It is frequently taken for granted that, because the Common Market in Western Europe places a good deal of emphasis upon the intensification of competition among existing European industries, a similar objective is valid for Latin America also.

But this places the emphasis in entirely the wrong place. In Western Europe, a massive industry already exists, and the main problem is to make it more productive and efficient. This objective can be secured by creating market conditions in which the more efficient firms will drive the less efficient ones out of business—or, at least, so the theory goes. There is no doubt a good deal of inefficiency in Latin American industry could also be removed through the stimulus or incentive of more intense competition. But this is only a small part of the problem. Much more important is the question of how to enlarge Latin American industry out of all recognition, notably through the establishment of entirely new industries in sectors where none presently exist. Doctrinaire emphasis on the need for greater competition is unlikely to contribute to the achievement of this broader objective to any very great extent. Indeed, there are many cases in which the prospect of competition might well deter new investment, whereas the guarantee of an assured market, free from competition, would be a powerful incentive. It is the latter type of logic that has been associated with the program of industrial development in Central America, through the Central American Industries Regime, under which there is specific provision for the creation of at least a temporary monopoly. Of course, monopoly brings its own problems, and these have to be dealt with effectively if the consumer is not to suffer. But free trade is not the only answer to monopoly, nor is it necessarily the most effective one.

At least equally important in slowing down the liberalization program has been the lack of any mechanism for dealing with prospective imbalances in intraregional trade. Countries experiencing pressure on their balance of payments have not unnaturally felt that they had to play safe in pulling down the barriers to trade. If there had been a Latin American payments union, or some other provision for credit facilities to ease the adjustment process should serious imbalances result from duty reductions or the relaxation of other trade restrictions, such countries would, no doubt, have felt less vulnerable and would have more readily undertaken to expand the scope of their trade negotiation with other members of LAFTA. But, in the face of strenuous outside opposition to any scheme that would provide automatic credit facilities to a country encountering balance-of-payments difficulties as a result of a liberalization program, LAFTA has, thus far, been unable to cope with the trade and payments problems inherent in the Treaty of Montevideo. The need to overcome these difficulties remains as pressing now as it was when these matters were first being considered in 1958 and 1959, and a resolution of the LAFTA members at the second meeting of the LAFTA Conference, held in Mexico City in late 1962, specifically calls for further study of this question.

The fact is that undue emphasis on free trade and currency convertibility as ultimate objectives of the Treaty of Montevideo could cause the whole program to come to grief. For, if the treaty means anything, it means cooperative development, particularly joint industrial development, on a region-wide basis. Simple solutions to the problem of Latin American development cannot be found in the principles of GATT or IMF as they stand. On this point, it is interesting to note that the report of a committee of experts, convened by the OAS in connection with the conference at Punta del Este, which established the Alliance for Progress, envisaged some important departures from orthodox GATT-IMF principles. For example, this committee foresaw the need for measures of "partial integration"—which are clearly inconsistent with Article 24 of GATT—and outlined its position as follows:

> . . . the diversity of conditions and vested interests are such that the road is not yet open to the total and immediate integration of the region. Integration must be gradual, both in coverage and degree. Moreover, partial integration, or a series of integration agreements that are partial either in terms of sectors or in terms of countries included or a combination of both, is not incompatible with an advance toward the general integration of the region, especially if an approach is made to some coordination of national development plans. This may perhaps be the best way of achieving progress towards general integration and of contributing to the development of all the countries of the region.
>
> The creation of partial and especially intimate ties may be justified by the proximity of the countries, the complementarity of their econ-

omies, the similarity of their development, their historical links and other factors.[1]

This is obviously a far cry from any approach to the economic development of the Latin American region that is based on the free-trade incentive alone. The same committee went on to devote a special chapter to the need of coordinating national economic-development plans. Pointing out that the freeing of trade could lead to advantageous specialization, but that a similar result could also be obtained by deliberate government intervention in the economy through joint planning, the committee made a number of constructive suggestions as to the way in which the coordination of plans could proceed. Given the need, in the committee's view, to reconcile the requirements for the optimum location of particular industries with the goal of developing Latin America as a whole, high priority was assigned to joint measures for building infrastructural facilities and to the establishment of new dynamic industries designed to complement existing ones, rather than to duplicate industrial facilities already available or in prospect. The same group of experts also noted that the rate of liberalization of trade was bound to be slow if payments arrangements were inadequate.

If there are grounds for concern about the rate of progress to date in implementing the objectives of the Montevideo Treaty, they are to be found not so much in the sphere of the reduction of restrictions on trade as in the area of joint development planning. If free trade were the key to economic development, we should not now be faced with the problem of underdevelopment over the greater part of the earth's surface. The fact is that free trade tends to bring about unequal rates of development in various parts of the world, and a correction of this tendency depends very largely upon deliberate intervention in the free market processes, with particular emphasis on the intelligent planning of future growth.

It stands to reason, however, that regional planning cannot begin until a firm foundation of national planning is laid. Much as one may deplore the obvious tendency of national planners to confine themselves to perspectives dictated by domestic market conditions and to overlook the possibilities for fruitful cooperation with other countries, the fact remains that there can be no meaningful planning for Latin America as a whole unless it is rooted in the national plans drawn up

[1] Organización de los Estados Americanos, *Integración económica de la América Latina: Informe del Grupo de Expertos* (Reunión Extraordinaria del Consejo Interamericano Económico y Social al Nivel Ministerial, Uruguay, Agosto de 1961) (Washington, D.C.: Pan American Union, 1961), p. 3.

and implemented by each of the Latin American countries individually.

One of the most arresting of Latin America's paradoxes is that, in the entire postwar period, this area has probably devoted more attention to questions of planning than has any other region outside Eastern Europe and China. The distinguished studies that have been made by the Secretariat of the Economic Commission for Latin America, under Raúl Prebisch, are very well known in this respect, and they have created a characteristic line and style that are well known all over the world. Indeed, for many years, the commission was vigorously attacked by critics in the developed countries for seeking to introduce planning techniques in Latin America for the solution of problems that, so it was felt, should be left entirely to the uninhibited operation of private enterprise. Many of these critics could see nothing but evil in the very concept of national planning, to say nothing of joint regional planning.

Since those days, of course, things have changed greatly. Indeed, it has recently become fashionable to attribute everything good in government economic policy to "planning." Under today's definitions, not only do countries like the Soviet Union and India plan their economies, but the countries of North America and Western Europe do so, too—and, in fact, probably always have. Moreover, whereas ten years ago the idea of planning was considered anathema in the underdeveloped countries, the preparation of an adequate development plan is beginning to be regarded as an indispensable prerequisite in securing economic aid. Thus, for example, under the Alliance for Progress, participating Latin American countries were called upon to formulate long-term development programs, if possible within eighteen months of the signing of the Punta del Este Charter on August 17, 1961. In response to this requirement, several Latin American countries have prepared such programs, and this already represents an important step forward on their part. It would be idle to pretend, however, that the adoption of a national development program by a government indicates, in itself, that economic planning has begun or is even about to begin. Quite apart from the question of whether the elaboration of such programs was undertaken, in some cases, merely in order to document a case for foreign aid, it must inevitably take time before the machinery of planning can be established and blueprints are translated into specific action by governments or private individuals.

If planning has yet to take concrete form in the domestic economies of the various Latin American countries, it stands to reason that region-wide planning, in any significant sense of the term, is even more remote. It is encouraging to note that Resolution 54 of the contracting parties to the Montevideo Treaty, approved in their second meeting in Mexico City, provided for a conference during 1963 of industrial-development planners in the various member countries. The first such meeting, held in Lima in April, 1963, laid the groundwork for action by exchanging information, studying past trends and future prospects, and confronting production targets with demand forecasts for the LAFTA countries as a whole. These proposals are all oriented in the right direction; but, once again, concrete action still lies in the future, and many difficulties will have to be overcome, at both technical and political levels, before one can really say that effective procedures have been devised for joint regional planning in Latin America. Yet, as was indicated above, in the absence of such measures the growth of mutually beneficial specialization and exchange within Latin America may prove to be very slow, quite possibly too slow.

It therefore becomes evident that, in any program for the development of Latin America as a whole, national and regional planning must go hand-in-hand with the reduction of trade barriers. Economic planning will not realize its full potential unless accompanied by the opening up of region-wide markets. And the lowering of trade barriers will provide insufficient stimulus to intraregional trade unless associated with the active coordination of national development programs.

Closely linked with the question of joint economic planning for the Latin American region as a whole is the problem of the treatment of the less-developed countries within the Latin American Free Trade Association. To their credit, the Latin American countries have recognized, from the very beginning of the common market program, that the development of the least-developed areas within the region could not be left simply to market forces operating within a framework of regional free-trade and *laissez faire*. Thus the Treaty of Montevideo made specific provision for special privileges and advantages to be granted to those countries which were likely to fall behind even further if their economies were opened up as fully to the forces of regional free trade as were those of their more-developed neighbors.

The special "advantages" envisaged by the Treaty of Montevideo have, in fact, been granted to Paraguay and Ecuador. The Paraguayan representative warned a LAFTA Conference in July, 1961, that, unless reasonable concessions were obtained from the other members, the free-trade area would become a dangerous experiment for his country's economy and finances. He maintained that the loss of customs revenue of the freed imports could, in itself, have serious consequences. In response to the Paraguayan case, LAFTA agreed, in September, 1961, to authorize participating countries to free their imports of primary and industrial products from Paraguay of all duties and restrictions for a period of nine years beginning January 1, 1963.

On the other hand, the special advantages offered to the less-developed countries have not yet prompted Bolivia to join LAFTA, although it has announced the intention of doing so. It will be recalled that Bolivia had participated in the discussions and negotiations leading up to the drafting of the Montevideo Treaty, and a place for that country as a founding member was kept open by the other signatories. The reason given by the Bolivian government for not acceding immediately to the treaty was that most of the nation's exports are marketed outside Latin America and that better and cheaper manufactures are available in North America and Western Europe than in Latin America. In other words, Bolivia objected to subsidizing industry in Argentina, Brazil, or Mexico by paying higher prices for imports from these countries than it would be charged for comparable products supplied by the industrially developed countries.

The Bolivian dilemma is a genuine one. On the one hand, Bolivia, no doubt, would like to play its part in the evolution of a prosperous Latin American economy and contribute to the success of the enterprise launched by the Montevideo Treaty; on the other, it is much too poor a country to be able to sacrifice the living standards of its people to regional ideals, however lofty. If Bolivia is to pay high prices for imports of manufactures from Argentina, Brazil, or Mexico, there must be some *quid pro quo*, i.e., assurance that a beginning will be made in her own industrial development.

Now, it is true that the special concessions granted by the other LAFTA members to Ecuador and Paraguay *may* prompt the establishment in those two countries of certain industries that would not otherwise have been developed there. However, such an outcome is far from certain, since it is by no means clear that the incentives afforded would be sufficient to persuade private industry to locate new plants in Ecuador or Paraguay, in preference to one of the more highly developed industrial centers elsewhere in Latin America. If inclined to hazard a guess, one would probably conclude that the especially favorable treatment given to imports from Ecuador and Paraguay, under the provision cited above, would, indeed, encourage their export trade in traditional products, but would probably not bring about any important measure of industrial development in the two countries. Generally speaking, industrialists considering the location of new plants are likely to attach more importance to such questions as the availability of skilled labor, the accessibility to fuels, raw materials, and intermediate products, and the general level of development of the area as a whole, than to the particular advantages that Ecuador and Paraguay have been granted by the other LAFTA participants. If this assessment is correct, Bolivian hesitation is well founded.

The real solution to the problem facing Ecuador and Paraguay (and, presumably, applicable to Bolivia as well) is an approved regional program in which these countries would be able to anticipate progress in terms of national economic development. In this respect, the Central American Industries Regime, established within the Central American Common Market, provides an important example and precedent. The particular significance of that system lies in the fact that it calls for joint industrial planning conducted in such a way as to provide adequate incentive for the less-developed, as well as the more-developed, countries participating in a regional integration program. Similar provision needs to be made in LAFTA, and this brings us back once again to the problem of joint planning. Without a carefully wrought plan of economic and industrial development for the region as a whole, agreed to by all the participating countries, great uncertainty is bound to persist as to whether countries like Bolivia, Ecuador, and Paraguay are really getting their fair share of whatever benefits the opening up of the regional market may bring.

One of the most interesting recent developments in LAFTA is the emergence of certain indications of a movement away from the free-trade-area concept toward that of a customs union.

In my book on prospects for a Latin American common market, written before the signing of the Montevideo Treaty, I devoted some attention to the question whether a common market in Latin America was likely to take the form of a customs union or free-trade area.[2] I pointed out that "a free-trade area is a rather odd and probably unstable arrangement over any long period, although it may have its uses during a period of transition." The reason for this is that the lack of a uniform external tariff in a free-trade area tends, to a greater or lesser extent, to defeat the whole purpose of economic integration. Within a free-trade area, the pattern of industrial development may well be distorted by the fact that the tariff imposed by one country on raw materials imports may be different from that imposed by another.

Let us assume, for example, that two countries within a free-trade area are manufacturing rubber boots, but that one of them exacts a much lower duty than the other on rubber imported from outside the area. In that case, the final product prices may fail to reflect the relative efficiencies of production in the two countries, simply because of the difference in duties charged on imported rubber. If the tariff differential is maintained, a less efficient industry in the low-tariff

[2] *Problemas de un mercado común en América Latina* (Mexico: CEMLA, 1959), pp. 83–89.

country could drive a more efficient industry in the high-tariff country out of business.

This sort of situation is bound to create pressure for harmonizing import duties on raw materials in all countries participating in a free-trade area. The same considerations, of course, apply to other goods needed in the production process, such as fuel, machinery, and equipment. Ultimately, even the tariffs on food and other consumer goods need to be harmonized, since intercountry discrepancies tend to be reflected in wage differentials. Other things being equal, manufacturers in high-tariff countries would probably have to pay higher wages than those in low-tariff countries; and this, again, would affect their competitive power in a region-wide market. In short, the very concept of a regional market to which all member countries have equal access implies the ultimate harmonization of customs duties applied to third parties, so that the location of manufacturing enterprise does not come to depend on chance differences in tariff levels instead of on productive efficiencies.

There is, however, another factor tending to push national tariffs into line, and that is the need to establish adequate and comparable margins of regional preference throughout the area. A member country with a low average level of tariffs obviously cannot grant as extensive an average margin of preference in favor of its high-tariff neighbor as the latter can—unless, of course, it raises its own tariffs against third parties to the level maintained by that neighbor.

Underdeveloped countries often maintain relatively low tariffs on goods that they do not produce for themselves and relatively high tariffs on those that they do. This means that they are in a position to grant substantial preference to their neighbors on the goods that they make at home (and which they are, consequently, not especially anxious to import), but that they cannot give much, if any, preferential encouragement to their neighbors on the products that they do not manufacture for themselves.

If this situation were to persist, underdeveloped countries would be able to grant one another significant tariff preferences only in respect of those goods that they are already producing for themselves. In practice, this would mean that LAFTA members would undertake cutthroat competition in the light industries producing textiles and other nondurable consumer goods, but that no significant mutual advantages could be extended in connection with some of the durable producer and consumer goods not now manufactured in the area, on which tariffs are likely to be low. If this were the effect of the Montevideo Treaty, operating within the terms of Article 24 of GATT, it would indeed be most unfortunate; for it would lead to economic—

and, ultimately, political—conflict between the Latin American countries without doing very much to raise the level of industrial development in the region.

These considerations suggest a need for tariff levels to move toward one another in such a way as to provide adequate regional incentives, not only in those industries in which Latin America already has some productive capacity, but also in those in which it does not. Where all or most member countries already do some manufacturing for themselves, as, for example, in the textile or other light industries, the need to harmonize preferential margins inevitably leads to the collateral requirement of the establishment of a common external tariff in the course of the transitional period.

On the other hand, where particular products are manufactured in only one or two of the member countries, or in none, the need for an adequate margin of regional preference throughout the area will usually imply a raising of tariff rates in some or all of the member countries. Once tariff rates on particular products have to be changed anyhow, it is natural to move them to the same level in all countries to obviate internal discrimination.

More generally, the advantages of a customs union over a free-trade area derive essentially from the need to establish the principle of internal nondiscrimination throughout the region. Such nondiscrimination means that no firm should be penalized by higher import duties charged by the country in which it happens to be located, and that the margins of regional preference on particular products should be standard in all member countries, again implying the eventual need for a common external tariff.

At least two of the resolutions adopted during the second meeting of the LAFTA Conference reflect the beginnings of a shift toward the closer forms of economic integration implied by a customs union as against a free-trade area.

Resolution 53 sets forth a basic interpretation of the treaty's intentions, comprising not only the freeing of trade among the signatories, but also the establishment of a "reasonable" margin of regional preference that would stimulate the gradual substitution of domestic output for imports. The resolution does not seek to define what a "reasonable" margin of preference might be, nor does it call for any raising of customs duties charged third parties at rates that are currently too low to afford a significant level of regional preference. It does, however, take a first step in maintaining the value of such preferences as have, in fact, been created by the annual negotiations for the mutual reduction of tariffs under the treaty. This is accomplished by enjoining the contracting parties to abstain from any action, including duty concessions to third parties, that would have the effect of reducing regional-preference margins. Thus, Resolution 53 seeks to guard against the danger that, under pressure from exporters in North America and Western Europe, LAFTA members may be induced to extend their mutual concessions to countries outside the region. To this extent, it makes initial inroads on the tariff autonomy implied in the concept of a free-trade area.

In Resolution 48, relating to complementary-industry agreements, customs-union concepts are introduced more directly, so as to provide for equality of treatment throughout the region. In the terms of the resolution, a complementary-industry agreement may provide for the harmonization of treatment accorded to imports from third countries, both of products covered by the agreement and of the raw materials and component parts used in their manufacture. The very first of these industrial agreements, announced in June, 1962, covered electronic tubes and asked that national tariffs and other restrictions on imports of these products from the rest of the world be brought to a common level as soon as possible.

The foregoing constitutes nothing more than a piecemeal approach. If the procedure described above with respect to electronic tubes were followed in every other industry, a customs union would ultimately emerge, but only as the combined result of a large number of separate agreements covering all industries. It may be, however, that once the process of harmonization has been successfully carried out in connection with a certain number of industries and products, countries may begin to consider a more coordinated and unified approach to the problem of a common tariff. For one thing, harmonization on an industry-by-industry basis has the drawback that it may lead not only to imbalance among industries but also to inequities among countries, depending on which industries happen to suit their local circumstances best. On such a basis, some industries may end up with a very high level of regional preference, others with a much lower level. An integrated approach, on the other hand, would make it possible to try to achieve some sort of balance in the advantages secured by the various countries for the particular industries in which they are currently or potentially interested. It is, therefore, not unreasonable to anticipate that, at some stage, the LAFTA countries may want to tackle the problem of a customs union head on, rather than indirectly through complementary-industry agreements.

Having said all this, one must not, of course, lose sight of the fact that a free-trade area offers certain advantages for the first stage of a Latin American common market—advantages that undoubtedly inspired the Montevideo Treaty in its present form. Most Latin American countries have been moving very cautiously toward acceptance of the idea of a common market and have not wanted to disturb the existing framework of trade with the rest of the world to any significant extent, pending a clearer understanding of the changes that a common market is likely to bring about and of the magnitude of the advantages that it is likely to yield. Latin American nations are understandably reluctant to face profound changes in the whole structure of their tariffs and other trade controls vis-à-vis the rest of the world simply for the sake of expanding their intraregional trade, which, after all, represents a very small portion of their total foreign sales. This may well be the most important single reason why a free-trade area has been considered the optimum form of regional economic organization for Latin America. Only as the advantages of regional economic integration show themselves more plainly than in the past will LAFTA countries be induced to undertake the major reorientation of foreign-trade strategy that would be required if they were to transform their association into a customs union, and perhaps, ultimately, into an economic union.

In this connection, I should like to comment on the general policy orientation inherent in a shift from a free-trade area to a customs union in Latin America. Some critics might maintain that such a shift would imply an "inward-looking" bias in the development of the region, since it would involve less concern with the region's trade with the rest of the world and a correspondingly greater concern with the development of intraregional commerce.

It has become commonplace in contemporary discussion of economic unions to say that such unions ought to be "outward-looking" and not "inward-looking." Indeed, the term "inward-looking" has become synonymous with everything that is evil in a regional economic association. Now, there is no doubt that this judgment has a certain validity when applied, say, to the regional groupings in Europe. For example, insofar as the European Economic Community follows unnecessarily protectionist policies in agriculture or other sectors, it damages both itself and the other countries of the world with which it trades. But it would be quite absurd to transfer this line of thinking automatically to economic unions among underdeveloped countries, for the trouble with underdeveloped countries is precisely that they are already too "outward-looking," in the sense that they are too much oriented toward their trade with the industrially developed countries and too little concerned with their domestic growth. They would, therefore, do well to look inward to their own development needs to a far greater extent than has been the case hitherto. There is no reason for them to be ashamed of such an attitude or to subordinate their own requirements to the trade objectives of the industrially developed countries. For LAFTA, a more coherent inward-looking policy would be a step forward, rather than backward, given the present economic circumstances of the Latin American region.

This is not to say, of course, that Latin American trade with the rest of the world is a matter of no consequence, or that it can be ignored in devising a regional economic policy. Any such idea would fly in the face of the obvious fact that nine-tenths of Latin America's trade is still carried on with North America and Western Europe and that geographic distribution is likely to continue for some time. What does emerge, however, is that the notions of inward-looking and outward-looking unions, so frequently discussed in connection with European economic integration, are subject to serious qualification when applied to the Latin American economic environment. Here, on the contrary, there is a presumption that joint economic development behind a common barrier of regional protection would be in the interest of Latin America as a whole and, ultimately, of the rest of the world as well; for a more prosperous and more rapidly growing Latin America is bound to be a more active trading partner for the world at large than a Latin America beset by the economic stagnation and retrogression of recent years.

Closely linked with the general economic strategy to be followed by the Latin American countries is the question of a common commercial policy vis-à-vis the rest of the world. Resolution 56, adopted at the second meeting of LAFTA Conference, provided for early meetings of commercial policy makers in the various member countries and called for the exchange of information and the continuing study of trade policy matters of mutual concern. This resolution is not indicative of any very great advance to date in the direction of a common commercial policy in Latin America—a circumstance that should not be too surprising, however, since progress on this front in the European Economic Community has also been quite slow. Although in theory the EEC Commission ought to be taking over responsibility for commercial policy from the national governments, in practice that agency remains very dependent upon the acquiescence of the member countries in anything it may do. This situation is likely to persist, especially if the French concept of *Europe des patries* gains general acceptance throughout the EEC.

For Latin America, however, the need to arrive at some common understanding in the field of commercial policy is, perhaps, even more urgent than in Western Europe, because the region's exports are seriously endangered by regional grouping of the advanced industrial countries. As the President of Uruguay stated during his opening address to a LAFTA conference in July, 1961: "The formation of a European common market and EFTA [European Free Trade Association] constitutes a state of near-war against Latin American exports. Therefore, we must reply to one integration with another one; to one increase of acquisitive power by internal enrichment with another; to the inter-European cooperation with inter-Latin American cooperation." [3]

A very significant report was submitted to ECLA on this matter in August, 1962, by four eminent Latin American consultants who recommended that their governments "should not rely exclusively on individual dealings; they should rather complement and strengthen bilateral action by swift and efficacious collective negotiation demonstrating solidarity, persistence and vigor which will reflect the real gravity of the situation more accurately." [4]

To this end, the above-mentioned experts urged further "the establishment of a Latin American agency to coordinate the trade policy of the countries in the region vis-à-vis the rest of the world, and, in addition, to deal on behalf of those countries as a whole, as and when appropriate, with countries or groups of countries in other regions and with international specialized agencies."

It is not necessary to enter here into the consultants' specific recommendations as to the way in which such a joint Latin American negotiating agency might be formed. They did not suggest that the LAFTA Secretariat should undertake these functions, presumably because that Secretariat remains a relatively weak one, with executive powers that do not even remotely approximate those of the European Economic Community Commission. (The Montevideo Treaty was clearly not intended to establish any kind of supranational agency for the political or economic unification of the region. Providing for a minimum of executive machinery at the center, the treaty bears a much greater resemblance to the Stockholm Convention that established EFTA.)

Nevertheless, the recommendations by specialists in the field clearly raise the issue of concerted action by the Latin American countries in their commercial policies vis-à-vis the rest of the world, and it is difficult to see how such policies could be coordinated effectively without due recognition of LAFTA's role. If the LAFTA Secretariat does not, at the present time, have the importance or strength to be able to negotiate commercial policy matters on behalf of the Latin American

[3] *The Observer* (London), July 30, 1961, p. 4.

[4] ECLA, *The Achievement of Coordination in Latin American Trade Policy: Relations with the European Economic Community* (Santiago, August, 1962; E/CN. 12/632).

countries as a whole, some *ad hoc* arrangement of the type envisaged by the consultants may well be necessary. But it is obviously not too early to begin thinking of a more dynamic central executive agency for LAFTA, and it is trusted that Resolution 56 represents a first step in that direction.

It should be said, finally, that LAFTA can succeed only within a general climate of economic and social change in Latin America. Economic progress in the region depends on much more than the lowering of the barriers to area trade. Reductions of tariffs and other obstacles to trade would be futile unless accompanied by reforms in land tenure and tax structure, plus an improvement in the distribution of income sufficient to persuade the mass of the population that they, too, may enjoy the fruits of economic advancement. Latin America cannot establish a meaningful common market in the midst of economic and social stagnation.

The fact that more rapid economic development in Latin America cannot result from a merely passive reliance upon the forces set in motion by a growth of regional trade may be illustrated from the Central American experience during the 1950's. From 1950 to 1960 trade among the five Central American countries increased almost fourfold, rising from a value of $8.6 million to $32.7 million. The rate of expansion was a little less than 9 per cent on the average from 1950 to 1955, but accelerated to as much as 20 per cent from 1955 to 1960. Exports of manufactures increased at an annual rate of 5 per cent in the first half of the period, accelerating to 22.5 per cent from 1955 to 1960.

Despite this impressive showing, in 1960 the share of industrial output in the total production of the Central American region remained at virtually the same level as ten years earlier—namely, 12 per cent. Even during the most recent period, when the agreements establishing the Central American Common Market began to take effect, industrial progress has been rather slow. Very striking also is the fact that there has been little change in the structure of the manufacturing industry during the past decade. The traditional types of manufacture, which had accounted for 80 per cent of that activity's total output in 1950, still represented as much as 77 per cent in 1960.

Thus, the outstanding successes of the Central American integration program, and the fact that a full-fledged customs union is expected to be realized in the area by 1966, by no means imply that any basic change has occurred in the economic outlook of the member countries. On the contrary, as the Secretariat of the Economic Commission for Latin America has pointed out, economic conditions in Central America have tended to deteriorate during the last few years.

While progress in establishing a common market has reached a high point and offers favorable prospects for the future, the economy has, in fact, been lagging. For the area as a whole, production is growing barely fast enough to offset the rate of increase in population; and, in some Central American nations, per capita output and income are actually declining.

It is, therefore, of the highest importance to keep in mind that economic unification is no panacea either for Central America or for the Latin American region as a whole. In an environment in which all forces are mobilized for economic growth and development, economic integration in Latin America can play a vital role. But without land reform where land reform is required, without the proper arrangements for economic planning, and without the many other measures that are needed in harnessing the region's resources and energies to the problem of development, the Treaty of Montevideo and the procedures it has set in motion are bound to remain sterile and unproductive. On the other hand, given the firm determination to undertake all the political, social, and economic changes required for more rapid economic development, economic integration can powerfully reinforce other measures by releasing the dynamic forces of regional specialization and exchange. Economic integration will not give Latin America an easy road to higher living standards or obviate the painful adjustment that the political and social circumstances of the region have shown to be necessary.

Once the economic forces of development are well and truly mobilized, economic integration can enhance their power, but under no circumstances can it substitute for them.

VII

GUSTAVO MAGARIÑOS

Integration Instruments and LAFTA Achievements

The Latin American Free Trade Association was born under the sign of gradual and progressive integration aimed at the formation of the Latin American common market as the final objective. Set forth in the Preamble and provisions of the Treaty of Montevideo, the principle of gradual and progressive integration is the fundamental guideline for the member countries in performing the tasks involved in the program's execution. Moreover, it constituted the source of inspiration for the ECLA-sponsored negotiations that marked the beginning of the LAFTA movement. Specifically, the objective has been to establish a system that will permit the gradual liberalization of trade and the parallel institution of preferential treatment for goods originating in the region.

The complexity of a process of this type; the difficult facts of economic life in Latin America, where a large number of countries are strongly dependent on international trade, but engage in regional trade to only a negligible extent; the differences in the degrees of industrial evolution of those nations; and the lack of theoretical tools and techniques—all have led to a concentration of effort on subregions. However, whereas in Central America the movement was held strictly within the corresponding geographic bounds, the initial idea of integrating the so-called southern cone of Latin America as the first step toward a broader association was soon ruled out by the adherence, first, of Mexico and, later, of Colombia and Ecuador. The choice of the free-trade-zone formula was dictated by practical politics. The experts did not believe it possible to convince the respective governments at the very start of the need to establish the legal bases for the setting up of a customs union. Consequently, the Montevideo conference in February, 1960, approved the only bases of integration that, at the time, were likely to meet with acceptance of a considerable number of Latin American republics.

To complete the integration process on which it has embarked, LAFTA must overcome enormous difficulties. One of these is traceable to the evident insufficiency of the technical and practical tools available to the Latin American nations and to the survival of certain patterns that are deep-rooted in the minds of the region's leaders. Traditionally, Latin America has depended on economic relations with the rest of the world and has not found an effective channel for strengthening its intraregional links. Since the expansion of the external sector of each country's economy has been a primary factor in its particular development, interest has generally been centered on marketing basic products—pitifully few in number—in the large centers of consumption. Consequently, commercial and financial networks, as well as marketing-research studies, have closely followed this peripheral circuit.

The attempt to diversify external action by diverting some of it to the regional sphere is greatly hampered by the prevailing lack of intraregional transportation, which is so inadequate that it is customary to ship merchandise indirectly between two points in Latin America (i.e., an intermediate stop is made outside the continent). An even more common hindrance is the use of outside financial services to settle such trade transactions. The scant importance of intrazonal commerce (except for a few instances of trade in certain products between two countries) makes it difficult to shift the almost exclusive concern with third-country relationships to the regional framework to any reasonable extent. The relative stability of the traditional trade flows has limited the possibilities for training experts able to tackle global foreign-trade problems. In many cases, foreign-trade measures are dictated by immediate circumstances, and judgment is based upon short-term considerations. The new approach imposed by the integration process, consequently, calls for a substantial change in each nation's attitudes toward foreign-trade problems; such change involves, in turn, a particularly lengthy and difficult educational effort on the part of the member governments.

From a technical standpoint, the requisite harmonization of policy instruments in support of the integration process faces sizable obstacles in almost every field. The more important of these problem areas are as follows: (1) customs policies, particularly with respect to tariff regimes; (2) agriculture; (3) industrial development, involving adequate complementarity agreements and location of manufacturing activities; and (4) financial and monetary policies, so obviously conditioned in Latin America by the critical ups and downs experienced by each national economy, particularly as regards the balance of payments.

The difficulties that stand in the way of any program to coordinate customs-policy instruments of the LAFTA member countries are considerable, and have to do with technical and administrative aspects, as well as with the actual duty rates. With respect to the former, the determination of appropriate bases for the standardization of the customs definitions, rulings, and procedures in effect in the region will be exceedingly complex; for, in many cases, there is no accurately compiled and systematic body of legal provisions. Quite the contrary, the various countries have, over time, adopted decisions dictated by immediate circumstances and introduced innovations (which have been carried over to the present) aimed at solving the problems of the moment. As a preliminary requisite, therefore, a thorough study will have to be made of the legal, regulatory, and administrative definitions applicable to the levy of import duties. In addition, data regarding the procedures directly or indirectly connected with the importation and exportation of merchandise must be gathered and analyzed. Although LAFTA's work in this field—that is, in the compilation of basic information on customs regimes, in line with a program initiated earlier by ECLA—is still in the initial phase, the need to make a choice between two courses of action is already in evidence. To achieve the desired standardization, would it be preferable to travel down the painstaking road of a comparative analysis of the regulations and procedures in force, so as to establish the bases for their later harmonization; or would it be more advisable to elaborate a common code that could be adopted simultaneously or multilaterally by the contracting parties, starting with the universally accepted definitions, regulations, and practices recommended by the specialized international agencies? Naturally, any decision in this case not only would depend on the degree of difficulty involved in adopting one system or the other but would also have to take into consideration the eventual disturbances that each might create, which would have to be coped with by the local administrations, whose good will and cooperation are essential to the success of the undertaking.

In the customs-tariff field, disparities noted between the duties charged by the nine countries that presently constitute LAFTA are highly important and extend to almost every aspect. In the first place, there are structural differences deriving from the fact that the respective tariffs have no common background and conform to no precise pattern. Lacking systematic classifications dictated by an appropriate methodological approach, the tariffs in force are a source of confusion with regard to the nature of the merchandise, as well as to the tariff schedule applicable in each case. In one instance, the tariff as it now stands has been built up during a lengthy historical process, involving successive stages characterized by the introduction of adjustments to new conditions created by the country's incipient industrial development.

In view of the foregoing circumstances, an appropriate technical base for the execution of the program aimed at constituting the Latin American free-trade zone has been lacking, and it is imperative that adequate common tools be constructed if more ambitious solutions for economic integration are to be attempted. To mitigate this difficulty, at least during the first operative phase of the process, the Montevideo Treaty called for the adoption of a standard basic nomenclature for purposes of statistical records and the realization of annual customs negotiations. In compliance with that provision, during the first meeting of the LAFTA Conference, the contracting parties used the Brussels Customs Nomenclature for reference purposes. Later, the Brussels nomenclature was supplemented by a systematic body of elucidative comment, for purposes of precise identification of the products incorporated in the liberalization program. The resultant Customs Nomenclature of the Latin American Free Trade Association, called NABALALC after the initials of the official title in Spanish, is the object of permanent examination with a view to periodic adjustment to the requirements of the integration process. The preparatory work on NABALALC revealed the deficiencies of the systems in force, with respect to commodity description and classification, and the disparities in the terminology and concepts employed by the LAFTA countries. At the same time, a joint effort was initiated in the direction of incorporating the Brussels nomenclature into the national customs tariffs. At present, the majority of countries have completed the corresponding conversion, or are in process of doing so; and, in this fashion, the respective tariff structures are being gradually brought into harmony.

As a first step in progressing from a free-trade zone to a future customs union, all the contracting parties must agree to adopt a common basic nomenclature that, based upon the Brussels listing, introduces the greatest possible number of subdivisions and has due regard for the joint interests of the members. Once this requirement has been met—and the contracting parties are well on the way to final solution in this matter—a choice must be made between approving NABA-LALC as the basis for the nomenclature of a future common tariff or incorporating it into the respective national tariffs, allowing for the possibility of the inclusion of additional subdivisions in response to each nation's foreign-trade peculiarities and the needs of its economy.

In the matter not only of custom duties but also of other charges having the equivalent effect (taxes applicable to the importation of merchandise and susceptible of quantification), the panorama presented by the foreign-trade systems of the LAFTA contracting parties is complex and chaotic. In the first place, a wide variety of tax concepts are employed. No accurate schedule of all the customs charges in effect in any one country is possible without use of a considerable number of columns. All the LAFTA tariffs, with the exception of Brazil's, apply both ad valorem and specific duties and, at times, a mixed levy. Several countries have recourse to a supplementary mechanism of foreign-exchange surcharges as a means of regulating foreign-trade transactions, with the aim of protecting domestic industry or defending the balance of payments. With a similar purpose in mind, they also resort to the tool of prior deposits. Additional ad valorem duties applied on dissimilar bases are also in common use.

Special taxes having primarily a fiscal objective cover a wide range and are based on varying taxation criteria. Prior to its last customs reform, which reduced the different import charges formerly in effect to a single levy consolidated on the basis of value, Argentina collected a "statistical" duty (i.e., one whose proceeds are used in financing statistical processing), a duty to finance the "forestry plan," and another corresponding to the "iron and steel plan." Brazil applies a special levy for customs handling, another that goes to a fund for port improvement, and yet another for the rehabilitation of the merchant marine. Chile enforces similar provisions through special import taxes under the "highway law" and the "unloading law"; it also maintains one relating to freight charges and one specifically covering chemical products. In Ecuador's tariff regime, there are special charges for "national defense," "electrification," "potable water supply," etc. Mexico levies on imports a special duty, expressed as a fixed percentage of invoice value, whose collection is devoted to the promotion of the export trade. Paraguay imposes, among other duties, a sales tax on all imported goods. In addition to her "maritime freight law," which establishes a percentage levy on freight charges, Peru has nine other provisions of a similar nature; and in Uruguay, apart from a tax on the transfer of funds abroad, charges on imports are established in special legislation.

To systematize information needed in the conduct of annual negotiations and to facilitate the harmonization effort in this field, LAFTA experts have divided all the foreign-trade charges into three categories: (1) fiscal charges, which cover duties, additional customs charges or surcharges, special taxes, and consular fees; (2) foreign-exchange taxes, which include foreign-exchange surcharges and taxes on the transfer of funds, on foreign exchange bought at official auctions, and on forward operations; and (3) monetary charges, consisting of prior deposits and similar requirements.

Difficulties engendered by such asymmetric and unsystematic structures are aggravated by the differing criteria employed in defining the tax charges themselves. At times, specific and ad valorem duties are applied simultaneously and thus become mixed duties. In other cases, the taxable commodities vary according to a specific tax objective. The units of measure utilized are dissimilar, in some instances corresponding to the metric system and its multiples (meter, kilogram, liter, etc.), and in others incorporating collateral definitions (gross kilogram, legal kilogram, net kilogram, etc.). Taxable value bases frequently differ: f.o.b.; c.i.f. (calculated by adding a fixed percentage to the f.o.b. value); the so-called domestic value, once a foreign commodity enters the country; appraised value (where the amount of the specific duties initially calculated must be converted into a "gold currency" equivalent by applying a fixed or variable factor); and "official" value (a price fixed in advance on each product and used as the basis for duty payment unless the invoice value happens to be bigger).

These factors make it difficult to effect comparative analysis of tax levels. Such a task would demand prior correlation of the national nomenclatures with the nomenclature used as the common base and the consolidation of the different duties into one. When this is done, evidence of unreasonably high customs levels and accentuated differences will often be uncovered with respect to similar products or products connected with the same economic activity. This statement is borne out by an examination of the new Argentine tariff, in which the different taxes formerly applied on the importation of each commodity have been consolidated in a single ad valorem figure.

For reasons of logic and objectivity, any effort aimed at harmonizing or unifying these highly variegated import-tax structures should be directed toward an independent criterion, based perhaps on the concept of ad valorem duty, in keeping with the most recent experience in the field and following the general outlines of the Brussels tariff system. In LAFTA's case, however, there is, as yet, no evidence of a definite orientation in this direction. Hence, the possibility should not be overlooked that the prospective common tariff, at least in minimum degree, will inherit certain features from the national tariffs and will set up specific duties of some kind for application to certain commodities.

Customs levels as between LAFTA countries also reveal very marked disparities, both from an over-all standpoint and in particular reference to certain products or groups of products. This problem was considered during the conference that formulated the Treaty of Montevideo. Article 10 of that treaty stipulates that customs negotiations must make allowances for the situation of those contracting parties whose duty levels and import restrictions are notably different from those of the other LAFTA associates.

The irrationality of many of the import taxes presently in effect and the disparate rates chargeable on the same product in the different countries make it well-nigh impossible to apply the average-calculation bases established by GATT for purposes of determining the duty levels of a common tariff. Even if it were susceptible of application, such a method would not comply with the provisions of Article 24 of the General Agreement on Tariffs and Trade, in the sense that the aggregate duties and restrictive regulations of the customs union should not entail a more burdensome incidence than that corresponding to the duties in force in the members' territories prior to the union's establishment. The use of simple averages, whatever the method employed, would produce an arbitrary external tariff whose rates would bear little or no relation to the essential factors that should be taken into account when drawing up a customs tariff.

The appropriate alternative would be to use the present tariffs solely as a source of reference for purposes of comparative analysis and choice of methodology and to apply more objective and independent criteria as the needs of the customs union may dictate. To obviate abrupt distortions in the national economies, once the presumably adequate tariff levels are fixed, union members might commit themselves to effect periodic approximations of their duty rates to a span of reference that would indicate the ideal duty rate, plus fixed tolerances above and below that ideal line. This span could be elastic (i.e., of variable width), depending on the special circumstantial differences pertaining to a given product or group of products. In any event, empirical methods for application during a certain number of years would appear to be in order for purposes of readjusting the tariff levels initially established to the future ideal level and of coping with unexpected situations that may arise during implementation of the common-tariff program.

Because of the LAFTA countries' dependence on their trade with the outside world, it may become necessary, at least for a reasonable period, to establish special provisions, designed to meet emergency problems of a general or individual nature, until such time as the various economic structures achieve an adequate degree of homogeneity. If provision is made for recourse to certain import restrictions and surcharges, approved in advance by the other member nations, the protection levels of any given country could be adjusted circumstantially to the ups and downs in the fortunes of its balance of payments.

In the field of direct import controls, Colombia and Mexico have instituted a fairly generalized use of the special import license. The quantitative restrictions, prohibitions, and administrative license systems in effect in certain of the other LAFTA countries do not, however, significantly influence their foreign trade, because these controls are restricted to a small number of products or regulate specific aspects of commercial activity.

Repeated reference has been made to the fact that governments applying the above-mentioned import-permit system are in a position to exercise strict control over trade with the remaining countries in the free-trade zone; to restrict the circulation of commodities on which duties have been rescinded or reduced; to regulate unilaterally their zonal payments position; and, at their discretion, to employ measures similar to those designed as safeguards in the treaty, but clearly intended for only highly exceptional use and contingent on special arrangements with the remaining contracting parties. On the other hand, if utilized as a tool to stimulate regional purchases, an import-licensing system can contribute powerfully to more effective trade discrimination in favor of the zone. However, all these considerations actually pertain only to the transition period of the program for reciprocal trade liberalization. As stipulated in the Montevideo Treaty, all import restrictions will have been eliminated by the time such a period comes to a close.

Perhaps the most important aspect of the matter under discussion is the theoretically possible use of the import-license mechanism as a means of persuasion in attracting investments to given fields of activity. In such a case, private firms would find themselves obliged to accept government directives in order to obviate the risk of having their importation possibilities seriously curtailed in the case of products that, in line with official policy, could be substituted by locally produced merchandise. When the country participates in an integration process, this coercive procedure could divert the natural flow of investment to that national territory or could channel such capital to areas of activity other than those agreed upon multilaterally.

The use of devices of this type has a considerable negative influence on efforts to harmonize foreign-trade policies of the member nations. In the first place, the customs-tariff levels of the respective countries are affected, since the necessary protection for local industry does not derive exclusively from fiscal measures. This is particularly true in Mexico, where importation problems are heightened by the long boundary line separating that country from so highly industrialized a nation as the United States. The problem thus arises of determining to what degree the economies of those countries can be compensated for the loss of the regulatory function of an import-licensing system by the duty rates incorporated into the common tariff.

Thus, it seems that the Latin American free-trade zone must evolve toward a customs union through diverse and complex stages. Completion of any one of these stages may change the outlook for the next, particularly in view of the possibility that other nations in the area may join the system.

As is the case elsewhere in the world, one area of activity that involves very significant difficulties is agriculture. Recognition of this circumstance is implicit in the Montevideo Treaty, which incorporates special provisions for this sector. The economies of LAFTA members depend, in large measure, on a number of agricultural pursuits carried out over an area of 6.5 million sq. mi. where the climate ranges from tropical to temperate. And although well-defined bases exist on which to build efforts for growing complementarity, certain fundamental difficulties stand in the way of encouraging free competition in agriculture. In the terms of the treaty, during the twelve-year transition period each country has the right to apply unilaterally measures to safeguard its economy, when the government considers that the trade concessions agreed upon result in, or may bring about, a substantial degree of economic harm. These clauses, which practically exempt agricultural commodities from certain basic commitments under the trade-freeing program, are offset, in theory, by the elimination of this special system once the time allotted for establishing the free-trade zone has elapsed. Since commerce in primary products, including agricultural commodities, will represent a substantial share of intraregional trade for a long time to come, the strict functioning of the treaty mechanisms will eventually subject the majority of such transactions to the rules of free competition.

However, a realistic approach to this situation would indicate the need for seeking a more feasible means of achieving agricultural integration of the zone. It does not seem possible, nor has it been possible, heretofore, in similar experiments in Europe, to establish free competition in farm production in a broadened market. On the contrary, if sizable distortions are to be avoided in the national economies, regulation of trade in agricultural commodities will be imperative. In that connection, it will be necessary to make an exhaustive study of the possibilities for agricultural complementarity and to create adequate conditions for the maximum utilization of the region's natural resources. The most logical solution would be to find a compromise between legitimate vested interests and organization of regional production in accordance with expert considerations.

The potential capacity of the agricultural sector for expansion is noteworthy. The initial increment will very probably derive from considerable possibilities open to import substitution. LAFTA countries annually import agricultural commodities worth $500 million, 47 per cent of which are supplied by third countries. It should be possible to substitute regional production for a sizable portion of commodities currently brought in from the outside. In addition, although the agricultural exports of LAFTA members comprise a very small number of commodities (which have been subjected to little or no processing), the efficient use of modern techniques could diversify external and regional marketing possibilities to a considerable extent.

The greatest difficulty in the path of any attempt to draw up a common agricultural program for LAFTA stems from the fact that there are no well-defined national policies and plans. The first requisite in accomplishing the desired objective would be to identify the general outlines of state agricultural policies in each of the member nations. This, in turn, calls for the compilation and analysis of provisions that are scattered through a tangled maze of legislative and administrative regulations. On many occasions, the measures taken have been inspired in the desire to solve circumstantial problems relating to a limited aspect or section of the agricultural economy. As a result, contradictory decisions have not been uncommon in relatively brief periods, sometimes within the same year. For this reason, it is very difficult to determine to what extent national agricultural-development aims conflict, and which factors are the best suited to the task of specialization for the greater collective benefit.

Despite the circumstances described above, any preliminary study on the subject would reveal the possibility of developing dynamic action aimed at satisfying the chronic deficits in foodstuffs and other agricultural commodity deficits in certain countries by using the surpluses customarily accumulated by others. As a matter of fact, even in cases in which producing zones do not, at present, have surpluses for export, the planned expansion of the corresponding activity, based on the assurance of an adequate market, could offset future shortages in the supply of these items in other parts of the area. A variety of processed agricultural commodities, whose commerce now accounts for only an insignificant share of intrazonal interchange as a whole, would subsequently be susceptible of an intensive rate of growth if common objectives were rationalized and the necessary commitments assumed.

Certain elements of judgment taken into consideration in examining the agricultural sector are also valid for focusing over-all national development programs in the direction of integration. The success of the Alliance for Progress plans aimed at the structural reorganization of the Latin American economies depends to a great extent on the realization, within a reasonable time, of a large-scale common market and the establishment of a greater degree of interdependence among the countries in the region. The economic and social objectives of the Alliance can be fully achieved only if the rate of industrial development is considerably accelerated and if, consequently, not only the existing bottlenecks are eliminated but, at the same time, the probability lessens that others as bad or worse can emerge. It is axiomatic that a market large enough to stimulate production on an adequate scale is essential to the expansion and diversification of manufacturing industries in Latin America.

The efficient implementation of the integration process to which LAFTA members are committed must be founded on intimate knowledge of the economic reality of each country; it also depends, in large measure, on the formulation of national plans that demonstrate due regard for the opportunities offered by the common market and, at the same time, discourage those investments which, although perhaps appropriate within the domestic environment exclusively, are not economically justified when projected to the regional level. Since LAFTA associates do not have sufficient capital to promote their development and, hence, must achieve optimum return on investment, it is imperative to avoid indiscriminate use of available financial resources, whether these are supplied out of national savings or originate in external aid.

If this scarce resource, capital, is to be adequately distributed, it is essential to make a careful analysis of each country's ability to develop the various industrial activities within the framework of the common market. The objective is to avoid undesirable duplication or multiplicity of effort in any one area, which would detract from investments in other fields offering a better relative return and might even create excessively rigorous conditions of competition. The consequences would be more serious still if each country were to plan expansion programs for its basic industrial activities with an eye exclusively to the internal market and without allowing for the certain, or very probable, inclusion of such commodities in the LAFTA liberalization program. Such an inclusion, apart from making a fundamental change in the size of the market, would nullify the protective barrier erected locally to support the productive activities involved. This last-mentioned effect is very important, for the planning process involves suggesting levels of protection in accordance with the projected increment in manufacturing output. On setting these levels, care should be taken, not only to protect internal industrial activity, but also to stimulate it by allowing reasonable external competition that will complement or replace, as the case may be, the internal competition that has diminished as a result of market conditions. In the case of commodities susceptible of placement in foreign markets, balanced protection is essential, since competition must be met abroad, as well as on the home front. If the national programs do not pay sufficient attention to the prospects and limitations inherent in integration, the policies for import substitution and export promotion included in such programs will be placed in jeopardy. As mentioned earlier, the problem of replacing imports and enhancing exports is intimately linked with the elaboration of a general foreign-trade policy.

Thus, the first essential in connection with the joint industrial development of LAFTA countries is the plotting of guidelines for the parallel or coordinated functioning of the national programs in such a way as to ensure their adaptation to integration objectives. Appropriate regional agencies are devoting themselves to this task at a time that is opportune, indeed, since most development plans in the area are still in the organization and project stage.

However, there are other problems of the utmost significance. It is important that common-market planning carefully weigh the objective of harmonious development of the area. This means that the expansion of manufacturing activities must not be permitted to rely exclusively on the spontaneous channeling of investments to areas that, for various reasons, are natural centers attracting capital. These reasons might include the existence of a more-developed industrial plant, involving a diversity of establishments capable of serving the large industrial complexes in subsidiary or complementary fashion; the greater flexibility and operational capacity of the corresponding financial market; and the size of the internal market itself, which, unquestionably, constitutes a basic guarantee for investment in the presence of any element of doubt with regard to the stability of the integration process.

LAFTA countries are persuaded of the need to devise formulas whose application will encourage the adequate location of activities in such a way that each nation will have a fair chance to accelerate its industrial development in harmony with that of the rest of the member states. Classified roughly in keeping with their relative degree of economic development, LAFTA associates lend themselves to division into three groups. Argentina, Brazil, and Mexico would constitute the highest classification, since they have an extensive and developed range of manufacturing activities and constitute the largest national markets in the area. The second group is made up of Colombia, Chile, Peru, and Uruguay; although their basic industries have attained a certain degree of development, insufficient demand has retarded and, on occasion, completely blocked the expansion of existing activities and the installation of new industrial facilities. Figuring in the third group are Ecuador and Paraguay, which qualify as beneficiaries of the special measures authorized by the Montevideo Treaty in favor of the less-developed nations in the zone.

The equitable distribution of opportunities, together with its corollaries in the areas of specialization and adequate division of labor, is one of the problems of primary concern to LAFTA. Its satisfactory resolution, involving the highly complex task of establishing workable norms in this field, is a prerequisite to the furtherance of the common market through the medium of balanced development of all the member countries.

Another crucial aspect of the LAFTA problem is to be found in the monetary field. In the short time that the contracting parties' reciprocal concessions have been in effect, in compliance with the liberalization mechanism provided for in the treaty, marked fluctuations in the value of the national currencies have had a disturbing influence on the trade prospects generated by the customs negotiations and even on the normal currents of intrazonal interchange. Deriving from successive devaluations in the recent past, abrupt changes in the par value of the monetary units of certain of the countries in the zone have distorted commercial relations and are obstructing the normal expansion of the export industries.

Any effort to solve this problem will inevitably encounter the basic difficulty that fluctuations in currency values are largely the result of circumstances typically present in an economy that is highly sensitive to the influence of its external sector and, hence, beyond the control of monetary and other national government authorities. By way of another negative influence, in terms of each country's over-all trade and balance-of-payments position, regional commerce is of relatively minor importance. In consequence, governments tend to disregard the effects of unstable exchange rates on zonal trade.

Action of any type aimed at establishing effective bases for avoiding this unsettling influence on regional economic relations should proceed gradually and with the utmost caution. The first step would be to constitute a committee of those responsible for the conduct of each country's monetary policy—the finance ministers or high-level central bank officials—and to assign them the task of evaluating the consequences of the measures adopted by the national authorities and analyzing the causes of the circumstantial instability of any given currency. As a second phase, this system of consultation could be extended to include all aspects of monetary policy. Once the habit of joint analysis of common problems is acquired, the confidence needed in essaying effective coordination of national policies in this field will, in time, follow.

The exposition of the problems involved in Latin America's integration process and the analysis of possible solutions could be extended to cover other fields having significant peculiarities, such as maritime, land, and air transport, labor policies, etc. The aim of the present essay has been simply to underscore certain aspects that are basic to an accurate appraisal of the achievements and deficiencies of the Latin American Free Trade Association. It is abundantly clear that, to be successful in this enterprise, the Latin American countries must start from scratch, creating everything from the most pedestrian (such as statistical methodology) to the most abstract (the "export psychology" for example). And that will take time, patience, and perseverance.

VIII

RAÚL PREBISCH

Surmounting Obstacles to a Latin American Common Market

Under the traditional (and now obsolete) pattern of international trade, which has been discussed elsewhere, the Latin American countries (as is still the case today) concentrated on commercial dealings with the large industrial centers. Their economic contact with one another was primarily limited to a small-scale interchange of certain primary commodities, and industrialization in the region developed in watertight national compartments. To serve the twofold aim of correcting the trend toward a foreign-trade bottleneck and promoting the economic feasibility of the industrialization process, the establishment of a common market is imperative.

Concerted with notable speed, LAFTA after only a few years of operation has easily surpassed the minimum liberalization commitments stipulated in the Montevideo Treaty. But owing to the sheer magnitude of the task the association is called upon to perform, there is a very real danger that its future rate of progress will become ponderous and hedged about by caution. Such a rate might be acceptable if we could turn back pages of history to those days in which the striking expansion of international trade lent steady impetus to the Latin American economies. As matters stand at present, however, when the serious obstacles of its development uncompromisingly demand of Latin America a new outlook, firm determination, and boldly constructive spirit, trade-liberalization progress (to date and in prospect) is woefully inadequate.

It would be a mistake to question the intrinsic efficacy of the instruments established under the Montevideo Treaty. Important policy decisions are required, however, before this efficacy can be reflected in concrete achievements, capable of counteracting the factors that can bring on early stagnation. The present system of periodical selective negotiations may find the climate becoming unpropitious, with the consequent risk that the entire endeavor may be reduced to a series of narrow and halfhearted preferential arrangements.

Goals for Regional Cooperation

Quantitative goals. This danger will persist until much clearer quantitative goals are established for the reduction and elimination of tariffs and other restrictions within a specific time limit. Failing that, the negotiations will be entirely lacking in the well-defined terms of reference that are requisite to success. These targets should not be set up in isolation, but should be accompanied by the groundwork for agreements for complementary functioning, under which industries of great importance for development strategy could be programmed. Before proceeding with these efforts, however, the concept of reciprocity must be clarified, and effective ways of ensuring it devised. Satisfactory achievement of this goal would, in turn, call for the establishment of agencies to promote reciprocal trade. All these interrelated matters necessitate the basic policy decisions referred to above.

Why is it so essential to fix these clearly defined quantitative targets? The LAFTA member governments have already assumed tariff-elimination commitments, particularly with regard to traditional commodities, in order to comply with GATT regulations. This is a relatively minor undertaking, however. Industrial products should also be covered, including not only those that are manufactured today but those that will inevitably have to be manufactured tomorrow through the application of increasingly difficult and costly techniques.

In order that LAFTA benefits may be gradually extended to the whole range of Latin American production, the quantitative targets must be established forthwith. Otherwise, the negotiations will rapidly cease to be binding and automatic, and the next step will be pressure from individual countries to obtain specific product concessions, which may often fail to coincide with the interests and claims of the other members. This, in turn, might retard the process of reducing and eliminating tariff duties and eventually bring it to a standstill. The establishment of quantitative targets would contribute to a radical change in such an attitude. Each country would have to make an effort to introduce a minimum number of reductions and eliminations every year, so that the goals agreed upon might gradually be attained.

Of what might these targets consist? Several formulas suggest themselves, but the simplest and most practicable is the arithmetic mean of tariff duties. I would recommend that, within a period of twelve years—perhaps slightly more or less, for the time limit is not the prime consideration—average duties applied by association members to their reciprocal trade be lowered to a maximum of 15 per cent and that all other restrictions of a protectionist nature be lifted.

The establishment of these goals should be combined with the obligation to reduce duties to a maximum of 30 per cent in the case of agricultural pursuits and industries developing at a natural rate of growth and to a maximum of 10 per cent in the case of dynamic industries. The rate-of-growth distinction was prompted by motives which will be expounded later.

It would be inexpedient to confine attention to the ultimate goal, without agreeing upon a gradual procedure with intermediary targets. Thus, at the halfway mark of the stipulated period, the tariff average should not exceed 30 per cent; maximum duties should not exceed 60 per cent for slow-growth industries and agriculture and 20 per cent for dynamic industries. Other restrictions would also have had to be reduced by one-half during the first six years; and, before the final twelve-year time limit was reached, a new agreement would have to be concluded on the basis of the experience acquired. In this way, a similar policy could be pursued during a second stage that it would be premature to attempt to envisage at this point.

Particular attention should be given to setting up a special procedure for very high tariffs, for example, those that are more than three times the maximum ultimately allowable for the group to which the product pertains (dynamic or slow-growth industries). The reduction from the present tariff level to a level three times as high as the final maximum (which was to be reached in two stages) would be effected proportionally and in the course of a very few years. When three times that maximum had been reached, the process of reduction would continue as described above.

Speed is essential in reducing the "excessive" portion of very high duties, so as to make way for market competition and spur on producer activities. In the case of commodities turned out by slow-growth industries, for example, a 90 per cent duty is felt to be conducive to salutary competition. If a special procedure were not adopted in such instances, the reduction of these very high duties might be completely inoperative from the standpoint of competition and trade throughout the greater part of the transitional period. The practical effects of such action would be felt only in the course of the final two or three years, with the result that not only would the advance toward integration be retarded, but a series of difficulties would accumulate that might engender strong opposition.

A policy decision does not require an exhaustive study of technical details. A standard nomenclature, of course, would have to be adopted; but this and other questions are ones on which technical experts would be expected to formulate recommendations for submission to the member governments. The essential point is that a high-level policy decision should fix the quantitative goals; for, in the absence of well-established targets, both intermediate and final, there is the distinct possibility that discussions will continue for years on end without significant progress.

Within the system of averages, different situations would arise. Whereas tariff duties on one series of products might be completely eliminated in the period agreed upon, in other instances it would be expedient to maintain a reasonable degree of protection. The time limits might be extended for countries at a relatively less advanced stage of development, in conformity with a principle that is fortunately embodied in the Montevideo Treaty.

Indubitably, the targets suggested will not seem very encouraging to those who would like to make straight for the common market by means of the total elimination of tariffs; at the other extreme, they will appear recklessly ambitious to those who give the name of "prudence" to the manifest imprudence of essaying only clumsy and hesitant steps in meeting the grave historic challenge of these as well as other structural reforms.

Those who advocate the immediate establishment of the common market through total tariff liberalization cherish the hope that the free interplay of economic forces will solve all problems without the need for planning of any kind. Planning is not incompatible with competition, which is an indispensable requisite for the efficacious operation of the economic system under which we live. Yet, paradoxical as it may seem, some intervention in the free interaction of economic forces is necessary in order to create a propitious climate for the operation of that competition: impersonal intervention on the part of the state, designed to guide, safeguard, and encourage, but not interfere with, the conduct of individuals in economic life, taking care to avoid the imposition of arbitrary restrictions.

Customs protection has been indulged in excessively, and, by limiting or completely eliminating competition from abroad, has frequently given rise to internal restrictive practices or monopolistic combines that weaken the incentive to attain satisfactory levels of productivity. Even without the advent of the Latin American Free Trade Association, it would have been advisable gradually to reduce protection to a reasonable level, had it not been for the frequent evidences of the chronic trend toward balance-of-payments disequilibrium.

The operation and limitations of competitive forces. Once the need for such action is recognized, the question is how to set about revitalizing competition. There are three main areas to consider: agriculture; slow-growth industries; and dynamic industries.

In agriculture, traditional exports are already the subject of a joint commitment for the complete abolishment of customs duties within the next ten years. However, it is not enough to engage in an undertaking of this nature and then simply await developments. Programs must be formulated for the rational distribution of production within the free-trade zone, taking into account not only present demand but the considerable increments anticipated in future, which will make it necessary to cultivate land of widely differing productivity. Such programs will, in some cases, require special regulatory measures. Only in this way can competition develop without creating serious disturbances; for productive land must not be allowed to lie idle (even if this means it must be used in a very different way than before), and manpower that can be absorbed either in some other area of agricutlure or elsewhere must not be left unemployed. The out-and-out abolition of customs duties could have this disastrous effect—underutilization of land and unemployment—on both traditional and other agricultural production.

The situation is similar as regards existing industries that have reached a vegetative stage of expansion, where demand increases only gradually, on a par with population growth. Income redistribution would undoubtedly provide a strong stimulus to these industries and facilitate their adaptation to the needs of the common market. To give them time to effect this adaptation, a gradual and well-planned system for the reduction and eventual elimination of import duties is essential. If the pace were too rapid, and the aim were total removal of protection in this first stage, a flood of new investment might seek to replace existing capital, with a view to increasing productivity at the expense of manpower absorption.

In fact, this is the main reason behind the "average" formula, which reduces some tariff charges to zero but permits others to continue their protective function in moderation. The question is actually one of degree, and the admissible flexibility should under no circumstances be used to hold customs duties higher than the 30 per cent maximum for longer than twelve months, in the case of slow-growth industries or primary production.

Dynamic industries ordinarily find themselves in very different circumstances, owing to their great development possibilities. This is particularly true of the new enterprises that will have to be established in the next few years to further the import-substitution policy, but this time within LAFTA's multilateral framework. In many of these cases compromising industries producing capital goods, durable consumer goods, and intermediate products, a total abolition of tariffs is required; in others, duties will have to be maintained, but at a level not exceeding the 10 per cent ceiling mentioned earlier.

Steps should also be taken for the early abrogation (e.g., within a six-year period) of duties applicable to basic raw materials, supplied either by agriculture or by the extractive industries and including petrochemicals. This measure is of the utmost importance, for the differences in industrial-goods prices from one country to another often derive from a variation in raw-materials costs. Some countries customarily protect marginal production of such materials; as a result, industry has to operate at a high cost level, even though its relative efficiency may be higher than that obtained in other countries, where industry has local access to inexpensive raw materials or can import them under low tariffs.

The countries belonging to the Latin American Free Trade Association produce practically all basic raw materials. If import duties on these commodities were abolished and a common tariff worked out to apply to third countries, it would be possible to effect large-scale substitution of imports from outside the area. A policy of this kind would, in some cases, almost certainly mean the end of marginal production, making it necessary to seek means of compensating workers and entrepreneurs for the resulting hardship. This could be one of the functions of the special fund described later.

Basic raw materials generally have a very low unit value, and transportation costs are so high that, in themselves, they constitute a form of protection for the production of the widely separated areas of Latin America. Consequently, the adjustment that will have to be made in these marginal sectors will, in all likelihood, be somewhat less drastic than that required in the rest of industry.

Industrial complementarity agreements. The dynamic industries are those which offer the greatest possibilities for agreements of this type—bringing us to the second point that calls for a high-level policy decision. In contrast to the slow-growth group, the dynamic industries are not so much in need of a renewal of existing capital as they are of investment in greatly expanded industrial plants in order to meet a rapidly rising demand. Here, the problem is to coordinate and distribute investments among the member countries in such way that all will receive equivalent benefits within the common market. Such benefits might derive from the integrated industries themselves or from other activities and would reflect the application of the principle of reciprocity already referred to. However, it should be emphasized that an equitable distribution of benefits cannot be expected to result from the mere interaction of economic forces. It will have to be ensured by programs for the complementary functioning of particular industries in the dynamic sector, and of those industries in conjunction with other activities.

There are various ways of achieving this distribution of industries. One would be to give exclusive export preference within the area to a country to which the program had assigned a particular industrial activity. But this might result in a patchwork of preferential treatment and might also lead to monopoly situations, at the expense of technical progress and of the consumer. The same would occur if member countries were forbidden to establish industries not allocated to them under the program. A time limit could be set on such privileges, of course, but there would be a risk that the industries thus sheltered would become accustomed to protection; and it would be difficult, if not impossible, to abandon preferential treatment at some later date and restore competition within the area.[1]

Does this mean that the activities established under a complementarity program would be exposed from the outset to competition from similar plants located in the same country or in other LAFTA members? If this were so, there would be an understandable reluctance to take part in a program that might founder within a short period. The solution is to provide incentives in the form of tax benefits, technical assistance, and long-term financing for the industries established under the program. During a given period, these benefits would not be extended to any similar plants that might want to go into business either in the same country or in other countries in the area. Thus, there would be an initial advantage for the program-based industries, but they would have to be prepared to face eventual competition from nonprogram plants. In the presence of this latent threat, they would be obliged to make use of their initial advantages, consolidate their technical and financial position, and produce at a reasonable cost level.

[1] These observations do not apply to Central America, where the establishment of a common market under particular conditions of industrial development is well advanced.

Arrangements for complementary functioning were anticipated in the Montevideo Treaty, but the system of incentives has not yet been organized. However, this is not the only reason why just one agreement has been reached to date, despite the very promising prospects involved. Apart from the excessive tariffs that already existed, the exorbitant restrictions that many Latin American countries have imposed, for balance-of-payments reasons, on certain imported goods have led private enterprise to follow the easy path of confining itself to the domestic market. Under these circumstances, production costs are very high, but profits are nonetheless substantial.

Recent events in the motor-vehicle industry are highly instructive. Not only are there a number of countries all trying to do the same thing, but there is also an incredible proliferation of anti-economic plants within a single country.[2] No matter how equitable a program for complementary functioning in the automotive industry or any other industry is, it is bound to encounter almost insuperable resistance unless there is a firm resolve to abolish restrictions and gradually to reduce duties between the member countries until moderate tariffs are reached (i.e., not in excess of the previously mentioned maximum of 10 per cent). In these circumstances, the experts asked to study a given program would not discuss whether arrangements for complementary functioning would be suitable for this or that industry, or whether tariffs ought to be reduced, but would devote themselves to finding ways and means of putting the governments' decisions into effect.

Although the case of the steel industry is quite different, it is clear that the industry is developing in each country on a completely autonomous basis, with the aim of producing the full range of products, whatever the cost. In justifying this state of affairs, a very odd argument tends to be used: "Let us first integrate within our own country and then think about multinational integration." By that time, it will, unfortunately, be too late. At present, Latin America has a production capacity of 5.5 million metric tons of steel ingots, and planned expansion will boost that figure to an estimated 18 million metric tons by 1970. However, 20 per cent of total consumption will still have to be supplied through imports. The equivalent of $3 billion will be needed to carry out these plans. Will this sizable amount of hard-earned

[2] Apart from Argentina and Brazil, countries that are already in production in the strict sense, there are four others—Chile, Colombia, Mexico, and Venezuela—that have vehicle assembly plants and are about to embark on production. The total Latin American market for passenger cars, estimated at slightly over 300,000 units a year, will have to be divided among something like forty existing and potential producers. Contrast this with the case of the major European producers, each of whom distributes some 250,000 to 500,000 units a year.

funds be invested on the basis of the steel production pattern now existing in each country, or will some form of specialization be sought?

There is a vast field for complementary-industry arrangements, which does not, by any means, exclude certain slow-growth sectors. Nevertheless, attention will have to be concentrated on a number of dynamic industries, since they do not face the same handicaps as the slow-growth activities when it comes to a policy of all-out tariff liberalization.

Certain difficulties are likely to arise if all member countries—on an equal footing insofar as their particular resources and industrial structure will permit—are to be allowed to go their own way in establishing within the same industry new production lines intended for the common market. In order to cope with this problem, it would be well for the complementarity agreements to be prepared and negotiated simultaneously for a wide range and variety of industrial activities. In this way, it will be easier for each country to obtain the essential reciprocity in the development of new industries capable of competing in the common market.

The principle of reciprocity. In the final analysis, the effectiveness of these arrangements and of the whole system under consideration will depend, in large measure, on the application of the principle of reciprocity. The interpretation of this principle, consecrated in the Montevideo Treaty, must be made crystal clear and can be stated in a few words: No member country can expect to derive more benefits than it offers. But the treaty does not stipulate what measures should be adopted to correct a persistent inequality of benefits deriving from its application.

The first thing to do, in this connection, is to provide for the technical and financial means to promote economic activity in the less-favored countries. This must be a collective commitment wholeheartedly supported by all the members of the association, in the manner explained below.

Second, the countries that consistently export more than they import from the area must take measures to restore a situation of equity. A more rapid reduction of import restrictions and duties, with a view to stimulating regional imports into countries having a trade surplus, might be effective *if accompanied by a reasonable margin of preferential treatment in favor of area products*. It is essential that this serious gap left in the treaty be filled. Lowering tariff barriers would be pointless if application to the rest of the world were to render preferential treatment inoperable or nullify it completely. Provision would thus have to be made for a minimum margin of preferential treatment for area members, covering any items on which duties have been lowered. Maximum margins must also be set, but the appropriate time for such action would be when the common external tariff is established.

Third, in extreme cases when all else fails, the less-favored countries might undertake trade-liberalization measures at a slower rate than the other LAFTA nations. However, this attempt to equalize benefits would not exempt the less-developed nations from instituting their own corrective measures. Special caution should be exercised as regards the overvaluation of currency, which could nullify the whole process of reciprocity. Monetary distortion of this or any other kind will have to be ruled out if the free-trade zone is to function properly.

A clear definition of the principle of reciprocity will help to dispel the misgivings entertained in some circles regarding plans for complementary industrial facilities. Since it will obviously not be feasible to arrive at an absolutely equal level of trade benefits in every arrangement or set of arrangements, recourse to other activities will be required. If equivalent benefits must be provided in each individual instance, the task of setting up agreements for complementary functioning might become long drawn out and complicated, when it should be precisely the opposite. In practical application, the principle of reciprocity will mean that each member country should have the assurance that, if the complementary-industry agreements and the reduction or elimination of duties do not provide equal benefits, other measures will be taken for that purpose. Although this obligation should be binding on all the regional associates, it is particularly important that it be adhered to by those countries that export more than they import.

From another standpoint, there appears to be some merit in the recommendation that the application of the principle of reciprocity be made to tie in with a payments arrangement. The effects of measures designed to ensure equal benefits might not be felt for some time; meanwhile, a country in a deficit position would have to spend dollars, usually in short supply, to pay its area creditors. Monetary authorities are understandably reluctant to support complementary-industry arrangements or competition-stimulating tariff reductions, if imbalances are apt to ensue that can be corrected only at long term. The debtor country must be given ample time to pay; and the creditor nation must be urged to use its surplus for additional imports from the area and, at the same time, to take measures aimed at preventing a continuance of the trend toward disequilibrium. All this would be done as specific expression of the principle of reciprocity. Of course, these strictly regional payments arrangements would become superfluous if an increase in exports to the rest of the world were to improve the balance of payments. In the meantime, they would stimulate the move toward the common market.

The Functioning of the Common Market

Promotional agencies. The need for promotional agencies within the common market is another important question that calls for top-level policy decisions. Before entering into a discussion of this point, however, we will digress briefly to touch on a subject that has a bearing not only on the common market but on economic development itself in its broadest sense: the technical and economical retardation of Latin American private enterprise in comparison with its counterpart in the major industrial centers. Unless an intensive and sustained effort is made gradually to narrow the gap between the two, we run the risk of building on quicksand.

The formation of the common market offers a peculiarly favorable opportunity for solving this problem. There is general concern that foreign enterprise, precisely because of its superiority and marketing knowledge, will make better use of the vast opportunities for trade that are emerging in the member countries and take the lead in the complementary-industry agreements and in the area in general. Unless this danger is averted, the entire undertaking will, in all probability, find its progress effectively blocked by heavy opposition. The fundamental solution is to support Latin American enterprise, so that it can achieve its full vigor in the formation of the common market and can stand up to foreign firms, either by making common cause with them or by competing on an equal footing. Competition on an unequal basis usually leads to the eventual liquidation of the weaker party, or, at the very least, subordination to the stronger.

Systematic support for Latin American enterprise in industry and agriculture is called for in three main areas: (1) complementary undertakings; (2) production for export, particularly in the countries that are less advanced and/or have not been granted reciprocal advantages; and (3) activities that require modification to meet competition, together with those needed to absorb the portion of the labor force thrown out of work in the adjustment process.

Approached from another angle, the promotion task should be carried out in the two fields of fiscal incentives and technical and financial action. On the technical side, a promotional agency should be set up to work in close contact with governments and private enterprise with a view to conducting the necessary studies for accomplishing the aims set forth above.

The experience that the ECLA Secretariat has acquired through contacts with the Latin American industrial community has convinced me of the need for technical promotion and the effective cooperation that can be elicited from that community. This is not to suggest that a vast and complex mechanism be set up to engage the services of a host of experts of various kinds. What is needed is preliminary coordination work, performed by experts who are already assigned to international or bilateral technical assistance programs or who are independently contracted.

A promotional agency of this kind could also assist by submitting applications for the requisite financing and preparing the concrete projects into which the proposals would be converted, once they were approved in principle. By channeling international technical assistance, both public and private, and combining it with local technical skills, the promotional agency would help to correct another of the weak points that have developed in the Latin American experience. Lastly, it could also undertake to engage the technical services needed in setting up initial plant operations. Its functions would, of course, be similar to those performed by development agencies in some of the Latin American countries. Although its sphere of action would extend to several countries, the promotional institution would work very closely with the national development agencies. In fact, for all practical purposes it would be the common-market development corporation.

Common-market support for Latin American enterprise must be complemented by suitable medium- and long-term financing. The Inter-American Development Bank (IDB) has repeatedly manifested its determination to take an active part in this endeavor. If the governments concerned lend strong impetus to the advance toward a common market by adopting the broad political decisions that are needed, the next question is whether the market's initial limited resources will permit it to assume the leading role for which it was destined in the region's grand design. Admittedly, there is no definite basis of judgment for determining the volume of additional resources needed to cover this special financing—apart from LAFTA's future requirements—but a $500 million figure is not considered excessive. The fund should be accumulated through a quota subscription system, with all due allowance for participation by private foreign capital in the arrangements for complementary industrial facilities.[3]

If confined to the agreement members, the political decision to create such a fund would obviously be merely symbolic. The United

[3] This type of financing for industries and other activities in the common market should not be confused with the system of export credits that is being put into practice by the IDB, although the two are closely related.

States has indicated a willingness to cooperate in the formation of the common market. That country's participation in this financing, quite apart from its intrinsic significance, would be clear proof that its attitude is primarily inspired not by the desire to open up new fields for U.S. private investment but to lend positive stimulus to Latin America's own capacity to develop.

Central America as an economic unit. The Central American countries have made significant progress toward the establishment of their regional common market. They have assumed firm commitments to bring this project to completion within a few years, and the governments are displaying an active interest in integrated industrial planning. Central America is thus moving toward economic unity, and, hence, will be able to join the free-trade area in a bloc, without in any way deterring the implementation of its own plans. Moreover, Central America will be eligible for the treatment established for an economic unit at a relatively less advanced stage of development and, therefore, will be able to reduce its customs duties vis-à-vis other members of the Latin American Free Trade Association at a slower rate than is expected of the more highly developed group.

Progress toward the common market: magnitude of the effort required. Well-planned and simultaneous action in all the fields mentioned above is imperative if automatically functioning elements are to be incorporated, without risk, in the system of targets proposed. However, the very fact of automatic functioning intensifies the urgency of laying down clearly defined guidelines for the gradual advance toward the common market. It is from such guidelines that the basic principles will be derived that are essential for the formulation of each country's economic-development plans. Planning itself, as it evolves, will gradually afford better criteria for application to common market problems. In other words, a reciprocal and active relationship must exist between the principles determining the allocation of resources under national plans and the measures establishing the common market.

All this calls for a more sustained and extensive effort than Latin America has ever yet essayed. The vast undertaking must be approached with foresight and courage, without which nothing great or lasting can be achieved in community life. Many formidable obstacles will have to be surmounted. Discipline will have to be imposed on competition; and competition conditioned by state intervention will necessitate major adjustments in economic activity, as tariffs are lowered or eliminated. However painful, these requirements are a *sine qua non* for the dynamic efficacy of the system.

Difficulties of another kind will also have to be faced. As a general rule, integration efforts are going forward independently of the planning task, and coordination will be indispensable. The proposals of the Latin American Free Trade Association in this connection are worthy of special note.[4] Similarly, the introduction of structural reforms and the choice of instruments for their implementation will have to give due consideration to integration efforts. In like manner, the commitments deriving from such efforts will have to be in line with the structural reforms.

In other words, the advance toward the common market will entail a continuous series of coordination efforts, which will not be spontaneously generated, but will grow out of carefully devised measures adopted at the national or international level, as the case may be. Internal economic policy will indubitably have to be subjected to discipline—a discipline that, in any event, is inescapable, irrespective of common-market considerations. Overvaluation or undervaluation of currencies will cause serious disruptions of reciprocal trade. This does not mean, however, that the common market cannot be made operative, but merely means that steps must be taken to correct such distortions, which harm not only intra-Latin American trade but trade in general, in addition to producing serious internal repercussions. Of a certainty, the need for a sound monetary policy adapted to development requirements will become even more imperative in the presence of a common market.

The task at hand is by no means an easy one, but present-day Latin America has too much at stake to tolerate shirking. Difficulties must be overcome on every front; and discouragement, indifference, and defeatism must not be allowed to gain a greater hold over those who fail to grasp the true significance of current events. The course of those events cannot be stayed, for there is a light on the horizon heralding the dawn of a new will to achieve. The new movement, perhaps in the not too distant future, will take up a great many necessary tasks that, at present, are being deliberately left undone in a futile endeavor to perpetuate a situation that is doomed to ultimate destruction because it no longer meets the test of dynamic progress. Let us with our own hands and in our own way form the demolition crew, here and now, when history beckons impatiently to Latin America and, in the midst of a world of antagonisms and anomalies, offer the region a unique opportunity to build anew, and to place its own vigorously authentic stamp on the ineluctable and sweeping process of change.

[4] Several problems of this type were discussed at a meeting held in Lima in April, 1963, of the representatives of the LAFTA agencies concerned with the planning, encouragement, and guidance of industrial development.

IX

PLÁCIDO GARCÍA REYNOSO

Problems of Regional Industrialization

Over a period of time, industrialization has become one of the most efficient tools to which developing countries can lay hand in the gradual attainment of their economic independence. In the presence of the earlier, and continuing, unfavorable effects on those countries from the instability of international markets for raw materials, industrialization helps lessen the impact of the factors that impede sustained economic growth in underdeveloped areas. In effect, the progressive shift from agricultural activities toward industry has resulted in greater and better-paid employment opportunities for labor; the processing of domestic raw materials within national territory, instead of their exportation in an unmanufactured state; and an improvement in the economic structure, in such a way as to provide a basis for import substitution and export diversification.

The Latin American Free Trade Association is distinguished from analogous regional economic cooperation systems operating in the world's industrial areas by one basic characteristic. Although the legal structure adopted might lead one to assume the contrary, the fundamental aim of the Treaty of Montevideo, which created the association, is not confined to increasing commercial interchange between the participating republics by means of mutually accorded customs-duty preferences. The treaty also seeks to accelerate the process of economic development in an area where most countries' economies are in a state of stagnation. In effect, the Preamble to this document declares that the countries that founded the Latin American Free Trade Association are "aware that economic development should be attained through the maximum utilization of available production factors and the more effective coordination of the development programs of the different production sectors."

Expressing this general objective in more concrete terms, Chapter 3 of the Treaty of Montevideo, entitled "Expansion of Trade and Economic Complementarity," stipulates that, by way of intensifying their economic integration and complementarity, the contracting parties will endeavor to coordinate their respective industrialization policies in gradual, but increasing, fashion. They will also sponsor private agreements among representatives of the economic interests involved and may, among themselves, enter into sectoral industrial-complementarity agreements. Such complementarity accords will establish the tariff-liberalization programs for application to products in the respective industrial branch and may incorporate provisions aimed at harmonizing tariffs on the raw materials and parts used in the manufacture of such commodities. The same chapter of the treaty goes beyond the industrial-complementarity agreements. In the terms of Article 15, to facilitate the integration and complementary functioning of their economies, the member countries commit themselves to undertake to harmonize their import and export regimes as well as the treatment of capital, goods, and services originating outside LAFTA.

Three years after the entry into force of the Montevideo Treaty, and independent of the increment in intraregional trade attributable to the progressive multilateral elimination of customs barriers and other restrictions, currents in favor of the coordination and complementary functioning of industrial activities in the zone are beginning to gather force. As emphasized in a recent report, presented to the Organization of American States:

> In an underdeveloped region, the freeing of trade alone is not likely to be sufficient to spark a great economic expansion, as was the case in industrially advanced Europe. The newly created opportunities and potentialities have to be exploited directly through a coordinated effort and new mechanisms because the existing financial and organizational resources within the individual countries tend to be inadequate to take maximum advantage of such new opportunities.[1]

However, coordinated regional effort and the performance of the new mechanisms required by industrial integration are hindered by (in addition to other difficulties) the nature of the process followed

[1] Harvey S. Perloff and Rómulo Almeida, "Regional Economic Integration in the Development of Latin America," *Economía Latinoamericana,* I, No. 2 (November, 1963), 154.

by Latin American industrialization in the last quarter of a century and by the pronounced differences among present levels of industrial activity in each of the countries in the region. The problem therefore arises of how to effect the simultaneous integration of the industrial structures of the more-developed countries—such as Argentina, Brazil, and Mexico—and, at the same time, create conditions that will permit the emergence of modern industry in the republics whose economic development has been relatively slower.[2]

During the first postwar decade, characterized by the relatively high rate of economic development in Latin America, the more developed countries of Latin America continued the industrialization programs they had undertaken during, or even before, World War II, and most of the other countries in the area initiated theirs. Thus it was that the first nondurable-consumer-goods-producing plants appeared, even in countries whose economic structures had not evolved to a very great extent. By the middle of the past decade, the region as a whole had achieved a very advanced level of import substitution in the case of consumer manufactures, while an increasing number of Latin American republics had started to produce capital goods. To give a quantitative idea of the level of Latin American industrial development at the time the region entered the stage of accelerated promotion of heavy industry (1954–56), suffice it to recall that, in the mid-1950's, regional production did not supply even 10 per cent of total regional demand for machinery and equipment, as against 75 per cent in chemicals, 62 per cent in paper and paperboard products, and 89 per cent in cotton textiles and yarns.[3]

However, in every country, industrialization to date—achieved in a majority of cases under the aegis of strong tariff protection—has been accompanied by high costs, low productivity, idle production capacity,

[2] Although the Montevideo Treaty makes the single distinction between nations having greater or lesser relative economic development, in actual fact LAFTA comprises three groups of countries: the two already mentioned, and one at an intermediate level. This middle classification corresponds to Colombia, Chile, Peru, and Uruguay, which have comparatively advanced consumer-goods industries and are entering the stage of more complex industrial undertakings. Passed at the third meeting of the LAFTA Conference which adjourned in December of 1963, Resolution 71 (III) recognizes that, to achieve balanced development of the zone, joint measures should be adopted with a view to promoting in the four countries mentioned above the establishment or expansion of productive activities whose development would be of zonal interest or for which the respective domestic markets are too small.

[3] ECLA, "Influence of the Common Market on Latin American Economic Development," *The Latin American Common Market* (United Nations, 1959; No. 59 II U.N.), pp. 53–92.

and, consequently, high prices to the consumer. In some instances, as emphasized by Dr. Raúl Prebisch in Chapter 8 of this volume, a situation has been reached that simply cannot be sustained in the long run. For example, in the automotive industry, which requires sizable investments, "not only are there [as Dr. Prebisch notes in his essay] a number of countries all trying to do the same thing, but there is also an incredible proliferation of anti-economic plants within single countries." There are six countries (Argentina, Brazil, Colombia, Chile, Mexico, and Venezuela) that are already producing motor vehicles, plan to manufacture them shortly, or have auto assembly plants. The over-all Latin American market, estimated at some 300,000 units per year, has about forty present and potential manufacturers, while the average European plant produces between 250,000 and 500,000 automobiles annually. Thus, the rational and coordinated use of resources available in the region is effectively blocked by each country's effort to establish its own integrated industries in response to balance-of-payments reasons or for prestige motives that disregard economies of scale. Such a situation is serious, indeed, in view of the shortage throughout the region of both internal and external financial resources—resources that must be supplied in ever-increasing volume to satisfy the need to establish new industries having a high capital density. An additional and sometimes acute problem is the scarcity of experts and technicians skilled in the design, installation, and operation of modern industrial plants.

However, the extent to which the possible progress of regional industrial development depends on the relatively limited Latin American markets should not be overestimated, for, in numerous activities, the optimum size of the plant is not necessarily larger than that which the present situation of such markets would dictate.[4] At the same time, it should be emphasized that adequate size, given conditions of reasonable tariff protection, is essential to the economic functioning of installations in the basic industries. At the close of the past decade, no Latin American country appeared to have an internal market large enough to permit it to take due advantage of modern mass-production techniques, although it is evident that some of the larger countries, such as Argentina, Brazil, and Mexico, had begun to offer favorable demand conditions in certain fields of basic industry. According to ECLA estimates prepared a few years ago, the largest national market

[4] See in this connection data gathered by Sidney S. Dell, *Problemas de un mercado común en América Latina* (Mexico: CEMLA, 1959), pp. 28–34; and by A. J. Brown, "Economic Separatism versus a Common Market in Developing Countries," *Yorkshire Bulletin of Economic and Social Research*, XIII, No. 1 (May, 1961), 33–40.

in Latin America at the halfway mark in the past decade had an annual purchasing power of some $13.2 billion.[5] In two other republics in the region, purchasing power amounted to some $10 billion yearly, while the individual markets of another four nations ranged from $2 billion to $5 billion per year, and those of four more were just over $500 million. Each of the remaining nine Latin American countries had an annual purchasing power of less than half a billion dollars. To determine what these figures really mean as an index to the region's industrial growth process, a comparison might be made, for example, with the size of the automobile market in the United States, which alone represents a purchasing power of some $7.5 billion annually.

The problem of industrialization on a national scale in developing countries is further complicated in industries where technological progress is rapid, or where there are frequent changes in marketing practices that affect consumer preferences. Both these circumstances have been present in the case of certain products manufactured by the chemical industry, for example. In this field, the process of import substitution of finished goods is well advanced in the larger countries and has begun in the republics having a lower development level. In 1959, on the eve of the signing of the Montevideo Treaty, total Latin American consumption of chemicals, including raw materials, intermediate goods, and finished products, was valued at slightly more than $3 billion. Of that amount, an estimated $2.2 billion represented chemicals that originated in the area, with the remainder (approximately $850 million) having been brought in from third countries. Argentina, Brazil, and Mexico jointly accounted for 76 per cent of Latin America's chemical production and 66 per cent of its consumption. In those three countries, imports (with the exception of heavy chemicals and various intermediate goods, such as synthetic rubber and certain synthetic resins and fibers) were substituted almost in their entirety by domestic production.[6] In 1959, imports represented only 14 per cent of Brazil's total consumption of chemical products, while the percentages for Argentina and Mexico were 17 per cent and 32 per cent, respectively.

This progress notwithstanding, demand for basic, intermediate, and finished chemicals continued to expand apace throughout Latin America, with particular emphasis on the new products in which the

[5] "Influence of the Common Market on Latin American Economic Development," p. 53.

[6] At present, Brazil consumes locally made synthetic rubber and even exports some surpluses to Mexico. Argentina produces certain types of this commodity, and construction work on installations for its manufacture will soon go forward in Mexico. Various synthetic resins and fibers are already in production in several countries in the zone.

Latin American consumer became interested as a result of the demonstration effect of consumption patterns in the more-advanced countries. Industrial expansion is reflected not only in greater demand for investment resources, but exerts constant pressure in the direction of product diversification. Preliminary studies in this field, for example, indicate that, in general, whenever a chemical industry is established to supply the region's global market, it will be assured of efficient operation, based on the application of steadily progressing technology, and can maintain an adequate margin of return. According to experts in the field, this regional industry could face up to international competition with a minimum of tariff protection in some cases and none at all in others.[7] On the other hand, in the absence of large-scale production tailored to the possibilities offered by the Latin American Free Trade Association and, hopefully, by the eventual establishment of a regional common market, the difference between Latin American costs and international prices would be such that the new branches of the chemical industry could not look forward to a reasonable profit margin. Having discarded the possibility of establishing the complete range of chemical plants on a national scale, for the reasons outlined above, there is the alternative of meeting domestic supply shortages out of imports. This proposal, however, must be rejected out of hand. There is no indication whatsoever in the international trade picture, at present or in the foreseeable future, that Latin America's capacity to import will expand sufficiently in the next ten or fifteen years to permit the region to embark on the indiscriminate importation of all the chemicals that might be in demand.

It has been affirmed that the progressive liberalization of inter-Latin American trade, by means of a gradual reduction in customs duties and the elimination of other restrictions, will automatically induce integration and industrial specialization and will, moreover, create strong incentives for the transfer of domestic savings to manufacturing and will encourage channeling to that activity of sizable amounts of external savings, in the form of foreign direct investment. Such an assertion appears to be accurate, but only up to a point. Obviously, when brought to bear on existing industries, the specialization process in a much-expanded market will result in a better location of individual firms, based on access to natural resources, availability of skilled labor, financing possibilities, and other factors. Both integration and industrial specialization would enable manufacturing firms to operate under conditions of greater efficiency, with higher productivity and optimum size (all of which, in turn, would result in lower

[7] CEPAL, *La industria química en América Latina* (New York: United Nations, 1963; 64. II. G. 7).

prices), provided that situations of monopoly or oligopoly are avoided.

However, since knowledge of the Latin American reality is as yet incomplete, and in view of the urgent need to accelerate the region's economic development, preferably in harmonious fashion, the task of changing the region's industrial structure should not be left to the free working of market forces, as they gradually emerge from the increasing liberalization of trade flows within Latin America. The problems that could arise from the free operation of these forces would be the probable concentration of industry in a small number of areas, the harmful impact of unbridled competition on the existing industrial structure, and the entirely justified demands on the part of the less-developed countries to participate in the dynamic industrialization processes generated by economic cooperation among the member countries of the Latin American Free Trade Association.[8]

To circumscribe the future development of regional industry—the primary instrument for promoting economic development—would be inconceivable to certain association members. All LAFTA participants should share in regional industrial progress. In effect, the Montevideo Treaty requires that zonal economic-development efforts conform to rules that reflect due regard for the interests of each and every association member. In other words, simply to open new markets in the area for the relatively more advanced countries is not the purpose of the cooperative endeavor sponsored by LAFTA. Such a situation would not only be unfair but would disregard a basic fact that, in order for those new regional markets to provide effective opportunities for enhanced commerce, the intermediate and smallest countries must vigorously expand their purchasing power by stepping up their export trade with the other zone members. "The strengthening of national economies," the Preamble to the Montevideo Treaty reads,

[8] Resolution 71, mentioned earlier, which aims at promoting industrialization in LAFTA members of intermediate economic development, and which extends this opportunity also to the least-developed countries, was adopted expressly as the result of justified pressures exerted by these two groups during the course of the third meeting of the LAFTA Conference. Resolution 73, passed by the conference in November, 1963, authorizes Ecuador to protect a number of domestically produced commodities against competition from the other associates for a period of as much as five years. The products involved are sulfuric acid, aluminum sulfate, chemical fertilizers, iron and steel, farm machinery and implements, and hand tools. As provided in Resolution 74, which also was approved during the same meeting of the LAFTA Conference, the contracting parties are obliged to take financial and technical measures aimed at accelerating economic development in general, and industrialization in particular, in the countries whose economies are relatively less developed.

"will contribute to the expansion of trade within Latin America and with the rest of the world. . . ."

It is the purpose of the Latin American Free Trade Association, not to accentuate the already wide differences in development levels in the area, but rather to stimulate economic growth and market diversification in all the member countries, on the basis of rational specialization and reciprocity of benefits. For this reason, priority attention should be given to planning zonal development at the government level and to introducing certain corrective regional mechanisms that will effectively block excessive concentration of industrial activities in a limited number of areas simply by virtue of the advantages offered by external economies.

However, an approach from another angle is equally valid. As mentioned earlier, pressing development needs and balance-of-payments problems created a situation in which present industrial structures at the national level were established independent of considerations of economic performance and, therefore, under conditions substantially different from those that characterize the industrial evolution of developed countries. The reorganization of these structures and the creation of the new multinational industrial complex could not be accomplished by recourse to the impersonal mechanisms of unlimited intraregional competition, particularly in view of the ever-present shortage of financial resources throughout Latin America. It is not the purpose of the Latin American economic integration program—nor would such action be feasible or advisable—to eliminate the less-efficient industrial producers at one blow and build on their remains a new, modern, competitive, and efficient manufacturing structure. Were this to happen, a regional industrial-reconversion program of almost impossible proportions would have to be executed, and there would be the risk that the Latin American industrial sector might fall into the hands of the large extraregional corporations with their ample financial resources and access to the latest findings of modern technology.

Given the existing industrial panorama and the need to achieve the region's development along equitable and realistic lines, a series of regional mechanisms in the industrial field are called for, some of which, in fact, have already been initiated. The primary objectives of such schemes should be as follows:

1. To facilitate the gradual adaptation of existing industries to the conditions and dimensions of a regional market, without exposing them to the excessive risks of competition from other firms, already in

operation or new, that may be attracted to the region by the changed circumstances of production and distribution and by the appeal of a market enhanced by a preferential customs regime.

2. Through progressive specialization on a national and regional scale, and also within each industrial branch, to extend the import-substitution process to sectors that are technologically more complex, require a higher initial investment, and are more advantageous from the standpoint of productivity and efficiency than those presently operating in the individual domestic markets.

3. To create favorable conditions so that existing firms, as well as those expressly established for exporting manufactured goods to third countries, will be equipped to compete with those operating in world industrial centers.

Over a longer term, this last point takes on added importance, because present international-trade trends reveal that world-wide demand for manufactured goods increases more rapidly than world-wide demand for primary commodities. The last-mentioned group is affected by low income elasticity, by the frequent appearance of substitutes that are the outgrowth of technological progress, and by increasing competition from certain industrial centers that have also developed into important producers and exporters of raw materials. Latin America's capacity to import from outside the area can obviously be reestablished and assured of continued growth by strengthening the region's position as an exporter of manufactured goods to world markets, beginning with commodities turned out by light industry.

Quite evidently, the realization of the program outlined here is no easy task. In the first place, although five years have gone by since the signing of the Montevideo Treaty, and the Punta del Este Charter is four years old, the idea of regional economic cooperation (to say nothing of the concept of industrial coordination) has not been sufficiently understood, nor has it received adequate political support on the part of governments or public-opinion-molding media in the countries belonging to the Latin American Free Trade Association. Nevertheless, the Latin American economists who were the authors of the Montevideo Treaty and the Central American Common Market, and certain national and regional agencies connected with integration, have been receiving increasing support from the most dynamic representatives of private enterprise in the region and from the new generation of public officials, who combine political acumen with a thorough knowledge of the internal and external aspects of the present-day Latin American economy. It is this united effort that can devise and implement new solutions to the industrial problems, which are becoming more acute with each passing day because of the lack of effective economic cooperation on a regional scale. Although complicated, such solutions are not impossible of attainment in the light of two significant circumstances: the Latin American economy is far from capitalistic in the orthodox sense of the term; and, as Professor Tinbergen so aptly observes, "Latin America has the advantage, unlike Europe and North America when they started their heavy industries, of living in the age of social and economic planning." [9] It would be wise, therefore, to schedule simultaneous action on several fronts. In line with the recommendations of the Montevideo Treaty, and keeping in mind the urgency of the task at hand, the suggestion should be made at the government level that the national planning authorities in the LAFTA countries, and particularly those responsible for industrial planning and development, should be brought into a progressively closer working arrangement. The first step in this direction was taken at the Meeting for the Planning, Promotion, and Guidance of Industrial Development, sponsored by LAFTA in the spring of 1963 in Lima. However, there has been a discouraging lack of concrete proposals aimed at coordinating industrial-development programs, notwithstanding the emergence of various bilateral groups for industrial cooperation between LAFTA members, notably the larger republics (Argentina, Brazil, and Mexico).

The next level of cooperation is suggested by the fact that, in most of the countries in the area, the state not only defines the general industrialization policy and goals and has a hand in their implementation by private enterprise but also participates directly in a series of basic industrial activities and ancillary services. Such a situation will presumably continue in future, for political reasons, in some instances, and, in others, because of the lack of domestic or external private resources. In connection with the duly planned integration of industrial enterprise of this type, the respective governments or state-controlled organizations might arrive at reciprocal and even multilateral agreements in the areas of production, trade, and technological research. Apart from eliminating unnecessary duplication and waste of investment, greater efficiency and higher productivity could be anticipated from the coordination of existing plants and those established in the future for purposes of industrial complementarity. An appropriate field for integration efforts of the type described would be the petroleum and petrochemical industries. In certain LAFTA republics, these enterprises belong to the state, and there are good possibilities for technical cooperation and complementary functioning,

[9] Jan Tinbergen, "Heavy Industry in the Latin American Common Market," Chapter X of this volume.

particularly with regard to basic commodities of petrochemical origin. With the exception of contacts made between the Mexican and Brazilian oil industries, no noteworthy progress has been made in this field to date, although it is here that joint accords at high government levels are destined to become increasingly effective.[10]

Private industry constitutes the third plane on which action should be taken. Coordinated on a regional scale, and with the support of international financial agencies, formulas should be adopted for the adequate and equitable, albeit not officially imposed, distribution of new private industrial undertakings within the zone. Such problems could be approached in various ways. One would be to exploit the possibility offered by the Montevideo Treaty of drawing up certain nondiscriminatory agreements among interested countries for the development of new manufacturing activities or for the interchange of their respective output. Consideration might also be given to supplying an incentive by making use of the mechanisms for promotion of new investments that already form a part of the industrial policy of almost every Latin American country. The only difference would be that, while up to now each country has endeavored to channel domestic investment to fields that carry a high priority from a national standpoint, and selectively to attract outside investment to its own territory, in the future association members would agree—on a compromise basis and with a view to regional specialization—to make their fiscal and financial incentive policies more or less uniform and applicable to designated industrial activities. These industries would be covered by conventions that combine criteria of harmonious economic development with those of availability of the requisite resources. Such regional cooperation obviously implies a considerable degree of rapport at the intergovernment level—specifically, periodic contact between the national planning authorities, particularly the technical personnel of the agencies responsible for industrial planning and promotion.

Regional cooperation of this type, involving the coordination of certain portions of national development programs and the fairly uniform use of incentives and directives addressed to private enterprise, has certain distinct advantages that were defined in a recent ECLA document in the following terms:

[10] An agreement was drawn up in May, 1963, between Petróleos Mexicanos and Petróleos Brasileiros, S.A., providing for the periodic exchange of statistical and technical information; the interchange of technical personnel; promotion of trade; a study of the development of the industry producing base petrochemicals; and an initial meeting, on petroleum exploration, production, refining, maritime transport, and marketing.

By establishing common guide lines on the structure of industry it would be possible to channel conveniently within an over-all framework the selective negotiation of complementarity agreements and to open the road for over-all commitments in the reduction of custom duties. It would also lead to a rational use of the opportunities that will arise from the widening of the market. Even without considering the effect of a common market, these opportunities are great, judging by projections to 1975 of the rate of growth in demand of the last fifteen years. Magnitudes of these projected figures alone suggest how large the possibilities are of industrial expansion and how ample the field for reaching agreements on sectoral complementation whose benefits would extend to all countries.[11]

Finally, there are the agreements for sectoral cooperation and complementary functioning among the private producers in the zone. These can be established on the initiative of the industrialists themselves, or the respective governments may wish to sponsor such arrangements by way of contributing to the execution of their industrial-development programs. According to ECLA experts, three types of agreements for industrial complementarity are possible: (1) agreements that are properly sectoral in scope and cover a complete branch of industrial activity in the participating countries; (2) agreements designed to eliminate customs duties on products in two or more interrelated industrial fields, with a view to facilitating participation by countries that are not, and do not plan to be, active in a given area of production; and (3) bilateral agreements providing for special marketing arrangements, whereby a country having an advanced industry would foster the establishment in another's territory of plants designed for the manufacture of given parts or pieces for use in the first country.

The sectoral agreements concluded in LAFTA from the middle of 1962 to the close of 1963 on electronic tubes and statistical machines, and the one on glassware, which has already been signed by the respective industrialists, fall within the first group. Using as an example the convention covering electronic tubes, negotiated in June, 1962, by representatives of the electronics industry in the five tube-producing LAFTA countries (Argentina, Brazil, Chile, Mexico, and Uruguay) and signed by the respective governments in November, 1963, at the close of the third conference, sectoral agreements have the following characteristics: They cover not only the product itself but the parts, other components, and raw materials designed for its

[11] ECLA, *Realizaciones y perspectivas en el proceso del mercado regional* (mimeographed; Mar del Plata, 1963; E/CN. 12/668), p. 71.

manufacture. They provide that imports by signatory nations of any products in the branch covered by the agreement will be exempt from customs duties and restrictions of any type, except those applicable to articles appearing on each country's reserved list. These lists of exceptions will be reviewed once yearly with a view to their progressive reduction, and the liberated products covered by the agreement will be included in a common list that will cover other LAFTA-negotiated commodities. Sectoral agreements further provide that, as soon as possible, the ratifying governments will standardize customs treatment applicable to the importation of the same goods from third countries; however, they may grant temporary import permits for the extrazonal supply of certain parts, components, and raw materials, when such items are not available under satisfactory terms within the zone. In the case of the convention subscribed to by the glass-manufacturing industry, there was an added proviso that the machinery utilized in glassware production must be made of materials of which at least 90 per cent were smelted or otherwise processed inside the zone.

To date, sectoral accords represent, at least in theory, a very useful contribution to the rational use of existing industrial capacity within LAFTA; moreover, they perform the important function of starting the free-trade-zone mechanism in the direction of a common market based on the establishment of a common customs tariff against the rest of the world. For several reasons, whose analysis is beyond the scope of the present essay, the Latin American countries have not shown themselves willing, as yet, to relinquish officially their divergent policies on trade with the rest of the world in favor of a common policy. If this idea could be made to prosper, the progressive establishment of sectoral common markets, in response to agreements for the complementary functioning of specific industrial branches, would bring the region gradually closer to a situation in which the operation of an over-all common market could become a tangible fact within a relatively short time.

The feasibility of this approach, however, depends on the speed with which successive complementary-industry agreements are concluded; for, if such agreements are held to a very small number, their advantages would accrue to certain countries only, probably the more industrialized ones, and would promote the formation of cartels, instead of constituting a step toward the regional common market.[12] As

[12] In accordance with Resolution 71 mentioned earlier, concerning greater industrialization of the intermediate countries, the contracting parties have espoused the firm purpose of assuring effective participation by Chile, Colombia, Peru, and Uruguay, as well as the countries classified as of less relative economic develop-

a further requisite that must be met if sectoral industrial-complementarity agreements are to be practicable and fulfill their intended function, LAFTA governments must give more dynamic support than they have heretofore to the industrial sectors interested in zonal complementation. For one thing, industrial-complementarity conventions should be subject to automatic ratification as soon as the LAFTA authorities have indicated that such arrangements are compatible with the principles and objectives of the Montevideo Treaty.

Of the comparatively few industrial-complementarity agreements concluded to date within the third group defined by ECLA, the best-known covers a Brazilian-Chilean integration program for the manufacture and assembly of automobiles. The paragraphs following summarize the principal recommendations formulated by the Joint Brazilian-Chilean Group for the plan's execution:

1. In Chile, a program will be promoted for the manufacture of automotive vehicles of several types that do not compete with one another and are among the makes presently in production in Brazil.

2. Chile is interested in developing four different types of vehicles in connection with the above program: diesel-powered trucks and buses; medium-sized gasoline buses and trucks; all-purpose vehicles; and a small-auto line.

3. In the execution of this program, Chile will import partial auto assemblies, parts, and pieces from Brazil, for final assembly in Chile. So as to balance the interchange, Brazil, in turn, will purchase mutually designated automotive parts and pieces from Chile.

4. The necessary stimuli will be provided for Brazilian cooperation in the development of Chile's automotive industry; the formation of joint-capital ventures will be fostered; and financial aid from public agencies will be actively encouraged.

5. Since Chilean industry will not immediately be in a position to equalize the interchange resulting from the integration program, automotive imports from Brazil may, for a maximum of three years, be offset by exports of items from Chile that have been subjected to a lesser degree of manufacture but are connected with the automotive industry.

6. For purposes of the program, both governments will consider the partial assemblies, parts, or pieces of automotive vehicles exchanged between the two countries just as though they were of domestic origin and will extend the same treatment to other countries that subscribe to the reciprocal integration system.

---

ment, in the complementary-industry agreements and in any other types of multinational arrangements designed to initiate or expand zonal productive activities.

7. Once perfected, the program will be open to participation by all LAFTA members.

Subsequently, Argentina and Chile arrived at an agreement in the automotive field along the general lines described above.

To encourage and accelerate the completion of industrial-complementarity agreements, and at the instance of the contracting parties, LAFTA's Secretariat has organized since mid-1963 a long series of sectoral meetings in manufacturing industry and allied fields, and also in transportation. The purpose of these gatherings is to establish contacts among the producers in the zone and thereby accomplish an exchange of information; more active participation by private enterprise in the problems involved in the annual tariff negotiations; investigation of the regional supply situation in regard to raw materials, machinery, and equipment; and the creation of adequate conditions for the urgent execution of industrial-development plans that take into consideration the magnitude of demand and the economies of scale. By way of collateral action to ensure continuity of these sectoral contacts, zonal agencies made up of representatives from each industrial branch have been promoted. During the year 1963, regional meetings along these lines were held in the following fields: petrochemicals; iron and steel; the mechanical industries; foodstuffs; pharmaceutical chemicals; and pulp and paper. In some cases, regional industrial associations were established and assigned preparatory work to pave the way for the subsequent formulation of industrial-complementarity agreements. It is safe to assume that these preliminary contacts not only will result in new sectoral arrangements but will bring strong pressure to bear on the Latin American governments, so that they orient their respective development programs toward a progressively integrated regional market and cooperate with one another, initiating whatever activities are needed to bring their national economies and economic policies out of their present state of isolated development.

The industrial-cooperation measures suggested here at the level of the national planning authorities, of the state-controlled enterprises, and by means of sectoral industrial-complementarity agreements, all designed to build a coherent and fairly uniform system of incentives for new regional-scope industrial activities, are only modest contributions to the solution of the problems of the huge disparities existing between general development levels in the region. By themselves, these measures cannot be expected to ensure the harmonious and equitable industrialization of all the LAFTA member countries. Also needed is a system of indirect incentives capable of attracting to the less-developed countries industrial investment from within and without the region. It is true that the Montevideo Treaty calls for preferential treatment of this group of countries to facilitate the task of expanding and perfecting integration; but, in order for such treatment to be relatively effective within a reasonable time, it must be supplemented by a direct policy for promoting investment and technical assistance, specifically designed to correct existing and future disparities.[13]

There is nothing new about the idea that rapid expansion of the Latin American economies on a regional scale, and particularly participation in this process by the relatively less developed countries, will be extremely difficult unless a strong regional development corporation is established—along the lines, for example, of the European Investment Bank. Over a period of several years, this conclusion has been drawn in the abundant literature published by ECLA and in contributions from outstanding economists from some of the countries in the area.[14] The establishment, in December, 1959, of the Inter-American Development Bank—an institution that could become a bank for Latin American integration, but has initiated its activities in this field only recently (with the creation of a fund to provide medium-term financing for inter-Latin American capital-goods exports)—will perhaps facilitate the establishment of a regional development corporation. The primary functions of the corporation would be fourfold: (1) to analyze the public, as well as private, investment possibilities in the less-developed countries from a regional perspective; (2) to endeavor to achieve a better and closer relationship between the less-developed and the more-advanced countries in the area; (3) to offer technical assistance in the preparation of concrete investment projects in the relatively backward nations, based on cooperation between entrepreneurs of these countries and those of other Latin American countries; and (4) to supply, on easy terms, a part of the financing needed in the realization of such projects. A corporation of this type would receive financial support from every republic in the area, since all would obtain advantages from the expansion and freeing of trade in the relatively less developed countries. This body would also seek access to external sources of financing.

Consideration should be given to direct participation by the regional development corporation (through stock ownership and repre-

[13] Resolutions 71 and 73 mentioned above pave the way for achieving the desired goals.

[14] Convincing arguments in favor of a regional development corporation are found in a very recent OAS study prepared by Harvey S. Perloff and Rómulo Almeida, *op. cit.*

sentation on the boards of directors) in the firms sponsored and assisted by it, so as to reduce the risks inherent in the location of such firms in a predominately underdeveloped environment. The operation and growth of new enterprises would be assured by access to financing under especially privileged terms and by the completely free entry accorded their products by the remaining LAFTA countries, the latter advantage being given in response to a special commitment entirely in keeping with the spirit of the Treaty of Montevideo. The establishment of a regional development corporation for such purposes has advantages that extend beyond the strictly economic field. It would represent certain and eloquent proof of the common will in the area to help the poorer neighboring countries. Furthermore, the psychological effect of such aid on the recipient nations should not be underestimated, nor should its influence on the attitudes of entrepreneurs within and without the Latin American free-trade zone. The criticism that is often so vehemently launched against the Central American Integration Industries Regime obviously does not apply here since there would be no attempt to divide the market and create monopoly situations. The aim would simply be to overcome the disadvantages that beset any industrial activity in the less-developed countries, by supplying financial resources under noncompetitive conditions, together with technical and managerial assistance, and, eventually, through unilateral customs concessions. It might be deemed advisable to apply the customs concessions on a temporary basis only, after the fashion of the fiscal exemption ordinarily established for new industrial firms locating in countries in process of development.

It will be no easy task to put into practice the regional industrialization program outlined in this essay. LAFTA's five years of operation and the limitations of the current structure of the Montevideo Treaty fully support this conclusion. The obstacles originating in the geographic extent of the Latin American free-trade zone and the absence of traditions of economic cooperation between the southern and northern countries in the region are added to, and perpetuated by, the inadequacy of government support—understandably enough, since national administrations often find it imperative to concentrate their attention on overwhelming short-term problems.[15] Regional industri-

[15] In April, 1963, the Brazilian and Chilean presidents expressed their dissatisfaction with the obstacles that are blocking the smooth and expeditious implementation of the Montevideo Treaty and pointed up economic cooperation as the appropriate tool for accelerating the region's development. With a view to remedying the situation, the two chiefs of state called a meeting of the foreign ministers of all the LAFTA countries. They had in mind the creation of a permanent consultation mechanism at the ministerial level and the adoption of measures

alization is also hampered by the anachronistic and negative attitudes still held by a sizable number of entrepreneurs operating within the zone. The pressure exerted by certain private groups against tariff concessions in competitive regional production fields, their lack of interest and reluctance to participate in the sectoral meetings for the preparation of industrial-complementarity agreements, and their eagerness to capture regional markets—unfortunately unaccompanied by a willingness to reciprocate by the way of imports—are factors that work against economic cooperation, in general, and are directly prejudicial to the region's industrial integration.

Granted that regional economic cooperation constituted one of the most effective instruments for recovering, and even improving on, the rate of economic growth in Latin America in the immediate postwar period (which later declined because of the world trade situation and some other factors), it is reasonable to exhort all the governments participating in the Latin American Free Trade Association to give political support to that mechanism and to promote the creation of a consultative body at the ministerial level. Through periodic meetings, the latter would make it possible to adopt government accords that give support to whatever concrete recommendations may be passed by the LAFTA Permanent Executive Committee. Moreover, LAFTA governments should lend new stimuli to the integration process, foster industrial-complementarity agreements as well as industrial integration, and revamp the tariff-negotiation machinery. These various points of support call for a series of efforts at a high governmental level on both the national and regional fronts.

As indicated at the beginning of this essay, the distinguishing feature of the Latin American Free Trade Association, when placed alongside other regional arrangements having a similar juridical structure but in operation in economically advanced regions, lies in the fact that the LAFTA-sponsoring Treaty of Montevideo seeks to accelerate the development process in a regional group of nations that, with few exceptions, are in a state of economic and social stagnation. To achieve this objective, the mechanisms for preferential commercial interchange must be reinforced by joint and vigorous action in the field of regional industrialization.

---

to step up the economic integration of the zone and streamline customs-concession negotiations beginning with the third meeting of the LAFTA Conference. The meeting of foreign ministers, originally called for August, 1963, and held in the autumn of 1965, adopted some of these proposals.

X

JAN TINBERGEN[1]

Heavy Industry in the Latin American Common Market

Latin America is entering upon an important phase of its development: the beginnings of a heavy industry have been created. Before World War I, the Latin American countries were primary producers, depending entirely on imports for the satisfaction of their demand for industrial goods. The interruptions of supply caused by both world wars stimulated the establishment of a number of manufacturing industries. The great depression made it clear that diversification of production was necessary in order to spread the risks of price movements, and it intensified the trend toward industrialization. Today, it is generally recognized that the most natural possibility for larger areas to increase their well-being is to industrialize, and Latin America is adopting this course. Obviously, the first industries were, and in fact the great majority of those in existence at present still are, of the light type. They are the natural extensions of primary production or handicrafts, or they are the consumer-goods industries, whose products were most needed during the interruptions of supply.

However, conditions for the development of heavy industry are gradually improving. On the one hand, demand for capital goods,

[1] The following essay was written by the author during his stay with the Secretariat of the Economic Commission for Latin America in September and October, 1959. It appeared originally in ECLA's *Economic Bulletin for Latin America*, V, No. 1 (March, 1960), 1–8, and is reproduced here with ECLA permission.

heavy chemicals, and so forth, is increasing as a consequence of the general process of development. On the other hand, experience in production and self-confidence have grown. Private capital formation, as well as more conscious public policies, opens up possibilities that did not exist before. Mineral reserves appear to be of many kinds and are substantial. A number of enterprises in the heavy industries are already in existence and further projects are in preparation.

This new phase in Latin American development is illustrated by the recently started implementation of the plans for regional economic integration. Proposals have been under discussion that make a distinction among three types of productive activity in the countries concerned. The first type constitutes primary production—i.e., agriculture and mining, being production essentially for exports. The second type consists of the light industries already in existence and having vested interests to protect. Here integration can only proceed slowly. It can proceed more easily in the third field, that of heavy industry, for the simple reason that this type of activity has only just started and vested interests in protection of one Latin American country against the others are not numerous.

The "take-off of heavy industry"—to coin a phrase based on W. W. Rostow's well-known expression—is sufficiently important to warrant special attention. Heavy industry is the most typical representative of those activities which, by their special features, challenge some well-established economic theories. Before dealing with them, it should be noted that Latin America has the advantage of entering this important phase of the development of heavy industry at a time when more is known about these features and their implications than was the case when Europe and North America were in a similar position. In other words, Latin America has the advantage, unlike Europe and North America when they started their heavy industries, of living in the age of social and economic planning. The techniques of this type of planning make it possible to study a number of implications of the creation of heavy industry before embarking upon its actual establishment. Alternative possibilities can be investigated, and their social and economic consequences appraised in order to choose the most attractive alternative and take the corresponding policy measures. These measures need not entail specific intervention in economic life, sometimes also indicated by the expression "planning"; what is meant here is planning of policy in the sense of preparing it with the aid of economic research on the future development of the economies concerned.

The question will no doubt be asked whether such planning is necessary, whether the most appropriate pattern of heavy industry does not develop by itself. It may even be suggested that Europe and North America were, in fact, better off in the days before forecasting and planning became so popular.

There is, of course, the well-known tenet of what economists refer to as welfare economics, namely, that the optimum situation will automatically develop if every single producer seeks to maximize his own profits. This may be called the decentralization thesis. The point is, however, that this thesis is valid only under specific conditions, and it is, in fact, doubtful that the special features of heavy industry satisfy these conditions. Recent analysis of the process of development makes it more and more probable that these features cause considerable deviations from automatic and optimal development.

This essay, therefore, deals with the two sides of the question, namely, how optimum development of heavy industry probably evolves, and whether it can be obtained by complete freedom to create enterprises in these branches.

With the aid of economic models, it is possible to determine the optimum pattern of an economy, particularly with regard to heavy industry. Such a pattern has many aspects, or "dimensions." It shows a certain distribution of productive activity over the various industries and processes; it indicates the size of the enterprises; and it gives information about their location. The ingredients to be used in the calculations are, as a minimum, figures about the inputs of the processes under consideration and about transport costs. A number of general economic parameters, such as demand elasticities in the most general sense, and world market prices will also be needed. The data on inputs are typically nonlinear, thus reflecting certain indivisibilities that are a characteristic of heavy industries in particular. Ideally, some knowledge of external effects also comes into play, although present knowledge of these phenomena is still very limited. It will be concealed in the assumptions made of labor productivity, government investments for infrastructure, and the like.

The models referred to above must be very complicated, as they must contain details in at least the three dimensions mentioned. Methodology may have to be primitive for that reason, consisting partly of trial-and-error calculations. Thus, the most appropriate location of some large units may simply be attempted. The advantage of using such calculations, even if primitive, lies in the fact that it is always better to make the trial, and especially the error, on paper than in actual practice.

The optimum pattern referred to depends, of course, on what the main aims of economic development and economic order generally are considered to be. To begin with, one very important aim will be a high level of income for the region as a whole. This aim will already determine some vital aspects of the optimum. But various distributive aspects are important aims, too. There must be a satisfactory distribution of income among countries and a satisfactory distribution among classes of the population. The distribution of income constitutes a particularly important aspect, as it relates to the topic under consideration. It goes without saying that the choice of locations for the most important enterprises exerts a considerable influence on the distribution of income among countries. It is precisely in this choice that the automatism of free enterprise may not work; this automatism may well lead to a maldistribution of heavy industry.

Assuming now that the optimum pattern of the heavy industries can be more or less estimated with the aid of the techniques outlined above, can it be expected that this pattern will automatically come into existence under a system, perhaps through some measures of commercial policy? It would seem doubtful, for three main reasons, all of them connected with the special features of heavy industry.

The first reason for doubting the effectiveness of a regime of free entrance to these industries is the relatively long construction period of the individual projects. This invalidates the accuracy of the market mechanism. Suppose there is a shortage of some product of heavy industry, which induces certain investors to increase the capacity of that industry. For quite some time after the project has been started, it will not yet contribute to production and the scarcity will persist. Prices will, therefore, not reflect the future equilibrium level, but only a temporary level. Before the project is finished, other investors may also have been attracted by these temporary prices and have duplicated the first project. Only after the first project is finished will the market reflect its existence, and then it will be too late to do anything about the second project. After both projects have been finished there may be overproduction and low prices, which will alarm investors. This may continue after the time has come for further investments, causing price rises beyond the equilibrium level. Because of the length of the gestation period, such prices lead to the well-known cycles in investment and production with all their disadvantages.

The second reason to doubt the effectiveness of a regime of free investment is the existence of indivisibilities. Rather large capital resources are required to establish plants of optimum size. Since these funds are often not available, there will be a trend toward unduly small plants, which will later be competed out of existence by larger units, when capital is more plentiful. The process necessarily implies waste of capital, which is particularly harmful for countries not endowed with large savings.

The third reason to doubt the usefulness of completely free decisions concerns the important question of location. Unlike most agricultural and mining activities, industrial activities can be carried out in many places, provided only that the transportation facilities are adequate. Where to begin is a matter of relative indifference to the private entrepreneur. Once he has started, moreover, the external effects and the infrastructure created will put a premium on new investments in the same center. These combined forces make the creation of centers of heavy industry under free enterprise a somewhat haphazard process. Some centers may, in the end, become too large from a special point of view, while in other very desirable locations heavy industry may not be set up at all. Market forces are no longer a clear and unambiguous guide to what is the most desirable distribution of heavy industry over the area under consideration.

The arguments briefly set out above may be checked by asking whether European and North American development have in fact been marked by the deficiencies just described. It is the author's contention that this is, indeed, the case.

First, free development in these older industrial areas has been characterized by the well-known heavy fluctuations called business cycles, which are partly due to the type of mechanism described: fluctuations as a consequence of long gestation periods, so clear from Aftalion's works.

Second, it is typical of European development that there should be smaller plants than is desirable from the viewpoint of maximum productivity. What is perhaps more significant is that, on the average, there are smaller plants in Europe than in the United States, even in those industries where the number of plants is large; i.e., the size of the market does not limit the size of the enterprise in a direct way. The greater scarcity of capital in Europe is the most likely explanation; and, if this is so, the condition will make itself felt even more in the case of Latin America.

Third, the question of location arises. It has long been contended that completely free enterprise does not necessarily lead to the most desirable location of industry. There was a feeling within Germany that regions too far removed from the big centers were underdeveloped and had to be helped by the well-known system of railway freight rates. It is now generally admitted, in Italy, that the entire industry moved north after free movement of goods and factors became possible through the unification of the country. Presently, with the European Common Market progressing, similar problems are emerging, and the European Investment Bank was created for the specific purpose of helping the development of regions that might suffer from the shifts expected. Moreover, similar problems are now being intensively debated and investigated in the United States.

From this evidence, it may be concluded that not only theoretical analysis but also practical experience call for caution. Latin America may profit from the more-advanced stage of our knowledge and may try to avoid some of the less desirable consequences of a completely free-enterprise pattern of development. It might be added that, for the world at large, it is now recognized that a policy of positive intervention must be adopted in order to attain greater harmony in the geographical distribution of industrialization. Would it not apply, then, to the problems of a single large continent?

What, then, would this intervention have to amount to? Certainly, it is not necessary, or even desirable, to think of the other extreme: complete regimentation. Moreover, one may choose among various instruments of policy. To begin with, "planning" will be very useful, in the sense of making calculations with regard to the optimum pattern. Since the structure of the whole continent would be at stake, and because of the remarkable work already done by ECLA, the author hopes that ECLA will be requested to undertake this task. Concrete numerical estimations of this character may already give some guidance to governments and to private business.

A second step might be an agreement among the governments of the region that the pattern resulting from the computation just discussed should be taken as the background of their policy. An element of flexibility in such a policy may be the periodic correction of the estimates in the light of new information.

The policies of the government may consist of indirect and direct instruments to influence private initiative. Indirect instruments may be financial assistance, as well as help in the construction of infrastructure. Conceivably, negative measures of this kind, such as taxes, can also be applied. Both can be used to induce private business to carry out the program agreed upon. Direct instruments may be the issuing of permits to establish new enterprises, while prohibiting the setting up of such enterprise without a permit. Although such direct interference is generally not attractive, not much harm will be done in the case of heavy industry, because the number of enterprises will, in any case, not be very large. (Financial help may also be of an international rather than a national character. Some of the international agencies might join the governments in an attempt to carry out the program.)

A point of some special interest is the precise shape to be given to financial help. From a theoretical point of view, a subsidy proportional to the number of workers to be engaged may be the best form, better than, say, the supply of capital at reduced rates. The true problem is not, however, to use capital, but rather to employ people. Subsidies of this kind might even make commercial policy instruments like protection superfluous. These questions will not be elaborated upon here, since they are not the subject under discussion. It may take more time to convince governments of the superiority of these instruments.

From the above arguments it will be clear, the author hopes, that there are some possibilities of giving guidance in the creation of an optimum pattern of heavy industry without resorting to detailed intervention. Such guidance, particularly in the field of heavy industry, may be of considerable importance to the well-being of the countries concerned.

XI

ENRIQUE ANGULO H.

Transportation and Intra-Latin American Trade

Latin America's underdevelopment is particularly in evidence when the region is observed from the standpoint of the economic relations among the constituent countries. If the concept of economic distance is applied, for example, we find that it disproportionately exceeds the geographic distance, which, in itself, is very great. Attributable to serious inadequacies and mismanagement in the transportation systems operating in the area, this phenomenon places difficult problems in the path of integration. With their present structure and operating systems, neither maritime and river navigation nor railway and highway transport facilities (air traffic, in this instance, being only of secondary importance) are capable of facilitating the normal—much less accelerated—growth of intrazonal trade. The fact that more than 90 per cent of such commerce is currently carried by sea clearly demonstrates the extent to which river and land media have been left abandoned over the years.

Although the following pages deal almost exclusively with maritime transportation, the author does not intend a disregard for the other means, where splendid opportunities for an increased trade flow between neighboring countries could be opened through comparatively simple expedients: the construction of a single bridge; the lengthening of a highway to form a junction with a general network; a bilateral agreement for railroad interconnection at a border point; an accord to facilitate international bus and truck traffic; the coordination of services among the tributaries forming the River Plate system; and, in general, projects for expansion and improvement. LAFTA, to date, has given understandable preference to ocean transport; however, it would be highly advisable for that intergovernmental body to begin to pay careful attention to the remaining aspects of the immense over-all problem of transportation in the zone.

Maritime traffic is a basic question, not only by virtue of absorbing so high a percentage of intrazonal trade, but also because of its susceptibility of a substantially augmented yield within a short time (provided a series of adequate measures are instituted), notwithstanding the complexity and deficiencies of present shipping and port facilities. In addition, sea transport has a bearing on the chronic balance-of-payments difficulties experienced by the countries in the region.

An ECLA study prepared in connection with the United Nations Conference on Trade and Development points out that, in 1961, Latin America had an unfavorable balance of $527 million on its freight account—an amount that increases to $657 million if insurance costs and other transportation charges are taken into account.[1] (This deficit is much greater than the ones for Africa and the Far East, for example.) Out of an estimated total of $1.9 billion in freight charges incurred in the same year for moving Latin America's international trade, only $207 million, or 11 per cent of the total, was paid to shipping lines in the area. On a tonnage basis, Latin American vessels carried no more than 6 per cent of the region's foreign commerce. In 1961, Argentinean and Chilean foreign trade was carried by extraregional vessels in the proportion of 71.9 per cent and 83.8 per cent, respectively, indicating a heavy expenditure of foreign exchange by the two countries. A study of Latin American economy in 1961 points out that "even in those countries where there exists a relatively large merchant fleet, the net balance from freight continues to be negative. In Colombia, in 1960, this deficit alone represented 20 per cent of total freightage but in Argentina and Brazil it reached 63 per cent and in Chile almost 78 per cent. In other countries the deficit was even larger." [2]

In Colombia's case, however, 1961 balance-of-payments data show that, thanks to the Flota Mercante Grancolombiana, income and outflow on this account were held in balance.[3] While Colombian im-

1 ECLA, *Latin America and the United Nations Conference on Trade and Development* (1963; ST/ECLA/CONF. 13/L.2), pp. 128–34.

2 Unión Panamericana, *Estudio económico y social de América Latina, 1961.* Documento preparado conjuntamente por las Secretarías de la OEA y de la CEPAL bajo la responsabilidad de la OEA (Provisional Doc. 5-A [español] Rev.) (Washington, D.C., 1962), pp. 169–70.

3 IMF, *Balance of Payments Yearbook*, XIV (1957–61).

ports carried on foreign ships occasioned an outlay on freight of $23.6 million, income derived from the Grancolombiana operations (including the portion corresponding to Ecuador and exclusive of insurance transactions) amounted to $29.6 million. The foregoing statistics would indicate that the development of the Latin American merchant marines would be sufficiently justified as a balance-of-payments defense measure, quite independent of other considerations.

Nevertheless, with respect to strictly intrazonal commerce, since the share that the zonal fleets have in its transport is rather high, the loss of foreign exchange for such commerce does not constitute sizable amounts. Thus, for example, according to partial data for different periods of 1963 and 1964, in the export to other LAFTA countries, the ships of zonal flags carried 71.4 per cent of the Argentine freight, 64.4 per cent of the Brazilian, almost 80 per cent of the Colombian, 72.3 per cent of the Mexican, more than 97 per cent of the Paraguayan, 55 per cent of the Peruvian, and almost 44 per cent of the Uruguayan. In importation from the zone, the average percentage was similar, the most striking cases being those of Uruguay, 93.7 per cent, and Brazil, 92.4 per cent. Consequently, for the LAFTA countries, the problem of the negative impact of freight account in the balance of payments is derived from the scant participation of their ships in commodity transport to and from extrazonal countries. This is an additional reason for coordinating their shipping resources and cooperatively expanding their merchant fleets through the process of economic integration, for, in this way, they could have available more ships to take care of traffic with extrazonal countries and could thus reduce their freight expenditure.

ECLA, OAS, and LAFTA have all devoted a good deal of time to a thorough study of the entire maritime transport problem in Latin America as a whole and, recently, in the free-trade zone. However, as was logical in view of the extrazonal orientation of Latin America's foreign trade up to that time, analyses made in the 1950's, although indubitably sound and excellently written, were useful solely in a premonitory sense. The topic appeared to be somewhat academic, and the recommendations made seldom went beyond the printed page. There is not a single reference to transportation in the Montevideo Treaty. The Punta del Este Charter does make mention of this problem, in terms to which we shall refer later, in Title 3 dealing with Latin American economic integration.

Insofar as concerns the Latin American Free Trade Association, except for some preliminary and preparatory statistical work, it was actually not until the second meeting of the Group of Experts on Transportation, held in July, 1962,—i.e., more than a year after the treaty went into effect, and two and a half years after it was signed—when the contracting parties gave serious consideration to maritime and port-service problems. By that time the first meeting of LAFTA Conference Contracting Parties had met, having paid little attention to this subject. The twenty-two recommendations forwarded by the Group of Experts to the LAFTA Permanent Executive Committee subsequently served as the basis for three resolutions (passed during the second meeting of the LAFTA Conference held in Mexico City, August-November, 1962), which for the first time defined LAFTA's general doctrine concerning maritime transportation.[4] This policy definition was unfortunately only embryonic, and its present content involves a number of loose ends that are of fundamental import and must be resolved by formal agreement among the member countries.

These resolutions sum up a series of basic principles indicating LAFTA's desire to make practical application of the ECLA-inspired concept that the prospective common market regime should be extended to the field of transportation. The aim here is to establish a preferential intrazonal system for the member countries' merchant marines by: (1) assigning a substantial quota of intrazonal cargo for the national vessels of the signatories and allotting a fixed percentage share of reciprocal trade to such vessels; and (2) ensuring that ships of signatory countries, carrying cargo and passengers between the member nations, "will receive equal treatment with the domestic vessels of the same class in each of said countries, insofar as concerns port, customs, and operational procedures, as well as in the payment of navigation tolls, sanitation, docking privileges, demurrage, pilotage, and other levies not pertaining to payment for services rendered the vessels."[5] In this way, the complementary function of maritime and river transport facilities will be promoted within the zone, with a view to their gradual integration. The stipulated privileges, moreover, will, by introducing the regional perspective, obviously reinforce the steps already taken by the contracting parties, or those in project, to stimulate the growth of their merchant marines. The assignment of cargo quotas is a procedure that has been in use in several Latin American nations by unilateral decision or through bilateral agreements, six of which are currently in effect.

To implement this policy, the resolutions under discussion provide for the following mechanisms: (1) a general agreement on maritime and inland waterway transportation; (2) an association of shipowners from the Latin American free-trade zone; and (3) a conference of

[4] LAFTA Resolutions 44, 45, and 46, reproduced in *En camino de la integración*, Supplement to *Comercio Exterior*, XII, No. 12 (December, 1962).

[5] LAFTA Resolution 46.

zonal shipping fleets. The operative agency in this case is the Advisory Commission on Transportation (Resolution 45) which, in common with all those of a similar nature, is an adjunct of the LAFTA Permanent Executive Committee.

At a meeting held in Viña del Mar, Chile, in July, 1963, representatives of state-owned and private shipping firms in the member countries formed the Latin American Shipowners Association (ALAMAR). A country-by-country breakdown of the membership shows, in April, 1964, twenty lines from Argentina, twelve from Brazil, nine from Chile, a joint Colombian-Ecuadorian enterprise, four firms from Mexico, two from Paraguay, five from Peru, and seven from Uruguay. The total dead-weight tonnage thus represented amounts to 3,525,000. As defined in the charter, ALAMAR will pursue the following general aims: to promote the development and intensification of maritime and inland-waterway transportation among the member countries; to cooperate with LAFTA and other agencies in constantly improving zonal transportation; to conduct research on problems relating to maritime, river, lake, and port activities (from the standpoint of zonal needs and with a view to cutting costs); and to sponsor the maritime conference system.

Several resolutions[6] adopted by ALAMAR on the occasion of its first assembly (held in Mexico City, November 25–30, 1963) attest to the intention of the Latin American shipowners to contribute to regional integration in their field. Two resolutions, for example, recommend that the associate shipowners give preference, under equal terms, to zonal shipyards when scheduling repairs, renovation, and the construction of new vessels. The preamble to another resolution on the subject of foreign trade declares that regional economic integration can suffer regrettable delays while the signatory countries lose a considerable amount of foreign exchange in freight payments when vessels under extrazonal flags are utilized, and that ALAMAR should, at an early date, undertake research on problems relating to maritime, river, and lake traffic and activities, for the specific purpose of avoiding such foreign exchange losses. Shipowners whose crews are not made up of their own nationals are urged to employ, insofar as possible, the services of seamen who are nationals of LAFTA countries. Finally, after pointing out that many Latin American shipowners have vessels that are lying idle for lack of cargo and that "it is perfectly feasible . . . for local concerns in the Latin American countries to carry out all maritime, river, and lake shipping activities between those countries," yet another resolution recommends that, in

6 ALAMAR resolutions reproduced in *Comercio Exterior*, XIII, No. 12 (December, 1963), pp. 920–21.

the event the associates need additional ships for the conduct of their business, they give preference, under equal terms, to the chartering or rental of vessels of any of the other members. For this purpose, associates having ships available are to so notify the ALAMAR Secretariat. During two extraordinary assemblies held in Uruguay (in late January and in early April, 1964), ALAMAR approved a declaration of principles summing up the association's shipping policy, and a draft agreement on water transportation. Both these documents were referred to the LAFTA Advisory Commission on Transportation.

In the matter of regional shipping conferences, at a meeting in Rio de Janeiro, in November, 1964, ALAMAR decided to support the formation of zonal freightage conferences. As a basis for understanding, the conferences would maintain relations with the producers, chambers of commerce, and business organizations, with a view to adopting necessary measures to favor the development of commercial interchange among the countries of the zone, through a system of consultations with the shippers that would keep their respective interests in mind.[7] The same meeting indicated the convenience of reorganizing the bilateral or zonal conferences in accord with whatever is definitely indicated in the agreements on maritime and river transport as the best practice for the transport of merchandise between the different countries of the zone. Maritime conferences constituted to date with exclusively Latin American participation are as follows: the Maritime Conference on Argentine-Chilean Traffic, which has been in operation for twelve years; the very effective Argentine-Brazilian Maritime Traffic Conference; and the Argentine-Peruvian Maritime Traffic Conference, as yet in the nascent stage.

LAFTA associates have not, as yet, been able to devise a mutually acceptable general convention on maritime and inland-waterway transportation. Early in its deliberations (June, 1963), the Advisory Commission on Transportation drew up a draft agreement, but its adoption was hedged about by so many substantive reservations, formulated by almost all the contracting parties, that from the very beginning it was obviously impracticable. During the third meeting of LAFTA Conference, held in Montevideo, from October to December, 1963, the sole resolution passed on transportation—No. 80—deals with inland-waterway problems and does not even make reference to the matter of the general convention. This was tabled once again until the following meeting of the Advisory Commission on Transportation, convened in the Uruguayan capital, in April, 1964. When re-

[7] See Enrique Angulo, "La Asociación Latinoamericana de Armadores examina los problemas del transporte marítimo en la Zona," *Comercio Exterior*, XIV, No. 12 (December, 1964), 861–64.

examining the question on this occasion, the commission referred to its initial draft proposal, plus others supplied by Argentina, Brazil, and ALAMAR. The discussions produced a second draft agreement, which was also accompanied by power-depleting reservations placed on record by several countries.

The major difference between the two drafts prepared by the Advisory Commission on Transportation has to do with the cargo preference, or preferential assignment of cargo.[8] The first assures member-country vessels of "free participation in the transportation of goods coming from and consigned to any of the contracting parties, without restrictions and under equal rights and treatment with the vessels of each contracting party," which is tantamount to a multilateral cargo preference. The second draft proposes a mixed system setting aside 80 per cent of the cargo for bilateral transportation, leaving 10 per cent as a multilateral reserve for zonal vessels, and allowing extrazonal shipping lines to handle the remaining 10 per cent. On the other hand, the two documents are in substantial agreement regarding the definition to be given a "national vessel"; and both provide that, within a maximum period of ninety days, the contracting parties are to promote the constitution of maritime conferences designed to standardize operational rulings, stimulate regularly scheduled service, fix rates and transportation terms, and guarantee compliance with the provisions concerning cargo preference and participation in shipping (subject to periodic adjustment when appropriate). As stipulated in both draft conventions, landlocked countries will be given whatever facilities they may require, in the matter of maritime and inland-waterway transport; and contracting-party national vessels carrying freight and/or passengers between the respective countries will receive the same treatment as each one's domestic ships engaged in intrazonal trade, in matters pertaining to port, customs, and operational procedures; payment of navigation tolls; sanitation; docking; and demurrage. The text drawn up at the 1964 meeting provides that the transport of petroleum and derivatives will continue to be regulated by the laws of each member country. Finally, the associate countries, in the terms of the second draft, are to meet annually to study the results of enforcement of the agreement, discuss eventual modification in reserved-cargo quotas, review the vessel-chartering system in effect in the zone, and decide on whatever amendments to the agreement as may be deemed necessary.

[8] ALALC, *Informes de la primera y de la segunda reunión de la Comisión Asesora de Transporte* (Montevideo, June 25, 1963; ALALC/CAT/I dt 1/Rev. 1), pp. 6–12; and (Montevideo, April 11, 1964; ALALC/CAT/II/Informe/Rev. 2), pp. 6–11.

In mapping out the above policy and fundamental institutional mechanisms, LAFTA's aim has been to introduce regional order in the prevailing confusion, to overcome obstacles, and to correct deficiencies. The elements of resistance opposing the association in this endeavor are both regional and extrazonal in origin. In the first place, maritime services are irregular, a fact which frequently makes it difficult to find cargo-carrying space at the opportune time and obtain a reasonable freight rate. Furthermore, intra-Latin American maritime transportation costs more than overseas shipping, owing to several circumstances: (1) high freight rates, which represent approximately 12.5 per cent of the c.i.f. value and 15 per cent of the f.o.b. value;[9] (2) uneven distribution of cargo moving in intrazonal trade; (3) surcharges on freightage (which, according to Chilean figures, represented an additional 5.5 per cent in the zone in 1961); (4) the chaotic situation prevailing at the ports (maritime conferences levy surcharges of up to 35 per cent of freight costs in Latin American ports, particularly in Brazil, Uruguay, and Argentina); and (5) excessive red tape in connection with shipping operations.

Even as precarious and deficient as they are, the maritime transportation media available to the member countries could go a long way toward serving LAFTA's purposes, if they were appropriately organized and coordinated. It is not so much the lack of elements as their utterly inadequate use that lies at the root of the worst difficulties. True enough, the Latin American merchant fleets, despite various plans for modernization, are, in most cases, ancient and of relatively small capacity. (The LAFTA members, as will be observed from the table in this chapter, account for less than 2.5 per cent of world merchant-shipping tonnage.) Nevertheless, available vessels would provide much better service than is presently the case if two plans were put into effect in synchronized fashion: (1) The shipping lines should reorient and combine operations, lengthening their currently short runs and taking advantage of opportunities for regular transshipment;[10] (2) Organized importers and exporters in each member coun-

[9] The lack of complete and adequate statistics can lead to serious error. To illustrate: LAFTA data show total 1960 interzonal imports worth $374.8 million; and ECLA has estimated in *Realizaciones y perspectivas en el proceso del mercado regional* (Mar del Plata, 1963; E/CN. 12/688), p. 32, that maritime freight payment on intrazonal trade in that year amounted to some $108 million. A comparison of the two figures gives a total freight cost that is more than double the amount ordinarily mentioned (which appears to have been based on Chilean calculations corresponding to 1961).

[10] The Argentine firm Empresa Líneas Marítimas Argentinas has a contract with the Grancolombiana line covering combined service involving transshipments at Callao, the latter's terminal port.

try should, as is entirely feasible, cooperate closely with ALAMAR and with the Transportation Committees within the LAFTA National Commissions, in order to schedule merchandise shipments in such way that the vessels are assured of a full cargo on the trip out, and on the return voyage as well, in keeping with a well-regulated system.

Shipping tariffs and, to a great extent, the availability of cargo space in the transport of Latin America's foreign trade are established by maritime conferences controlled by foreign interests. The following are the principal ones operating in Latin America: Magellan and South Pacific Conference, United States–Brazil–River Plate Conference, Outward Freight Conference, South American Reefer Conference, Coffee Pool Agreement, and the European–River Plate Conference. The only four Latin American firms of international standing at present participating in extraregional maritime conferences —in a decidedly minority capacity—are Empresa Líneas Marítimas Argentinas (ELMA), Lloyd Brasileiro, Flota Mercante Grancolombiana, and Compañía Sudamericana de Vapores. Since the system of majority vote prevails in the maritime conferences, the Latin American shipping lines can do very little to influence decisions regarding freight rates and the distribution of available cargo-carrying space.[11] At

[11] ECLA has pointed up the lack of precise information on the system used in setting freight rates on regional traffic, owing to the many types of maritime carriers: maritime conferences, companies belonging to such conferences, independent firms, regularly scheduled services and those that are only occasional, tramps, etc. See ECLA, *Transport Problems in Latin America: Possible Studies Bearing on the Common Market* (Santiago, March 28, 1959; E/CN. 12/C. 1/14), p. 8.

For its part, the U.N. Economic Commission for Asia and the Far East (ECAFE) indicates, "The developing countries in the region have pointed out that by reason of the virtual monopolistic control exercised by the conferences, and the tying arrangements entered into by them with the shippers, ECAFE countries and their shippers have little say in the determination of the freight rates." See ECAFE, *Problems of Shipping and Ocean Freight Rates in the ECAFE Region* (Geneva, January 14, 1964; E/Conf. 46/26), p. 48. Document submitted to the United Nations Conference on Trade and Development.

Along the same line, another study presented to the UNCTAD calls attention to freight charges between ports in areas in process of development and cites the following facts: Freightage charged by the conferences on cargo carried from Liberia to other West African ports makes very little allowance for the short length of the runs, for it is only slightly less than that applicable to cargo transported to Europe and the United States. Such tariffs are an obstacle to greater cooperation among the African countries and, hence, to their industrialization, which is tailored to the needs of a broader regional market. Similar cases of relatively high freight rates appear to be applicable to commodities moved between Latin American ports. Although the tariffs cannot be strictly proportionate to the distances involved (among other reasons, because the amount of port costs is independent of that factor), causes of unduly high rates call for urgent investigation, since they obviously can constitute a significant obstacle in the path of expanding regional

best, they are able to exert some slight pressure in favor of moderation. Latin American companies find that the simple act of joining an international conference is a laborious and difficult task: in some instances, long years of insistence were necessary, plus the effect of the new situations that arose when the countries in the zone took measures to encourage shipping in domestic vessels. The most recent example is the invitation extended to Uruguayan shipowners (following certain merchant-marine protective measures instituted by the government) to join the European–River Plate Conference, with the offer that 20 per cent of the maritime transportation of Uruguay's foreign trade on the corresponding route would be reserved for the local interests. Retaliation was threatened in the event the proposal was not accepted.

The circumstances outlined above explain why absurd situations arise, as attested to in official documents or in statements by authorized sources. Merchandise sent from Porto Alegre to Montevideo arrives sooner if routed through Hamburg than if shipped direct. Freight costs from Buenos Aires to a Mexican port on the Gulf of Mexico are lower by more than 25 per cent if the shipment is routed through Southampton. Uruguayan wool consigned to the United States goes first from Montevideo to Hamburg, despite the presence in port of domestic vessels that make direct runs to New York.

The subject of maritime conferences intrudes forcibly upon our attention and obliges a digression at this point. It must be examined, if only in a few lines, because of Latin America's long and sad experience, together with the bitter response to protectionism from the great maritime powers and the conflict inherent in that situation. In combination, these two factors justify the fear that regional plans for the complementary functioning of maritime transport facilities will encounter dangerous obstacles of an external nature. In every instance in history, when Latin American countries have endeavored to further the development of their national merchant marines through preferential-treatment policies involving subsidies and exemptions, foreign pressure has unfailingly been brought to bear. This pressure has been exerted by both private and government sources abroad, acting singly or in concert, and has sought to block the use of protective measures, notwithstanding the fact that preferential practices have been, and are, common to all maritime countries. Indeed, their seafaring suc-

---

trade. See Economist Intelligence Unit, London, *Improvement of the Invisible Trade of Developing Countries: Ocean Shipping and Freight Rates and Developing Countries*. Document prepared at the request of the General Secretariat of the United Nations Conference on Trade and Development (Geneva, January 28, 1964; E/Conf. 46/27), pp. 233–34.

cess over the years is largely attributable to just such measures. One may cite two examples. In response to energetic and reiterated protests by foreign shipping interests, the Ecuadorian government agreed to repeal its law on consular fees, which gave local importers a saving incentive of 2.5 per cent to utilize the transport services of the Grancolombiana fleet. Beginning in the year 1959, as reported by the fleet's board of directors, the withdrawal of the 2.5 per cent margin occasioned a steady and very substantial decline in the tonnage of commodities shipped to Ecuador on ships of that fleet and, consequently, in freight earnings. The decrease in importation was calculated at some $1.2 million.[12] In the second instance under discussion, the executive branch of the Uruguayan government decreed in June of 1963 that merchandise imported in domestic ships would enjoy certain reductions and exemptions in connection with customary duties and surcharges. Reacting promptly, the European–River Plate Conference, with headquarters in London, advised all its members that shipping on given vessels flying the Uruguayan flag and bound for Montevideo would be considered a "breach of contract." Conference representatives threatened to paralyze transportation to Uruguay, and the question had repercussions in official British circles, whence a note emerged characterizing the decree as most disturbing and indicating that representations would be made to the Uruguayan government. There was a further indication that Great Britain was watching the situation closely and keeping in contact with other European governments. Eventually, five nations presented memoranda and formal protests to the Uruguayan authorities: Great Britain, Italy, Norway, Sweden, and Belgium. During the course of this conflict, certain highly censurable discriminatory tactics have come to light that are used against Uruguayan vessels by foreign charterers operating with the conference. There was, for example, the practice of delaying cargo deliveries in port, when a Uruguayan ship was anchored, and expediting handling, when a vessel of the conference lay alongside the dock.

Later, in September, 1964, when the conflict with the European countries had been alleviated, the U.S. Federal Maritime Commission (FMC) announced that, because the decree was discriminatory against the U.S. shipping companies and in view of the failure of the negotiations carried on during fifteen months with the authorities of Uruguay, it had decided to exercise reprisals consisting of a surcharge on U.S. merchandise exported to that country on Uruguayan ships. The commission fixed a period of thirty days, starting in early Decem-

[12] Flota Mercante Grancolombiana, S.A., *Informe de Labores, 1961* (Bogotá, 1962), p. 18.

ber, 1964, for enforcement of the measure. But this application was suspended the following month, in view of the fact that, in terms of a notification of the Federal Maritime Commission, Uruguay had informed the United States that it was preparing to present to its congress a new law regarding maritime shipping, the purpose of which was to support and promote its merchant marine, without adopting measures that meant discrimination against U.S.-flag ships.

The general feeling of the European authorities with regard to the whole problem of what they consider to be "flag discrimination" is clearly depicted in the following excerpt from a document prepared by the Maritime Transport Committee of the Organization for Economic Cooperation and Development (OECD):

> Many governments continue to follow discriminatory practices of various kinds in order to protect their national shipping without regard to ordinary commercial considerations . . . such practices are detrimental not only to the maritime countries, but also to the efficient and economic conduct of world trade. The governments of a number of important maritime countries, mostly members of OECD, have continued to take such action as was open to them to resist the growth of these practices, and some of them have considered the question of possible countermeasures to deal with flag discrimination. The Government of the Federal Republic of Germany has in fact obtained powers which would enable restrictions to be imposed on the employment of ships belonging to countries which practice discrimination against German shipping.[13]

Even more significant than all the foregoing, however, and also more disquieting, is the public reaction on the part of several important U.S. shipping lines that participate in the maritime transport of intra-Latin American commerce, as well as the attitude taken by U.S. authorities—in this case, the Federal Maritime Commission, the Department of State, and the Senate. In connection with the drafts of a general agreement on maritime and inland-waterway transport and the resolutions adopted by ALAMAR, the U.S. firms (among them Moore-McCormack Lines, Inc.; Delta Steamship Lines, Inc.; Gulf and South American Steamship Company; Grace Line; and Lykes Brothers Steamship Company) have publicly voiced energetic protests, in which they maintain that the LAFTA countries plan to follow discriminatory practices against U.S. private shipping interests. The position was confirmed, at the meeting held by ALAMAR in Rio de Janeiro, in November, 1964, by observers representing the five com-

[13] OECD, *Maritime Transport, 1961: A Study by the Maritime Transport Committee* (Paris, 1962), pp. 46–47.

panies just named. They indicated to the Latin American shipowners that any LAFTA agreement that would not guarantee the participation of their enterprises in the shipping equal to that which it had traditionally enjoyed, would bring about retaliations on the part of the United States against the fleets of the associated countries. At the same time, they have requested that the Federal Maritime Commission intervene by officially urging State Department action through diplomatic channels. According to releases from the specialized press in the United States, in July of 1963 the Department of State instructed the U.S. Embassies in the LAFTA member countries to present notes to the respective governments, outlining U.S. objections to the plans for establishing a preferential regional system for maritime transportation in the free-trade zone. This report was confirmed by the FMC Chairman, Rear Admiral John Harllee, who also stated that appropriate U.S. Government departments were following this matter very closely and were prepared to undertake whatever action might be necessary to ensure that U.S. shipping concerns continue to enjoy equal opportunity. The Senate Interstate and Foreign Commerce Committee has also discussed the problem and has requested that the U.S. Department of State keep it fully informed. In U.S. shipping circles, mention has been made of the possibility of recourse to reprisals, the first of which might be to prevent vessels of any of the Montevideo Treaty contracting parties from transporting goods to the United States from any of the other LAFTA countries. Thus, for example, Argentine ships would be excluded from the Brazil-U.S. coffee traffic.

The above digression will throw some light on the extrazonal factors that enter into play. From their almost prepotent vantage point in the international maritime market—which, far from free, is regulated to suit their purposes—these outside elements can effectively frustrate regional integration plans in the field of ocean transportation. Here, then, as in other LAFTA spheres, only through close solidarity can the member countries make progress and defend the common interests of the zone with some probability of success. The fact that the opinion of the contracting parties appears to be divided on several essential questions dealt with in the draft general agreement is an element of weakness that should be overcome with dispatch. It is imperative that the members conclude the formal agreements referred to in the discussion of LAFTA's general doctrine on maritime transportation. In the absence of such accords, the members will be unable to form the solidly united front that is a prerequisite to the institution of the prospective preferential system; they cannot expect to function as a bloc in negotiating better terms from the foreign-controlled maritime conferences; and, finally, the rapid evolution of the complementary functioning of maritime transportation will be impossible.

All in all, the associated countries should make new proposals covering the general agreement on water transport, removing the matter of cargo preference from the key prominence it had assumed and placing it in a rational framework. It would be necessary to: (1) give priority to the coordination of the maritime policies of the LAFTA countries, creating the proper agencies (national maritime and port commissions and a zonal maritime and port commission); (2) subscribe to a clearly worded protocol regarding harbor improvement (installations and operational systems) and regarding standards that would assure the ships of all the associate countries the same advantages as nationals; (3) coordinate the lines and ships available in the zone, rearranging their itineraries to the extent required to assure all the countries of regular service in accordance with their needs, under acceptable conditions of quality and cost; (4) agree to a common policy that would permit the growth of the shipping industry according to a regional plan, with a view toward establishing a LAFTA fleet that would operate, first, on intrazonal level and, later, in world trade; (5) sign an agreement in the field of shipbuilding, supported by both national and international financing (the first sectorial meeting of shipbuilders was to be called by LAFTA in the year 1965); (6) create a regional freight conference, under government control, through a LAFTA maritime and port commission; (7) adopt, in principle, multilateral cargo preference, putting it into practice gradually in the light of future conditions (the existing systems would for the moment continue to exist, those of bilateral cargo preference as well as those of free cargo, but would be subject to a process of adaptation to the system adopted in principle); (8) proceed to make a study of the present ties of shipping lines of the associate countries with foreign companies and with international maritime conferences for the purpose of having a true picture of the situation, which would permit the carrying out of the necessary negotiations between LAFTA and extrazonal interests.[14]

The urgent need for countries in process of development to reach basic agreements was underscored in one of the studies on the promotion of invisible trade of those countries, prepared for the United Nations Conference on Trade and Development.[15] The study strongly

[14] See Enrique Angulo and Javier Alejo, *La integración regional del transporte marítimo y el caso de México*, Supplement to *Comercio Exterior*, XIV, No. 11 (November, 1964), 22–27.

[15] Economist Intelligence Unit, *op. cit.*, p. 80.

urges developing nations to give absolute priority to measures that will equip them with a "countervailing power," through the creation or reinforcement of bargaining mechanisms, on a national or regional base, for use in dealings between the national associations of exporters and importers and the international maritime conferences. Countries under development are also exhorted to continue their efforts to expand their merchant marines, primarily by means of regional agreements.

The gross inadequacies found in Latin American port installations have been the subject, over a long period, of literature in abundance. Physical and legal deficiencies have been analyzed, as well as those deriving from operational methods. ECLA and, most notably, OAS (through its Permanent Technical Committee on Ports and the Inter-American Ports Conferences) have both done their best to make the countries in the region understand the serious repercussions of insufficient and badly managed port services and have urged that this situation be corrected without delay. However, judging by the *Report on Port Activities* submitted to the annual IA-ECOSOC meeting held in Mexico in October, 1962, progress has been disappointing, to say the least. The trend, in fact, has been in the opposite direction. As the report points out: "A brief review of the condition of the ports in Latin America today indicates that instead of gaining in capacity and efficiency, they have deteriorated." [16] The equipment breaks down for lack of maintenance; there is a personnel shortage, and labor disputes are frequent; procedures and paper work constitute an almost hopeless tangle; dreadful traffic jams occur, involving onshore trucks as well as the vessels in the harbor; loading and unloading operations are dragged out day after day.

The problem is of vital import to the free-trade zone. According to OAS, more than 66 per cent of the cost of transporting intraregional commerce by sea has to do with the handling of cargo and forms a part of the expenditures effected at the ports. Under these circumstances, it is obvious that the ports are the most suitable place for reducing maritime transport costs.[17] The improvement in port facilities (which, in a substantial number of cases, has prompted the maritime conferences to eliminate surcharges initially imposed on specific maritime runs) can become a very useful instrument in negotiating conference freight-rate reductions.

In view of the scant tonnage represented by the Latin American merchant fleets, any plan for reorienting maritime shipping in favor

[16] Pan American Union, *Report on Port Activities* (OAS Secretariat, July 10, 1962; Doc. 18-C [English]), p. 13.

[17] *Ibid.*, p. 2.

of zonal service would apparently presuppose the sacrifice of some of the present routes to the outside world, although coordination will permit the obtaining of greater results from the same number of units. This is yet another reason why LAFTA associates must undertake the inescapable task of increasing the capacity of their merchant marines. Programs for this purpose are already under way, or in project, in most of these nations. Under these circumstances, serious thought should be given the possibility of constituting a Latin American or zonal fleet, keeping in mind that additional local-flag vessels will be needed to carry an ever increasing proportion of the region's ocean trade. Apart from serving the specific objectives of regional integration, such a fleet would represent an economy measure. As pointed out in one of the studies presented to the United Nations Conference on Trade and Development, if all or a substantial majority of the countries in process of development were to try to expand their own merchant marines, a sizable capital outlay would be required and individual operating costs would, very probably, be quite high.[18] The study concludes that it might be advisable, in many instances, for such nations to approach the merchant-marine expansion problem from a regional point of view, whose practical expression might be operational agreements or zonal-scale shipping concerns with multinational membership.

In support of those who believe in bold solutions, it might be well, at this point, to quote a paragraph from the Punta del Este Charter mentioned earlier. Title 3, paragraph 11, reads as follows: "The promotion and coordination of transportation and communications systems is an effective way to accelerate the integration process. In order to counteract abusive practices in relation to freight rates and tariffs, it is advisable to encourage the establishment of multinational transport and communication enterprises in the Latin American countries, or to find other appropriate solutions." [19] Going a step further, at the second American interparliamentary conference held in Santiago, Chile, in 1961, a unanimously approved Brazilian proposal suggested that the countries in the zone study ways and means of organizing a government-controlled Latin American merchant fleet. For its part, the Uruguayan delegation to the Group of Experts on Transportation recommended that a single-flag Latin American fleet be created, organized as an international mixed-capital enterprise. Vessels engaged

[18] Economist Intelligence Unit, *op. cit.*, p. 223.

[19] Pan American Union, OAS General Secretariat, *Alliance for Progress*, Official Documents Emanating from the Special Meeting of the IA-ECOSOC at the Ministerial Level, held in Punta del Este, August 5–17, 1961, p. 19.

in international transportation would constitute the fleet, in keeping with certain administrative provisions, but would continue to be the property of the local shipping interests in the associate countries.

It would be the task of the public sectors to promote the formation of a Latin American fleet and, by means of appropriate incentives and regulatory measures, to channel shipping activity toward a policy designed to further regional purposes. The number of maritime firms under state control in the associate countries provides the respective governments with the solid base needed in accomplishing the task of reorienting and integrating shipping lines.

In theory, the Brazilian proposal has the most merit. A government-owned Latin American merchant marine would be the most flexible and appropriate instrument for use in adapting to the dictates of the common interest, beyond the limitations of a narrow profit motive, and, hence, would be best suited to contribute to the growth of intrazonal trade. The record of the Grancolombiana line, which has so eminently served the economies of the two co-owner governments, would argue in favor of a solution of this type. However, there is the very real danger that it will not be congruent with the prevailing tendency among governing groups in a majority of the member countries and will, moreover, be roundly rejected by vigorous vested interests. A Latin American fleet having mixed ownership and management, on the order of the Uruguayan idea, might find a more favorable climate, but its establishment would entail prolonged and complex negotiations. If events support these predictions, it would be well for the governments, if possible with the support of private enterprise, to undertake a provisional and intermediate solution, consisting of assigning a nucleus of ships of different nationalities to zonal traffic. In the measure that the trade volume expands, new vessels built in regional shipyards, and multilaterally financed, could be added. In any event, the associate countries must become aware of the need for increasing, at the same time, tonnage available for extrazonal transport.

The development of the merchant marines according to a regional plan, with a view to meeting the demands of intrazonal interchange as well as those of commerce with the outside world, to the maximum extent possible, necessarily involves an investment problem. At the IA-ECOSOC meeting referred to earlier, the cautious and reluctant thesis propounded by experts from the OAS (which has shown a certain hypersensitivity to the investment obstacle) was refuted by several Latin American delegations in a lively debate. The delegations pointed out that investments in ships can be recovered at very short term, can generate foreign-exchange earnings or permit a savings in foreign exchange, and can enhance the political and economic independence of the investing nations. The experts' argument that few opportunities for employment are created by investment of this nature was considered relatively unimportant, and it was emphasized that the purchase of foreign-made vessels requires a cash payment of only 20 per cent of the value in each case.

As indicated earlier, almost all the LAFTA members are endeavoring to rehabilitate and develop their fleets. Most of the resources they devote to that purpose, however, cover work contracted with extra-regional shipyards, while some of the zone's shipbuilding facilities are lying completely or partially idle and their situation is critical. The lack of resources to finance exports is unquestionably the major reason why sales of locally built vessels are almost nonexistent in the zone. Latin American shipbuilders cannot possibly compete with the powerful companies in the maritime nations in the matter of time payments and other credit terms. Under these circumstances, it is not uncommon for the shipyards in a member country to be deprived by extrazonal competition of the opportunity to build units for domestic shipping lines. The Inter-American Development Bank program for medium-term financing of intra-Latin American capital-goods exports may be expected to contribute to the solution of this problem. In any case, the example given by Mexico by ordering from Brazilian shipbuilders four merchant ships—an operation that involves some $8 million—establishes the necessary precedent for the shipbuilders of the zone to continue the same road. An initial positive reaction was visible at the meeting of ALAMAR held at Rio de Janeiro.

Any national plan for the development of the merchant fleet must incorporate the shipbuilding industry. Brazil's experience in this regard merits thorough study, for it embodies positive results achieved by implementing a well-planned and far-reaching program.[20] In a scant four years, Brazil has created a shipbuilding industry equipped with six international-type shipyards, some of which were financed by joint capital, while others are wholly Brazilian-owned. Their combined annual production capacity amounts to 150,000 metric tons, gross measurement. This has been accomplished within an appropriate institutional framework through the application of a series of measures and mechanisms for assembling resources and stimulating both national and foreign investment in the field. In keeping with the principle that the development of the merchant marine and of the nation's shipyards are inseparable phases of a single process, the Brazilian authorities have followed a policy of intelligent protectionism.

[20] Seminário de Planejamento Industrial, *Documento informativo do Grupo Executivo da Indústria Naval* (São Paulo, 1963; Doc. Inf. No. 5) p. 39.

LAFTA: Evolution of Merchant Fleets, 1949–63

Country	1949 [a]		1953 [a]		1958 [a]		1962 [b]		1963 [b]	
	Number of vessels	(In thousands of dead-weight tons)	Number of vessels	(In thousands of dead-weight tons)	Number of vessels	(In thousands of dead-weight tons)	Number of vessels	(In thousands of dead-weight tons)	Number of vessels	(In thousands of dead-weight tons)
Argentina	117	932	146	1,170	146	1,185	235	1,592	215	1,574
Brazil	169	896	196	1,096	201	1,121	285	1,568	295	1,673
Colombia	10	39	16	72	24	129	29	165	29	165
Chile	42	212	44	252	49	271	55	334	55	352
Ecuador	5	20	8	22	7	27	9	34	9	34
Mexico	21	160	29	213	30	228	43	245	51	355
Paraguay	4	4	4	4	4	4	24	20	25	21
Peru	19	102	23	115	23	125	39	187	43	232
Uruguay	11	104	9	81	15	97	19	139	18	137
Total	398	2,469	475	3,025	499	3,187	738	4,284	740	4,543
World Total	12,868	103,461	14,370	119,427	16,966	158,047	23,347	190,400	. . .	203,083 [c]
LAFTA As Percentage of World Total	2.4		2.5		2.0		2.3		2.2	

Based on CEPAL, *Economic Survey of Latin America,* 1963 (E/CN.12/696/add. 1), II, 146.

Sources: For 1949, 1953, and 1958, U.S. Department of Commerce, *The Handbook of Merchant Shipping Statistics* (Washington, D.C.: Government Printing Office, 1958). For 1962 and 1963, the figures were prepared on the basis of information from the main Latin American shipping companies, the Instituto de Estudios de la Marina Mercante Argentina, the Comissão de Marina Mercante do Brasil, the Asociación Nacional de Armadores de Chile, and Lloyd's Register of Shipping 1962–63.

[a] Only vessels of 1000 gross tons or over.

[b] Only vessels of 500 gross tons or over.

[c] Estimated.

XII

RAYMOND F. MIKESELL

External Financing and Regional Integration

Officials of most external assistance agencies concerned with Latin America have indicated on numerous occasions that a primary objective of their aid is the promotion of Latin American economic integration. Moreover, the promotion of economic integration is a stated objective of the Inter-American Development Bank and of the Punta del Este Charter, which sets forth the aims and implementing machinery of the Alliance for Progress. This paper examines the role of external financing in assisting regional activities (i.e., those directly involving the interests of two or more Latin American countries), and in supporting national projects or programs designed to promote or complement regional economic integration. No attempt will be made to catalogue all of the various types of assistance that have real or imagined implications for economic integration. Rather, I shall concentrate on certain problems and policy issues arising out of the employment of external assistance in support of the principle of regional economic integration in Latin America.

We may distinguish several categories of external financing that promotes, or claims to promote, regional economic integration:

1. Infrastructure projects, such as highways, railroads, and power, financed and executed more or less simultaneously in more than one country. An example would be a multiple-use river development, involving power, irrigation, and flood control, for streams that bound or

flow through two or more countries. Such a case would, of course, require joint planning and simultaneous financing and execution of specific, interrelated projects in more than one country. It is quite possible that the physical extension of some of these undertakings will take in areas that overlap national boundary lines.

2. Industrial and agricultural activities that involve regional trade or otherwise influence regional economic activity. In these instances, external financing may be direct or channeled through regional intermediaries. Thus, for example, a major objective of the Central American Bank for Economic Integration is the financing of firms selling in that regional market. In some cases, these lending activities are in support of regional plans for industrial and agricultural development.

3. Intraregional trade. The proposed system of medium-term export credits, to be administered by the Inter-American Development Bank, falls in this category.

4. Joint planning by national governments or quasi-public or private entities, in areas where such planning will presumably facilitate regional integration.

5. Purely national operations financed either directly by the external agencies or through regional financial or technical-assistance intermediaries and aimed at achieving a certain standardization of services or governmental practices (e.g., education, health, censuses, and cadastral surveys), or the uniform development of given fields of economic and social activity. When undertaken on a regional basis, these endeavors are alleged to lend direct or indirect support to economic, political, and social integration.

Regional Financing of Infrastructure

Regional integration can most obviously be served by external financing when the funds are channeled to international highways and railroads, power facilities, and multiple-use river facilities involving expenditures in, and benefits for, more than one country. Since external agencies make loans to individual governments or to firms domiciled within a single country, blanket credits covering projects of this kind would present certain difficulties. Although it should be possible to work out arrangements whereby each country would be responsible for servicing a portion of the loan, a project of this nature requires joint planning, a more or less simultaneous passage of enabling legislation, and the provision of local currencies to supplement the external financing. However, single loans are not an indispensable requisite for joint projects. What is necessary is the simultaneous authorization of funds for loans by external agencies, acting singly or in combination, to aid countries engaged in joint, or closely interdependent, projects.

A prime example of a joint project that could profit from a series of approximately simultaneous loan authorizations is the inter-American highway that has been under construction through the Latin American states over a long period. To date, the planning, financing, and implementation of this project has been piecemeal and far from integrated. Although various external agencies have, over several years, extended many loans to individual Latin American countries for the construction or improvement of various parts of this highway, simultaneous loan authorizations involving more than one country are conspicuously absent.

In addition to the lack of joint planning of infrastructure projects suitable for external financing, there is the possibility that an external agency may consider one of the countries involved an unsatisfactory credit risk, either because of a limited external-debt-service capacity or for other reasons. This obstacle could, of course, be overcome by the coordinated provision of loan funds from two or more external credit agencies. As a matter of fact, if the problem is simply a difference in the individual countries' capacity to service loans, several international finance agencies, including the World Bank and the Inter-American Development Bank, have both hard- and soft-currency loan windows.

A case can certainly be made for better coordination of the activities of the various external lending agencies at both the national and regional levels. However, the existing structure of those institutions does not impose any significant obstacles to the external financing of regional infrastructure projects; hence, it should not be necessary to create special regional institutions for this purpose. Nevertheless, the existence of regional financing agencies does not ensure priority consideration for infrastructure financing. A review of some thirty loans made to 1963 by the Central American Bank for Economic Integration shows that no credits whatsoever have been extended for regional infrastructure projects.

External Financing of Regional Industrial Integration

With the establishment of the Latin American Free Trade Association and the negotiation of agreements for a Central American Common Market, a number of questions have arisen regarding external financing of the industrial-development aims of those regional integration endeavors. The regional approach to outside financing in the industrial field derives from four basic objectives set forth in the Montevideo Treaty, which created LAFTA,[1] and echoed in the several treaties establishing the Central American integration system:[2]

1. Financing should be made available for new or expanded plants capable of producing for regional markets.

2. Funds should be devoted to complementary operations involving firms in different countries of the integrated regions.

3. Care should be taken to avoid the creation of excess production capacity within the regional market.

4. "Balanced development" should be achieved. Disparities in the rates of growth of member countries should be discouraged, as should increased trade imbalances arising from the trade-liberalization program.

Although the Montevideo Treaty does not provide for a specific institution for channeling or coordinating external assistance for members, Articles 15 and 32(e) of that document outline collective arrangements for outside financial or technical aid in support of "industrial complementarity" and balanced industrial growth.[3] For their part, the Central American countries have established the Central American Bank for Economic Integration for mobilizing both external and internal resources for use in financing industrial and agricultural projects; and the U.S. Agency for International Development (AID) has established a Regional Office for Central America and Panama Affairs (ROCAP) for coordinating U.S. financial and technical assistance to the area. Both AID and the Inter-American Development Bank have provided substantial financial support for the Central American Bank for Economic Integration.

The basic objective of assigning a high priority to financing firms capable of producing for a regional, rather than a national, market raises significant questions with respect to external lending policy and the allocation of capital. Hinging on the existence or nonexistence of regional free trade, the rationale appears to be approximately as follows: If free-trade conditions are actually or potentially present within the region, external lending agencies should consider the loan application of an industrial concern from the standpoint of its ability to perform efficiently as a *regional* producer and distributor. (In the ab-

[1] *Multilateral Economic Cooperation in Latin America*, I: *Texts and Documents* (New York: United Nations, 1962), I, 57–66.

[2] *Ibid.* pp. 5–31. For the text and analysis of the basic Central American treaties, see also Joseph Pincus, *The Central American Common Market* (Guatemala City: Regional Office for Central America and Panama Affairs, Agency for International Development, 1962).

[3] *Multilateral Economic Cooperation in Latin America*, I, 59 and 61.

sence of regional free trade, the credit institution would weigh the comparative advantages of financing production for domestic use, and possibly for export to the rest of the world, against having the commodity supplied from abroad.) The group of countries constituting a regional organization under a free-trade system would be regarded by the external financing agency as a single economy. The lending institution would still have to consider whether the commodity in question ought to be produced within the region or imported, but the existence of the free-trading regime adds a new dimension to its appraisal.

In response to economies of scale and the possibility of the more or less simultaneous establishment of complementary industrial facilities, the range of products that might be produced economically for a regional market will presumably be considerably broader than that which would be limited to the demand generated in a single national market.

On the other hand, production for the regional market should not be regarded as an end in itself or as sufficient justification for external financing. In the first place, if destined for a regional market, many commodities could be produced only at high cost and sold behind a high tariff wall. Such operations would have no net trade-creating effect, and would constitute a misallocation of resources, with a consequent loss of welfare for the region as a whole. Second, there are a number of high-priority industries that would not enter into intraregional trade because of high transportation costs. Building materials are a case in point. Third, there are certain industries that cater to world markets in preference to regional ones, and it would be unfortunate if the countries of a region were to neglect these industries in favor of those producing solely or largely to supply regional needs. This is especially important in the case of countries and regions whose exports of traditional primary commodities to the rest of the world are expanding at a slower pace than that demanded by rising calls on foreign-exchange reserves to finance imports and debt service. Although greater intraregional specialization and trade may promote substitution of regionally produced goods for imports from the rest of the world, the accelerated pace of industrial development will progressively enhance the demand for imports from outside the region.

External financing for planned complementary industry within a regional trading area may also have some merit, provided the complementary functioning of industry can meet reasonable tests of economic efficiency. For example, the development in one country of low-grade iron ore or coal, which could find a market only if an uneconomical steel plant were established in another country in the same region, would obviously be indefensible. The fact that a commodity could be produced with regional materials or components and thereby contribute to "complementarity" does not necessarily make it economical or representative of a wise allocation of investment resources. The foregoing notwithstanding, there are undoubtedly opportunities for intraregional specialization which *are* economical and merit coordinated effort on the part of agencies for external financial assistance.

External Financing and "Balanced Development"

Unqualified acceptance of the objectives of avoiding excess capacity and achieving "balanced development" is subject to serious question from the standpoint of both economic philosophy and the administration of external assistance.

With respect to the avoidance of excess regional capacity as a policy objective for endorsement by external lending agencies, a distinction should be drawn between two general situations: (1) restricted industrial enterprise, where official intraregional action directly or indirectly limits the number of firms in a given branch of industry; and (2) unrestricted industrial enterprise, referring to specific fields that are open to all comers.

Restricted industrial enterprise. Perhaps the best example of the limitation imposed on an industry's capacity by governmental accord among the countries constituting an integrated region is the Convention on the Regime of Central American Integration Industries. Under the terms of this document, a designated Central American plant, or group of plants, is assured of immediate intrazonal free-trade treatment for its output, whereas similar items produced in "nonintegrated" operations would have to wait ten years for duty-free status. Apart from the preferred regional-market position thus conferred on "integrated" operations, they would also enjoy external tariff advantages.[4] Although discriminatory treatment in intra-Latin American trade as a means of restricting freedom of entry into industry is not specifically provided for in the Montevideo Treaty, Articles 15, 16, and 17 confer the requisite authority for the negotiation of formal arrangements designed to accomplish that purpose.

In cases where monopolistic enterprises are fostered by regional groups (either by discriminatory trade treatment or otherwise), exter-

[4] The text of the Convention on the Regime of Central American Integration Industries, signed on June 10, 1958, by Guatemala, El Salvador, Honduras, Nicaragua, and Costa Rica, is reproduced in *Multilateral Economic Cooperation in Latin America*, I, 23–26. For a discussion of the significance of this convention, see Pincus, *op. cit.*, pp. 82–87 and 102–8.

nal credit agencies may be unwilling to provide financing for the favored few, on grounds that such action would promote the perpetuation of a monopoly situation and constitute a collaboration that discriminates against other investors, both local and foreign. As a matter of fact, both the Inter-American Development Bank and AID have refused to sanction the use of the funds they have loaned the Central American Bank for Economic Integration in financing firms given preferential treatment within the Central American Common Market by virtue of being designated as "integrated industries." These external agencies maintain that eligibility for entry on nondiscriminatory terms is essential for the operation of competition and the realization of the corresponding benefits of improved efficiency and lower prices.

Those who oppose this position argue that free entry on equal terms would lead to wasteful duplication or overcapacity, or, somewhat paradoxically, to a dearth of new enterprise because of the unwillingness of domestic and foreign investors to build plants of economical size unless they are assured of all or a large part of the regional market, at least for a certain period. Where the total regional market is small in any case, the argument continues, investment must be planned, or at least guided; and the unfettered operation of competitive forces is a luxury the less-developed nations cannot afford. Thus, we are faced with a difference in economic philosophy whose full discussion unfortunately exceeds the terms of reference of the present paper.

Unrestricted industrial enterprise. Where the regional economic group makes no provision for restricting the entry of firms into an industry, external financing agencies, in deciding on loan applications, must still take into account existing or planned productive capacity in relation to the regional market. In fact, this is one of the criteria applied by the Central American Bank for Economic Integration (some of whose funds are supplied by external lending agencies) when considering credit applications from firms operating within the Central American market. Let us assume that a firm already in operation has sufficient capacity to satisfy three-fourths of effective regional demand for its product at the going price. Now assume that a second company proposes to build a plant with an equal or greater capacity and applies for a loan from an external financing agency. The introduction of a new, and perhaps more efficient, plant may force down the price of the product. If the demand for the commodity is fairly elastic, the market might be able to absorb the output of both plants; or, conceivably, the less efficient firm might be forced out of business or, at any rate, obliged to take steps to reduce its costs. These and other considerations most certainly merit careful investigation when deciding whether to honor the new firm's loan request.

We turn now to the relationship between external financing and the principle of "balanced development" for members of an integrated region. Present in both the LAFTA treaty and the Central American economic-integration program, this principle lends itself to several interpretations, none of which are entirely acceptable to international or regional financial institutions whose operations are meant to conform to a particular approach.[5]

Throughout the long history of negotiations that culminated in LAFTA and the Central American Common Market, in both of which ECLA was the prime mover, ECLA has tended to interpret balanced development in terms of more or less equal rates of industrial growth and the expansion of member-country commodity exports to the region. Thus, the attainment of balanced industrial growth would be reflected in an improved regional balance-of-payments position for each participating country, especially as regards trade in industrial commodities.[6] As envisioned by the Montevideo Treaty, balanced industrial growth is to be achieved mainly through trade liberalization designed to discriminate in favor of the countries that are less developed industrially. Moreover, as provided in Article 32(e), collectively sponsored financial or technical arrangements are to be made in favor of such countries, so as to bring about the expansion of their "existing productive activities or to encourage new activities, particularly those intended for the industrial processing of their raw materials." In the Central American Common Market, balanced development will presumably result from the establishment of certain "integrated industries" in each member country, which, for a time at least, would enjoy a monopoly position within the region.

Comment is in order at this point concerning the publicly avowed policy of the Inter-American Development Bank with regard to balanced development. In the words of the bank's President, Felipe Herrera, that policy is "to evaluate the condition of the areas having a lower rate of growth and those where underdevelopment is most notable. The Bank is not only tending to give priority attention to low-income countries but is also operating in certain zones belonging to medium and large countries which on the whole do not require large-

[5] See Pincus, *op. cit.*, p. 102.

[6] Raymond F. Mikesell, "The Movement Toward Regional Trading Groups in Latin America," in Albert O. Hirschmann (ed.), *Latin American Issues: Essays and Comments* (New York: Twentieth Century Fund, 1961), pp. 139–40.

scale foreign action for the improvement of prevailing living conditions." [7]

On the one hand, we have the above-noted ECLA interpretation of balanced development, which is reflected in the plan for establishing in each Central American country monopoly industries that will enjoy special privileges in the regional market. On the other, there is the balanced-development approach that seeks to give less-developed members special consideration with respect to whatever financial and technical assistance is made available to the region, but without violating the principle of comparative advantage or disturbing the operation of competitive forces. Between the two interpretations there is a significant difference, as outlined below.

It is certainly true that inherent in the creation of regional markets is the danger of intensifying economic and social "dualism" in less-developed areas. Given free entry into industry and free trade within a region, there will be a tendency for both domestic and foreign capital, as well as skilled labor, to gravitate toward the more industrially advanced centers. External and regional financing institutions alike will ordinarily provide the greatest amount of financing to those areas or countries whose projects best fulfill the eligibility standards of those agencies. Moreover, the most economical industrial projects will be formulated in areas having the greatest concentration of external economies. Finally, if, like the Central American Bank for Economic Integration, the external financing institution is under a basic obligation to provide financing for those firms capable of producing for a regional market, it is apt to find such firms concentrated in certain countries and industrial centers. There is, then, an inherent contradiction between the principle of balanced development among the members of an integrated region and the principle of comparative advantage in the promotion of firms oriented toward regional markets. To a degree, at least, these conflicting objectives can be dealt with by means of technical assistance, by giving high priorities for essential infrastructure projects to less-advanced areas, and, perhaps, by special tax and other incentives which will attract both regional and external capital to those areas. In addition, unbalanced industrial growth within a region can be compensated, to some extent, by the development of an efficient agriculture and the improved marketing of farm commodities within and without the area.

What, then, should be the role of external financing in facilitating

[7] See IDB press release, October 23, 1962, "Address delivered by Felipe Herrera, President of the Inter-American Bank, at the Second Plenary Session of the First Annual Meeting of the Inter-American Economic and Social Council held in Mexico City, October 23, 1962."

regional integration in the field of industrialization and trade? The answer obviously depends on the degree to which industrialization is subject to joint government planning or is left to the operation of competitive forces based on free entry into regional markets. If certain industries are reserved for the public sector by all countries within the integrated region, external or regional financing could facilitate the establishment of these industries, once their nature and location has been determined by the joint planning machinery. However, external financing agencies may be unwilling to finance government-controlled industrial enterprises for which domestic or foreign private capital is available. In some instances, of course, the industrial undertakings designated as public enterprise by the regional planners may hold little attraction for the private investor. Such might be the case of steel mills, for example, which would then be eligible for financial aid from external agencies, provided the specific project had a sound economic base. Finally, the joint planning authorities might desire to attract domestic or foreign capital to certain industries by offering loan capital from external or regional financial agencies, along with other inducements. External agencies are likely to be reluctant, however, to provide capital, either directly or through regional credit institutions, under conditions that involve favoritism or limitations on the free entry of other firms in the same industry. In other words, it is important to differentiate between activities designed by the regional planners to induce investment in certain fields and those aimed at the creation of monopolies.

In the field of agricultural development, especially insofar as concerns commodities destined for regional, rather than export, markets, external financing can make a significant contribution to regional integration. The expansion of agricultural output for local consumption very often requires governmental assistance of various types: production credits to enable farmers to obtain equipment, seed, and fertilizer; the construction of feeder roads and storage facilities; and the supply of transport equipment. It is quite possible that markets that are potentially the most readily accessible may be across national boundaries. Even under free-trade conditions, however, an opportunity to serve these markets may depend upon the existence of transportation and storage facilities and, perhaps, processing plants in neighboring communities on the other side of the border. In such a situation, coordinated external financing may be essential to implement joint planning in the field of agriculture. Even in the case of export agriculture, it may make economic sense to develop production in one country and ship the commodity to another for processing and export.

One may conclude, therefore, that there are a number of situations in which external financing can play a significant role in regional integration in the field of infrastructure, industry, and agriculture. The extent and nature of this contribution will depend, in large measure, on the region's economic structure and the character and efficiency of regional planning. It might also be observed at this point that, although limited amounts of outside financial and technical assistance may encourage the creation of the basic conditions for regional integration (such as the freeing of intraregional trade; the unrestricted movement of capital, labor, and business enterprise; and joint economic planning by public authorities, including inducements for private-sector operations), the mission of external financing is largely circumscribed to *facilitating* rather than *inducing* or initiating regional integration. In the absence of direct cooperation among the governments themselves and among the firms in the private sector, external financing is not likely to achieve "balanced development," nor can external or regional credit agencies be expected to allocate resources in such a way as to realize the objectives of regional planning.

Regional Financial Institutions

The only institution that qualifies as a regional financial agency in Latin America is the Central American Bank for Economic Integration. Proposals have been made for a development bank to serve LAFTA integration efforts. However, since the member countries can by no stretch of the imagination be regarded as constituting an economic region, and since the LAFTA treaty does not even provide for a complete freeing of intra-LAFTA trade in the foreseeable future—to say nothing of other basic elements of regional integration, such as a customs union and the free movement of capital, labor, and business enterprise—the creation of a LAFTA development bank would simply duplicate the facilities of the Inter-American Development Bank. Despite its avowed objective of prompting Latin American integration, the IDB—thus far, at least—has been merely one of several international credit institutions that have made loans to individual Latin American countries. Its lending activities have paralleled, and sometimes competed with, those of the Export-Import Bank, the IBRD and its subsidiaries, AID, and European financial agencies. To examine the role and usefulness of a regional financial institution in facilitating regional integration we must turn, then, to the Central American Bank for Economic Integration.

CABEI obtained its initial capital from the five member countries (Costa Rica, El Salvador, Guatemala, Honduras, and Nicaragua), each of which subscribed $4 million, and is also the recipient of grants and loans from AID and the IDB, plus credit lines from the Bank of Mexico and the Bank of America.

The first question that suggests itself is what function is served by pooling the financial resources of the member countries, all of which are themselves in need of, and receiving, external assistance for development purposes. There are several possible answers.

First, it might be argued that, since CABEI is designed to finance only regionally significant infrastructure projects, services, industry, and agriculture, it will allocate its pool of funds in a manner that will contribute to the general regional welfare, in which all members will share, and presumably, share alike. To cite a case in point, however, it is doubtful that a $1.5 million loan the CABEI has made to a Honduran cement plant, whose output is expected to be sold regionally, will provide equal benefits to all members. In fact, the common tariff set up on cement strongly suggests that members not producing this building material might otherwise buy it at a lower price from outside the region. In other words, countries receiving the largest share of the pooled funds will, in all likelihood, receive the greatest benefits. Exceptions to this statement would be infrastructural projects that complement projects in neighboring countries, or those few cases where the creation of an industry in one country will provide an important market for the products of another.

The second argument for making loans out of a regionally contributed pool is that it will facilitate joint economic planning by providing a readily available source of funds to assure that projects involving expenditures in more than one country can be financed without delay. This argument assumes that under other circumstances financing would constitute a major obstacle in the path of coordinated investment activities.

The third reason adduced is that CABEI loans will be channeled preferably to firms producing for the regional market, thereby facilitating intraregional trade and specialization. Here, the implication is that individual countries, either because of a lack of capital or for administrative reasons, would not be disposed to give a high priority to financing firms capable of serving regional markets.

A fourth argument, which is related to the first, is that funds will be allocated in accordance with the principle of comparative advantage within the region and hence promote the optimum use of regional resources.

A fifth argument, written into the CABEI charter but not necessarily reflected in its policies, is that the bank, in allocating funds within the region, will promote balanced development. (The system is likened to that followed by the U.S. Government, by which expenditures in, or loans to, a given state are not tied to the amount of federal revenues derived from that state. In some cases, the federal authorities may give more than they get; in others, the situation is reversed.) The application of this tenet, however, may well be in contradiction to the optimum use of capital resources in accordance with the principle of comparative advantage. On the other hand, CABEI could fulfill an important need by helping members to adjust to the regional free-trade regime.

It is maintained, finally, that access to the regional pool of funds constitutes a powerful inducement for countries to undertake the commercial policy obligations of membership in a regional customs union; further, had it not been for CABEI, the Central American Common Market might not have come into existence. (In addition to providing long-term development financing, the bank also operates a clearing house for regional payments involving the extension of a limited amount of short-term credits to members.)

Assuming for the moment the desirability of the basic objectives sought in the pooling of regional funds, it is difficult to assess these arguments in the aggregate. There is at least some validity in most of them, while others are questionable or even contradictory. An examination of some thirty CABEI loans, most of which have been to firms that are present or potential regional-market producers, does not reveal a clear superiority of regional financing, as compared with funds supplied through local development banks, assuming that regional free-trade is a present or future reality. There is already considerable evidence of dissension among the member states with respect to the distribution of loan funds. As of June 6, 1963, nearly 40 per cent of the loans had been made to one member, Honduras, while Nicaragua had received only 16 per cent. Also, charges of logrolling in the allocation of loan funds are frequently heard in Central America. (In noting these charges, the author is not suggesting that they are valid, and he is personally convinced of the integrity of the bank's President, Enrique Delgado.)

CABEI enjoys one rather singular advantage, which is perhaps more political than economic: The fact that each member country contributed to the initial capital has apparently facilitated credit calls on external sources such as AID and the IDB. Had CABEI not been created, these institutions presumably would not have made the same amount of funds available to the individual countries. Given the broad acceptance by external financing agencies and the U.S. Government of the desirability of region-oriented financing—indeed, any proposal advanced in the name of integration seems to have taken on a well-nigh fatal charm for many officials—it is quite likely that the device of a regional financing institution has, in effect, succeeded in attracting additional external capital.

Let us turn now to a comparison of the respective merits of external financing through regional institutions and financial assistance supplied directly to individual member countries of a group seeking regional integration. Arguments advanced in favor of channeling external funds through the regional institution, rather than making them available on an individual basis to members of the regionally integrated group, very substantially echo those adduced in behalf of pooling regional resources for administration by a regional credit agency. The same limitations as those observed earlier naturally apply, including a possible conflict of objectives (e.g., balanced development versus optimum allocation of regional resources). However, certain additional problems arise whenever external financing of a regional lending agency is involved. If funds are borrowed from abroad, service payments must be made in foreign currencies and should be taken into account in the regional investment pattern. This fact notwithstanding, the agreement establishing the Central American Bank for Economic Integration places the principal emphasis on the financing of projects intended to enhance intraregional trade.[8] The bank has no control over member countries' internal policies and hence cannot influence the comparative attractiveness of export industries over regionally oriented industries. (For example, the CABEI has no jurisdiction over the level of the common tariff, exchange rates, or inducements to export-oriented industries.) Thus, there is no mechanism for coordinating CABEI's external borrowing operations with the region's aggregate balance-of-payments position with the outside world —unless, of course, this is accomplished through regional planning.

Another problem arising out of the channeling of external financing to regional institutions is the end user's reluctance to assume the exchange risk involved in foreign-currency obligations. In the case of loans made to national development banks, the exchange risk is frequently assumed by the central bank or treasury of the beneficiary country, and the commitment made by private borrowers specifies payment in local currency. CABEI has noted a tendency on the part of loan applicants to request that their credit needs be met only out of that portion of the bank's assets that are carried in regional currencies,

[8] CABEI may, however, make loans for projects designed to expand extra-regional exports. Article 2(b) prohibits CABEI's financing of investment in "essentially local industries."

since they do not want to assume the exchange risk involved in borrowing foreign currencies.[9] This preference persists in spite of the higher interest rates for regional-currency loans than for those extended in a foreign currency. This situation has been cited as one of the reasons why CABEI has been slow to use the resources made available to it by external lending agencies.

If the regional group does not take steps to coordinate the internal and external financial policies of its members, outside financing of regional financial institutions complicates the problem of assessing the borrower's debt-servicing capacity and makes it difficult to exert pressure in behalf of measures that will tend to improve that country's balance-of-payments position. This function could, of course, be undertaken by the regional financing institution itself. However, in the absence of a high degree of economic and financial coordination among member states, the credit agency cannot aspire to any very great influence on members' internal policies. It should be pointed out that no balance-of-payments problems will ensue as long as each member of the regional group seeks to maintain an over-all balance-of-payments equilibrium. (Under these circumstances, any deficit with the region would be compensated by a surplus with the rest of the world.) The danger lies in the possibility that each country may assume that, so long as a favorable regional trade balance offsets its debt-service payments to the regional financing agency, little regard need be given to the impact of such payments on the country's balance with the rest of the world, and it can therefore continue to finance its investments with impunity out of funds supplied by the regional credit institution. The general adoption of such policies would obviously work to the region's ultimate harm, since all members cannot simultaneously increase their positive regional trade balance; for its part, the regional bank cannot meet its external debt obligations unless the region improves its net balance with the rest of the world. Thus, there are inherent dangers in channeling external loan funds through a regional banking institution whose overriding purpose is to direct investment into industries that produce for a regional market. The situation could be remedied, of course, by deliberate efforts to give high priority to industry and agriculture oriented toward world markets. As mentioned earlier, however, a review of the CABEI loan portfolio as of June, 1963, indicates that virtually all of its industrial

[9] CABEI is protected against a devaluation-induced depreciation in the dollar value of the capital subscriptions of individual members. This is accomplished by a clause that requires any member whose currency has been devalued to maintain the dollar value of its capital contribution by paying in whatever additional local currency may be necessary. See Article 5 of its charter.

and agricultural credits are in support of enterprises producing for the regional market.

The proponents of development through reliance on import substitution, rather than on export expansion, argue that foreign-exchange-saving investments directed toward import substitution can achieve regional industrialization even when the export trade in traditional commodities is at a standstill or increasing only very slowly. But experience has shown that, as a consequence of the high import component of investment expenditures and the rising debt service, this approach has failed to achieve balance-of-payments equilibrium; furthermore, it stringently limits the range of industrial commodities that optimum-size plants can produce for markets as limited as the one comprising the whole of Central America.[10]

Other External Financing of Activities Designed to Promote Regional Integration

Space will not permit mention of more than a few additional external financing activities, current and proposed, that seek to promote regional integration in Latin America. Important among these is a proposal for a regional system of medium-term financing of Latin American exports, now under implementation by the Inter-American Development Bank.[11] The absence of medium-term export financing facilities in Latin American countries and the consequent restriction on the development of export markets argue in favor of the establishment of such a system by the IDB. The feature of the proposed program with which I would take issue, however, is the limitation of the medium-term financing to exports moving in intra-Latin American trade. The reason given for this restriction, intended to remain in effect at least during the initial stages of the program, is that "one of the principal purposes of the system would be to encourage the promotion of economic integration in Latin America." [12]

A variety of proposals for facilitating intra-Latin American payments have been put forward over the years. Including payments unions, clearing arrangements, and facilities for rediscounting commercial paper, some of these schemes anticipate external financing; but whatever contribution external financing can make to these and other Latin American economic integration efforts depends chiefly on the

[10] Raymond F. Mikesell, *U.S. Private and Government Investment Abroad* (Eugene, Ore.: University of Oregon Press, 1962), chap. xiv.

[11] *Study on the Financing of Exports in Latin America* (Washington, D.C.: Inter-American Development Bank, 1963).

[12] *Ibid.*, p. 28.

merits of the proposals themselves.[13] These questions are discussed elsewhere in this volume. It is important to keep one fact uppermost, however: Regional economic integration is not an end in itself, but a means intended for the promotion of social and economic development.

Finally, there are a number of external financial and technical assistance activities that are being undertaken in the name of regional integration but whose relationship to that goal is rather farfetched. By way of a recent example, one of the aims sought by the IDB in lending $2.9 million out of its Social Progress Trust Fund to five Central American universities was to give "support to the Central American university integration movement being fostered by the Higher Central American University Council." [14] Although advantages undoubtedly will accrue to specialization in higher education in Central America, enabling each university to develop strong faculties in certain fields and thereby attract students from all parts of the region, an adequate system of student exchange and transferability of academic credits has yet to be established. However desirable the stated objective, external financial assistance cannot be effective in the absence of genuine planning and coordination among the universities.

Similarly, activities sponsored by AID's Regional Organization for Central America and Panama (e.g., the Mobile Rural Health Program and the Cadastral Survey and Economic Mapping Program) appear to be content with providing approximately equal and standardized services for the five Central American states rather than lending support to meaningful economic integration. Finally, programs for technical assistance and financial support of joint planning activities in Central America have been harassed by a planning philosophy conflict that has arisen among the countries themselves and among the external agencies, including ECLA and the U.S. Government. In the author's view it would be far wiser to concentrate on joint planning and cooperation in specific regional activities, such as highway development, power, and perhaps higher education, plus the establishment of agricultural and industrial research centers, instead of attempting to coordinate all-inclusive long-range national plans reflecting different governmental policies and employing programming techniques of doubtful efficacy.

13 The author's views on payments arrangements for Latin America have been set forth in "Algunos problemas y posibles formas de abordar la solución del problema de pagos dentro de la ALALC," *Cooperación financiera en América Latina* (Mexico City: Centro de Estudios Monetarios Latinoamericanos, 1963), pp. 118–45; and in "The Movement Toward Regional Trading Groups in Latin America," pp. 147–48.

14 See IDB press release of September 23, 1962.

Some Tentative Conclusions and Unresolved Questions

Insistent emphasis on regional integration in the semantics of economic development has resulted in a tendency to devise external financing and technical assistance programs whose principal justification is that they support "economic integration," however vaguely conceived. Such activities should be subjected to a more rigorous analysis as to exactly what they expect to accomplish within the political and economic environment of the countries concerned. Sound economic and social development, rather than the promotion of integration, should be the primary purpose of external financing. Regional institutions that owe their existence to external sponsorship or imposition are mushrooming; but economic, political, and administrative conditions essential for their operation are conspicuously lacking. The creation of these conditions depends upon governmental determination and competence and, even more important, upon the support of the public, in general, and of key private institutions, in particular. Neither economic integration nor basic social and economic change can be imposed from the outside. Since they have not even achieved *national* integration, most Latin American countries have a long way to go before being able to essay genuine cooperative action with their neighbors. At its most meaningful, Latin American economic integration must begin with freedom of movement of commodities, capital, enterprise, labor, and ideas. Seeking to mesh activities at the governmental level is highly impracticable, particularly in view of the degree of internal disorganization so often in evidence in the majority of governments in the region.

I also believe that the provision of external assistance through regional financial institutions such as CABEI warrants re-examination. Some of CABEI's difficulties have derived from major policy disputes, in which the member countries, as well as the external financing agencies, have become involved. In addition, administrative snags have occasioned serious delays in the approval of loan applications.[15] Nevertheless, CABEI has unquestionably been an important factor in the establishment of the Central American Common Market, and if it

[15] In conversations with the President of the Central American Bank for Economic Integration, the author learned that although AID's regional branch, ROCAP, is supposed to have the authority to approve loans made by CABEI out of AID funds, CABEI has experienced delays of as much as five months in obtaining approval of financing for regional firms (which had already been passed by its own board) because ROCAP was obliged to submit the loan proposals to AID, in Washington, D.C. In this case, then, the new regional machinery served only to add yet another administrative layer to the external assistance process.

can be prevailed upon to forgo the "integrated industries" scheme for creating regional monopolies, this agency should be given strong external support.

On the other hand, the basic aims of economic integration in the case of LAFTA would, it seems to me, be better served by the establishment of effective machinery for coordination at the regional level of the activities of the several external financial and technical assistance agencies, including AID, the IDB, the IBRD and its subsidiaries, and the U.N. Special Fund.

The experience thus far in Central America contains valuable lessons that can be applied to good advantage when considering proposals for external financing designed to support economic integration in LAFTA or other areas. Given effective coordination of their activities, there is no reason why the external lending and technical assistance agencies could not handle directly any specific project requiring the simultaneous extension of loan funds to two or more countries. In addition, regional coordination among the external financial institutions would enable the implementation of basic credit policies, established in consultation with regional organizations and embodying a system of priorities.

Advocates of financing by regional agencies may be quick to argue —and with reason—that, despite outside loan assistance, some of the national development banks have not operated effectively. As a matter of fact, some of these banks have not been able to avail themselves of already authorized external credit lines, even after several years.[16] I seriously question, however, whether the incompetent management demonstrated by individual governments can be corrected or offset by regional institutions staffed by administrators drawn from these same governments.

One further point of significance in regard to external financing of programs sponsored by LAFTA. It is clear from the CABEI experience that external agencies will not finance enterprises that aspire to a monopoly status within the free-trade area; nor will they lend assistance to "fenced in" areas of activity involving restrictions on freedom of entry. LAFTA would therefore be well advised to subject its poli-

[16] For example, as of June, 1963, out of the $5 million authorized by the Export-Import Bank in December, 1959, for use by Guatemalan banks in financing local industrial enterprises, only $1 million had been used. This circumstance is primarily attributable to Guatemalan administrative difficulties, which have occasioned similar delays in the utilization of other loans. Judging from CABEI's experience, however, regional credit institutions face the same problem: As of July 1, 1963, CABEI had not availed itself of any of the $5 million loan authorized by the Development Loan Fund (AID) in July, 1961, or the $6 million credit line approved by the IDB in April, 1963.

cies to conscientious review insofar as they may affect the availability of external financing. Specifically, policy harmonization should be effected between LAFTA and the IDB, and should be carried over also to the other external assistance agencies on whom LAFTA may have occasion to call.

XIII

FELIPE HERRERA

The Inter-American Development Bank and Latin American Integration

Since its creation, the Inter-American Development Bank has actively participated in the formulation of practical solutions relating to the Latin American integration process. In the different aspects of its activities and in public statements by its directors, the IDB gives daily expression to its permanent concern with accelerating that process. The bank's interest in this case stems from the conviction that, in the absence of economic integration, it will be impossible to remove some of the fundamental obstructions to the economic and social development of the Latin American countries.

Whereas the aspiration to the political reintegration of Latin America—that large and scattered family—implies a return to tradition and the possibility of essaying a universally projected common destiny, from a technical standpoint economic integration is the only way open to all the peoples of the region for the realistic initiation or acceleration of an autonomous movement, in which many presently unsolvable problems can be satisfactorily overcome in the broader framework of a common market, a free-trade zone, or simply special sectoral complementarity agreements.

At a time when self-centered, exclusion-bent nationalism is yielding in all the world to a federalism in which the different communities constitute themselves in regional units, Latin America must not continue in its present dismembered state. Quite apart from the requirements growing out of the current coalescence of forces on the international political front, internal exigencies, resulting from the very dynamics of the growth process, create the need for integration as the sole possibility of taking advantage of a broadened market and making better use of productive resources.

On the other hand, it should be remembered that national integration, both economic and political, is a prior condition to Latin American integration and that the latter should not be considered an alternative for the urgent structural transformation that some of our countries need to initiate and others, to complete. Integration should be based on the dynamic function performed by each of the constituent parties. It will constitute the harmonization of diverse efforts, not the sum of passive attitudes. Hence, the integration process must begin with each country's success in the direction of ensuring equality of opportunity for all its citizens. Integration has a vertical dimension, in depth, which does not oppose, but rather of necessity precedes, the horizontal, geographic dimension of the movement for the coordination and complementary functioning of multinational endeavor. Thus, when the IDB, through its lending or technical-assistance operations, contributes to promoting or consolidating structural and institutional reforms that enable a better use of internal resources, it is furthering the general integration process (even though the results may be apparent only inside the boundaries of the national or provincial community). For, if the final objective of this process is the "realization of the long-sought Western ideal of equality of opportunity," as Gunnar Myrdal says, integration will not be able to mobilize the productive capability of the great majorities until they regard integration not only as a prospective common market but the enlargement of their hopes to encompass definite horizons of material well-being and cultural advancement.

Integration will not become a collective cause if it grows out of the decision of minority groups that care not whether they perpetuate the vast, empty distance separating them from the masses. It is important to emphasize again that Latin American integration will complement and accelerate the national development process, but that, as evidenced by the European experience, in no case can it serve as a substitute. There are those who, devoid of the creative will, proclaim the hope that a movement "from outside" will compensate for the lack of internal impetus. Neither a free-trade zone, nor a common market, nor the constitution of agencies for collective political representation will solve the problem of Latin American retardation unless, simultaneously with the creation or perfecting of such institutions, each country wages war against the causes of its own misery. Integration in itself is no talisman that will deliver Latin America from stagnation, just as political independence and the promulgation of liberal constitutions did not automatically ensure a consolidation of democracy in all Latin American countries.

Criterion of Integration

At the time the Inter-American Development Bank was founded, in December, 1959, the economic integration process was not being urged on by the clear determinations that today lend it impetus. That fact notwithstanding, the agreement establishing the IDB assigned the new institution the fundamental objective of contributing "to the acceleration of the process of economic development of the member countries, individually and *collectively* [italics added]."[1] The search for common solutions was established in the definition of an agency that, in itself, brought to fruition the age-old aspirations of the Latin American community.

Although from the beginning of its activities the IDB gave special attention to the possibility of financing projects having a bearing on the integration process, as evidenced by the support given the Central American Bank for Economic Integration, during the first stage of its lending operations efforts were concentrated primarily on specific projects in each country. During this period, the IDB followed traditional international banking practices, with the exception that priority projects were selected in fields that, up to that time, had not been favored by external financing. The precepts of the Punta del Este Charter, which promoted the formulation of national development plans, made it possible for the IDB to finance projects adjusted to an over-all and coordinated view of each member country's economic growth. The criterion of natural priority was thus gradually replaced by criteria of eligibility in which the level of priority established by the national development plan carried the most weight. The wisdom of the project was, in itself, no longer the sole point at issue; consideration was also given its relationship to the country's balanced growth.

Some time ago, IDB operating policy entered into a third stage that will bring the agency's profile into sharper focus and project it well into the future. This stage is characterized by the recognition of a new dimension: regional integration. As a result, specific projects and national plans are analyzed from a broader perspective. The merits of the transaction are no longer judged solely in terms of the project

[1] Agreement establishing the Inter-American Development Bank, Article 1, Section 1.

itself or its influence on the national plan. If it helps strengthen the integration process, the project is assigned an additional priority that has a decisive effect on the bank's action. The "integration component"—destined to become an increasingly important element among the eligibility criteria—is considered principally in connection with projects for the establishment of industrial plants or the expansion and diversification of agricultural production, but has a bearing also on other fields, such as transportation, communications, and power. By giving preferential consideration to projects having the "integration component," the IDB daily reaffirms in practice its long-held conviction that experience accumulated in the formulation of national development plans should bear fruit, at short term, in the preparation of regional plans, particularly through the coordination of specific areas of economic activity. Two experiences, one Latin American and the other European, support these statements. With respect to the first, it is abundantly clear that planning on a regional scale in Central America has lent greater precision to national planning. In the matter of coordination by sectors, suffice it to recall that the European Common Market had its origin in the European Coal and Steel Community, which acted as a centripetal force over against other fields of production.

Because direct contact with Latin America's financial problems has convinced the IDB that the objective of integration cannot be attained unless recourse is had to regional planning, the bank gave its full support to the resolution passed at the São Paulo meeting of the Inter-American Economic and Social Council of the OAS, enjoining all Alliance for Progress agencies and mechanisms to promote regional planning. In similar fashion, on the board of the Latin American Economic and Social Planning Institute, to which it gives financial assistance, IDB has advocated conducting research on the relationships existing between the regional integration process and planning at the national level.

IDB-financed national-scale projects that have met the additional priority requirement by virtue of their potentially favorable influence on the integration process have been several in number and varied in scope. Mention might be made, for example, of loans to industries that will be in a position to expand their exports to other Latin American countries and of the financing of several infrastructure projects designed to improve communications systems between neighboring countries.

In company with national projects whose repercussions will be felt beyond the boundaries of the country in which the works program is executed, loans in support of multinational programs are particularly worthy of note. To cite two examples: the $6 million credit line established for the Central American Bank for Economic Integration; and the loan for $3 million made available, through the same institution, to the national universities of the five Central American countries for financing an over-all program of basic sciences, in the interest of technological development within the framework of regional integration.

Based on the experience it has accumulated thus far in the matter of credit-policy orientation, the IDB may be expected to devote an increasing volume of its resources to financing national or multinational projects that directly accelerate the regional integration process.

Technical Assistance and Integration

To reach any goal, however modest, in the Latin American integration movement means reformulating an endless number of problems, finding solutions, outlining new conceptual molds and techniques, modifying habits of thought and consumption, etc. Although each of the Latin American countries has long cherished the hope of a definitive reunion in the political field and a joint endeavor in economic matters, such an ambition could never survive the lack of physical and spiritual communication that, until very recently, has kept those countries apart. Notwithstanding 150 years of independent political life, their mutual relationships continued to develop for the most part within a colonial system, in which the interests of the dependent territories, like the radii of a circle, bore no direct relationship with one another, but came to a central point in a far-distant metropolis.

In order to modify the channels through which the flow of individuals, goods, and services has been directed in the past—traditionally toward the outside of the region—a coherent series of measures of various types will be needed, based on a thorough knowledge of present reality and future possibilities. In the field of trade and investment, for example, reciprocal concessions between LAFTA members, the suppression of customs duties on most of the products exchanged between the signatories of the General Treaty for Central American Economic Integration, and the advantages offered the investor by the Regime of Integration Industries on the isthmus present advantageous conditions that can be put to good use. A series of studies and promotion efforts must be undertaken, however, to channel these already existing incentives in such a way that they provide a stronger stimulus to integration. This is a new and previously unexplored field, which calls for the type of imaginative technical assistance that the IDB has begun to lend and will intensify in future. At the ministerial-level meeting called by the Inter-American Economic and Social Council in Mexico City in October, 1962, the Inter-American Development Bank officially announced its decision to initiate a program for integration research and promotion, as an important part of its technical-assistance activities.

For the purpose of orienting the above program toward the more immediate needs and possibilities of integration, the bank called a meeting of representatives of the various institutions interested in such problems. One of the recommendations of the working group was that the IDB serve as liaison for the systematic exchange of information on work being done in this field by the different institutions. It is safe to assume, then, that future technical assistance by the IDB in behalf of the integration process will involve a working arrangement with other institutions, with whom human and financial resources will be mobilized in common.

The principal objective of the bank's technical-assistance program is to promote development projects that are of interest to two or more Latin American countries and contribute to facilitating the integration of their economies, through the collective exploitation of shared natural resources, the realization of possibilities for complementary trade dealings, or the creation of an adequate infrastructure in border areas. In this connection, the IDB has conducted a promotion campaign that has already begun to crystallize in concrete projects. As indicated in the report presented to the IDB Board of Governors during the April, 1961, meeting in Rio de Janeiro:

> The reality of geographical economic zones overlapping several countries has perforce required these nations to take coordinated action. The Inter-American Bank may well be an efficient device for promoting the economic and regional integration so urgently needed and thus benefiting vast population sectors through the exercise of multilateral efforts. These ideas suggest the possibility of an integrated development of the resources of the countries adjoining the vast river network of the Paraná and Paraguay rivers; the prospects of joint development of southern Peru and northern Chile, where farming and water-power resources are limited; the economic-social development of the Andean Indian communities, particularly in Bolivia and Peru; the possibility of planning a coordinated campaign to develop Chilean and Argentine Patagonia; and the combined development by the Amazon countries of that valley which can make such an important contribution to humanity. Programs of this sort would enable us to overcome the tragic coincidence of our border areas with the most extreme underdevelopment. Through the course of the years we have become accustomed, like neighbors on poor terms, to turn our backs on each other. We may be confident that the

future will transform isolated military cantons into focal points from which a progress without boundaries will issue.[2]

Among the multinational programs to which the IDB is directly contributing technical assistance, the integrated development of the Colombian and Venezuelan border zones merits special mention. The program will promote the development of these boundary areas by means of the improved utilization of both natural and human resources and through the creation or improvement of essential infrastructure projects. Technical assistance granted, free of charge, to the governments of Bolivia, Colombia, Ecuador, and Peru to enable a feasibility study of a highway running along the jungle's edge on the Eastern slopes of the Andes is another example of the multinational projects to whose investigation and financing the bank is willing to make a significant contribution.

One aspect that is perhaps not so well known, but is nonetheless important from the standpoint of what it can mean for the future, is the stimulus that the IDB has given the organization of Latin American consultant firms and the use it has made of the services of experts from the member countries. More than 50 per cent of the project proposals presented for the IDB's consideration have been prepared from start to finish by technicians from the region. In this way, IDB lending and technical-assistance activities, as well as the special courses organized for officials and technical personnel by its training division, are contributing to the formation of a fund of first-hand knowledge that relies on the close examination of the varied regional experience and thereby affords Latin American professionals a broader and more thorough insight into Latin American problems—all of which will facilitate the search for collective solutions.

Purchasing Policy and Export Financing

As pointed out earlier, when weighing what might be termed a given project's "integration component," the IDB gives preference to the financing of industries that are potential contributors to the export trade with other Latin American countries. It should be emphasized, further, that the bank also subjects project proposals to detailed scrutiny to determine the possibilities that can be generated thereby

[2] Address by Felipe Herrera, President of the Inter-American Bank, at the second plenary session, held on April 11, 1961, in Inter-American Development Bank, *Proceedings of the Second Meeting of the Board of Governors* (Rio de Janeiro: IDB, 1961), pp. 36–37.

for imports from other Latin American countries. The policy that has gradually been evolved in support of the acquisition of commodities produced in the region has already perceptibly increased the intra-Latin American trade flow. Eleven Latin American countries are shipping out goods designed for the execution of IDB-financed projects elsewhere in the area. This gradual process of replacing traditionally extraregional sources of supply will be accentuated in the future, not only as a result of the bank's continuing promotion work and the increasing volume of projects in progress, but because such a purchasing policy will forge strong links between regional exporters and importers and create consumption habits in favor of articles of Latin American manufacture.

Of all the programs instituted by IDB up to now, however, the one that unquestionably will have the greatest repercussions on the economic-integration process is the financing of intraregional exports of capital goods. Endowed with agility and flexibility, the program pursues the primary objective of encouraging the development of basic industry in Latin America through an increase in intraregional commerce. Its immediate practical goal is to enable the Latin American exporter to compete with suppliers from other areas in the matter of financing.

The amount of $30 million out of the bank's ordinary resources was initially earmarked for this program. Eligibility for IDB financing is tied in with the Latin American origin of the goods for export. In this connection, goods qualify as originating in a Latin American country when they are produced or manufactured in that country from raw materials or components that are national or *regional* in origin. Any item containing components imported from outside the area is also considered to be of local origin when the exporting country has added the final processing that imposes a new individuality on the merchandise, and provided further that the c.i.f. value of the part imported from outside the region is less than 50 per cent of the f.o.b. price of the finished article.

Given the important fact that financing will not be limited to the finishing of capital goods, but will be made extensive also to the components that figure in their manufacture, trade currents stimulated by the program will be much broader than those reflected in figures covering the interchange of capital goods.

The program grants medium-term financing, i.e., between 180 days and, ordinarily, 5 years. This flexibility, which will ensure efficient functioning as well as adaptability to marketing conditions, extends also to the maximum time limit on export loans. In effect, the regulations provide that "such [financing] periods may extend beyond 5 years in order to allow the member countries to adjust to the variations which may exist in international competition." [3]

The IDB may finance up to 70 per cent of the invoice value of the export. The importer will normally make a cash down-payment amounting to at least 20 per cent. For his part, the exporter must assume and sustain financial responsibility for at least 15 per cent of the importer's indebtedness.

Although the volume of inter-Latin American trade in capital goods is presently quite small, there is every indication that such commerce will increase notably in the next few years. For this reason, and in view of the limited funds initially set aside for the program, the IDB has endeavored to mobilize resources from both the importing and exporting countries, and looks forward to the employment of operational methods that will enable the procurement of additional resources on the international capital markets.

With the launching of the program to finance intraregional capital-good exports, IDB has taken a decisive step under its policy of stimulating the complementary functioning of industry and the expansion of trade among the countries in the region.

It is difficult to forecast, with any accuracy, the effect the program will have on the economic-integration process. The least that may be expected to happen, however, is that the Latin American countries will open new channels for their foreign trade and gradually modify their production patterns. By contributing to that result, the Inter-American Development Bank, a determined and active advocate of Latin American integration, is complying with the express assignment outlined in its charter, which provides that, among other functions, the institution shall "cooperate with the member countries to orient their development policies towards a better utilization of their resources in a manner consistent with the objectives of making their economies more complementary and of fostering the orderly growth of their foreign trade." [4]

[3] Article 8 of Regulations for the Financing of Exports of Capital Goods, in "Inter-American Development Bank," *Program for the Financing of Intraregional Exports of Capital Goods* (Washington, D.C.: IDB, 1964), p. 19.

[4] Article 1, Section 2 (IV) of the Agreement establishing the Inter-American Development Bank.

XIV

ERNANE GALVEAS

Financing Latin American Exports

Structural changes in the international capital markets beginning with the great depression practically did away with traditional forms of financing international trade, which had relied mainly on the use of systems involving bank acceptances and medium- and long-term credits for the importation of machinery and equipment. Since there was no tie-in between the merchandise and the credit for financing its purchase, importers automatically obtained a double benefit: Not only was the transaction financed in the capital market where credit was cheapest, but merchandise purchases were channeled to countries offering the lowest prices.

The subsequent system—of direct supplier credit—often tended to deform the external debt structure of the importing countries by committing an excessive proportion of their foreign borrowing in obligations at shorter terms than the nature of the investment warranted. At the same time, a direct link was forged between the purchase and its financing, in such way that the buying decision was shifted more in the direction of credit-term considerations than toward product price and quality.

The stage immediately following consisted of the institution of national systems for export financing. In various European countries—notably, France, Great Britain, and Germany—official institutions and mechanisms were created, with government support and sponsorship, to facilitate the extension of credits of this type. New official facilities for medium-term export financing were also established and speedily developed in Canada, Japan, and the United States. Of these, the Export-Import Bank of the United States provides a good example.

Such a solution is, of course, far from ideal—a fact that has been recognized by several authorities. Paul Rosenstein-Rodan, for example, points out that no perfect competition exists in international markets for capital goods.[1] Many producers lose out in the struggle, even when their sales offers are completely competitive in terms of price and delivery dates. In this connection, Rosenstein-Rodan suggests the establishment of an international institution to rediscount export documents carrying terms of up to four years and covering machinery and equipment consigned to underdeveloped countries. The resources needed by such an agency—some $100 million to $200 million—might be supplied by the International Bank for Reconstruction and Development (IBRD), the International Monetary Fund, and the United States Government, seconded by private Swiss and U.S. banks.

Other international experts maintain that the basic problem consists not of doing away with export credit (which has so efficiently promoted foreign trade and investment in countries in process of development), but of finding ways and means to establish a broader mechanism designed to eliminate undesirable bilateral effects in this field. One of these experts, Claudio Segré, considers that the negative aspects of the present system could be obviated through closer international cooperation and suggests two possible solutions: (1) the creation of a rediscount system, obviously intended for some somewhat distant date, to be managed by an international banking consortium or by a multinational agency in which all beneficiary countries have representation; or (2) the establishment of a finance agency designed to administer a broad system of direct credit grants to importers at "medium" terms of five, ten, and as much as fifteen years.[2]

Assuming that an international organization were created, the member countries would subscribe the institution's capital, but would effectively pay in only a portion of it. On the basis of the capital subscription, the agency might be in a position to float bond issues on the international capital markets and also call on the money markets for subsequent financing. To ensure the degree of liquidity needed by the institution, the export-credit guarantee would have to be utilized. Under Segré's first suggestion, the export-credit document, on its presentation for rediscount, would already carry the guarantee of the ex-

[1] P. N. Rosenstein-Rodan: "The Need for International Financing of Exports" (mimeographed; Washington, D.C., 1953).

[2] Claudio Segré, *El financiamiento a plazo medio de las exportaciones* (Mexico City: CEMLA, 1961).

porter's bank. In the second instance, the constitution of a joint guarantee covering the risks of the operation would be in order.

In Search of a Solution for Latin America

In recent years, export-financing problems have become a matter of concern for international institutions, as well as for Latin American technicians and governments. Finding a solution is of the utmost urgency, since present-day Latin America as a whole is confronted with the following series of difficulties, which form a veritable bottleneck in its economic-development process:

1. The region's economic development depends fundamentally on its industrial production capacity, on which the importation of capital goods, in turn, has a direct bearing.
2. The stagnation of the export trade has made it impossible to import machinery and equipment in sufficient volume to take care of Latin American investment needs. In addition, the process of substituting local production for consumer-goods imports has just about run its course, and it is logical to assume that further development gains will depend on whatever possibilities may exist for producing capital goods.
3. In the face of export-limiting trends, Latin America as a whole will have to look to intraregional sources for the production and supply of a substantial portion of its machinery and equipment requirements.
4. On an immediate and generalized basis, capital-goods production in the area calls for the establishment of installations, taking into consideration the economies of scale, which invariably exceed the absorption possibilities of the narrow domestic markets, considered individually.
5. Production of machinery and equipment in the Latin American countries has, furthermore, encountered difficulties in serving markets, both at home and abroad, because of the lack of financing of a magnitude that would enable competition (at least insofar as credit terms are concerned) with offers from the giant enterprises of Western Europe, the United States, Canada, and Japan.

The above considerations have long been taken into account in research and discussions on the need for accelerating the growth process in Latin America. ECLA, for example, has been advocating, since 1956, the creation of a payments and credit system in Latin America and has suggested, on several occasions, that an agency be established to finance inter-Latin American exports and thereby serve as a highly useful instrument in fostering trade in the region. Even prior to the establishment of the Inter-American Development Bank, it was felt that one of the specific functions of such an institution might be the financing of capital-goods exports.[3]

Indeed, when a meeting was eventually convened in January-April, 1959, to draw up the charter of the Inter-American Development Bank, this matter was raised immediately. Brazil proposed that all operations in which the prospective bank would be empowered to engage be enumerated in detail, and urged that specific reference be made to export financing. Considering that such an enumeration might be limitative in its effects, however, the meeting decided in favor of a broad and flexible wording submitted by the United States.

Suggestions and proposals of this type took on greater consistency at subsequent regional gatherings. In April of 1961, on the occasion of the second annual meeting of the IDB Board of Governors, in Rio de Janeiro, Argentina strongly advocated the adoption of a program for financing the exportation of manufactures and capital goods within the Latin American Free Trade Association. Supported by Brazil and Mexico, Argentina formally proposed that a special fund be created to rediscount documents presented by countries in the region and covering capital-goods exports.

In May, 1961, at the ninth session of ECLA, an express recommendation was made to the effect that international finance agencies study the problem of medium- and long-term credit for the placement of capital goods produced in Latin America. In August of the same year, on instituting the Alliance for Progress, the Punta del Este Charter indicated that Alliance resources could be used to encourage Latin America's expanding trade in industrial goods. Unfortunately, however, the vague terms in which this provision was couched rendered it quite ineffective.

Finally, in Buenos Aires, in April of 1962, during the third annual meeting of the IDB Board of Governors, Brazil—whose original intention had been to suggest that the bank's charter be modified in such a way as to enable the institution to finance exports—ended up by proposing that the bank management, on the basis of a broad interpretation of the initial constitutive agreement, draw up regulations for a special export-credit system that could be put in operation at an early date, Brazil's proposal elicited express recognition, on the part of the IDR Board of Governors, of the urgent need for the establishment in Latin America of a system to finance certain exports, with particular emphasis on capital goods. The bank's management was assigned the task of designing the most adequate mechanism to achieve that objec-

[3] ECLA, Second Meeting of the Central Bank Working Group (Santiago, 1958).

tive.[4] The meeting also passed an Argentine motion that a study be made of the feasibility of setting up a regional export-credit insurance system.

The Inter-American Development Bank referred the entire matter for study to a group of member-country technicians, who were assisted by an impressive array of U.S. and European specialists. The preliminary version of the group's report was discussed—and heartily approved—at the seventh operational meeting of the Center for Latin American Monetary Studies (CEMLA), convened in Mexico City in September of 1962. General recognition was once again given to the urgent need for establishing a regional system for financing Latin American exports, primarily for the purpose of contributing to: (1) economic development of the region; (2) progress toward economic integration, which, in itself, constitutes a development factor; (3) diversification of the economic structure of the Latin American nations; (4) mobilization of internal and external resources; and (5) improvement in the competitive position of Latin American exports over against those supplied by the highly industrialized countries.

In the interest of maximum efficacy, it was felt that a regional system of this type should be built upon a composite base, consisting of a domestic agency in each of the Latin American countries and a regional institution—the Inter-American Development Bank.

Domestic-level agencies would have the basic function of financing exporters (either directly or through the banking system) by discounting credit instruments deriving from the export of goods eligible for medium-term financing under regional-system standards. The domestic agency, in turn, would have the right of recourse to the regional institution in order to refinance a substantial portion of its export-loan portfolio.

The domestic agency, in each case, would be a public or semipublic institution—perhaps the central bank or a national foreign-trade bank fully backed by the state, in line with IDB requirements. Furthermore, to facilitate simple and adequate coordination of the operations of the regional system, relations between the central agency and each of the participating countries would be conducted solely through the designated domestic institution.

Finally, it would be up to the domestic agencies to exercise constant vigilance to assure strict compliance with the rules established by the regional system, as well as to assure the legitimate use of the medium-term export credits.

The most important functions of the regional agency would be: (1)

[4] Resolution AG 5/62, adopted at the Third Meeting of the Board of Governors of the Inter-American Development Bank, Buenos Aires, April, 1962.

to determine what types of goods are susceptible of financing and to establish the corresponding credit terms and exportation requirements; (2) to refinance a portion of domestic-agency credit grants to exporters, in line with regulations drawn up by the regional institution; (3) to promote the mobilization of international financial resources by utilizing outstanding balances on the credit instruments originating in the export transactions refinanced by the regional organization; and (4) to establish uniform terms for financing intraregional exports and to help standardize export credits in international trade in general.

In connection with the first function mentioned, the regional agency would draw up lists of the types of exports eligible for regional system refinancing. At the same time, it would determine how much the importer should pay down and would establish the characteristics of the credit instruments covering the portion of the transaction payable on time. The regional institution would be committed to refinancing the exportation of approved goods, in the proportion permitted by available resources.

From the very outset, it would be necessary to establish uniform credit terms on intraregional exports and effectively to support efforts aimed at the gradual standardization of this type of financing in international trade generally. The first-mentioned objective would be readily attained, since the regional agency would refinance only such exports as conformed to the system's general standards.

To strengthen the bargaining power of the regional system, the study group deemed it advisable to ensure that the regional agency carry the representation of all the Latin American countries in their dealings with other export-financing and credit-insurance systems operating in the international market.

In view of the low level of intrazonal trade in capital goods and other durable manufactures, it was anticipated that relatively modest financial resources—some $30 million—would suffice initially for launching the regional export-credit system.

At the first LAFTA central bank and trade-policy meeting, held in Bogotá in early April, 1963, further recognition was given the fact that the lack of a finance mechanism is frustrating inter-Latin American production and trade possibilities in various important merchandise lines. Exporters in the region cannot compete with producers in other areas, for the decision of the Latin American importer is basically influenced by the possibility of obtaining financing for the transaction. In the light of this circumstance, combined with the fact that medium-term credit in the region is in short supply, delegates to the

Bogotá meeting concurred in the need for a substantial mobilization of external resources.

To safeguard the interests of countries that, at present, are not in a position to export capital goods, it was considered that provision should be made for them to obtain financing for the exportation of other types of commodities, quite independent of the increasing inflow of funds for encouraging productive activities, in the terms of Article 32 of the Treaty of Montevideo.

By way of an additional guarantee of balanced benefits for each of the contracting parties, export credits might be geared to the total amount of benefits extended the individual countries by the Inter-American Development Bank, and the imports thus financed could figure as one of the reciprocity mechanisms envisioned in the Montevideo Treaty.

All the major considerations discussed at regional meetings in recent years, including the selection of the institution that will perform the regional-agency functions, were incorporated in the final document on the subject, which was approved by the fourth meeting of the IDB Board of Governors, convened in Caracas in April, 1963.[5] On that occasion, IDB authorities were enjoined to adopt an IDB-administered intraregional system for financing capital-goods exports. This was to be accomplished prior to September 30, 1963, and financed out of a limited amount of ordinary capital resources, plus any others that might come to hand, with the exception of those earmarked for the Fund for Special Operations.[6] The IDB program for financing the regional trade in capital goods started working shortly afterward.

Special Features of a Credit System for Latin American Exports

Given the wide range of economic conditions in the various Latin American countries and their disparate development levels, it will not be an easy matter to establish a system for financing regional exports completely satisfactory to all LAFTA members.

A case in point: The strict limitation of financing to capital goods met with strong initial opposition on the part of the relatively less

[5] Inter-American Development Bank, *Study on Export Financing in Latin America* (Washington, D.C.: IDB, 1962; Doc. DED 63/5-Rev).

[6] On September 30, 1963, IDB's Executive Board approved a set of Regulations for Financing Capital Goods Exports. See CEMLA, *Suplemento Mensual al Boletín Quincenal,* October, 1963, pp. 350–52.

developed countries, who argued that it was impossible for them to use the system and that its benefits would therefore accrue exclusively to nations that had made greater industrial progress. This objection, however, has little or no validity in view of the arguments outlined below:

1. It would not be feasible to establish a system for financing all of Latin America's export trade. No particular problem attaches to credit for the raw materials that make up the bulk of regional exports to the outside world, since such financing is being reasonably well attended to—generally, at terms of less than one year—by the local and foreign banking community.

2. An effort would be made to broaden the definition of capital goods to make it extensive to intermediate commodities and construction materials, thereby affording an opportunity to almost all the member countries to use the system.

3. Financing would be limited to intraregional exports and would therefore benefit both the capital-goods importing and exporting countries.

4. Apart from drawing on new resources, for the most part supplied by the capital markets, export financing would under no circumstances be detrimental to national investment programs. Credit grants would be computed as part of the exporting country's "quota"; the use of such funds would be scaled to the total allocation for that nation of IDB recourses intended to cover both investment financing and export credits.

Another widely discussed feature of the proposed system has to do with financial needs and sources of funds. An investigation of 1959 and 1960 exports by the seven most-developed countries in the region (Argentina, Brazil, Chile, Colombia, Mexico, Peru, and Venezuela) showed that the annual average of intraregional trade in capital goods and intermediate products amounted to a scant $45 million. On this basis, it was estimated and finally agreed that the system would initially require no more than $30 million, which might be expanded to some $100 million later on.

Although the basic resources were to be supplied out of ordinary IDB capital, the project also called for participation by the importing country (payment by the importer against sight drafts covering 10 per cent to 15 per cent of the total purchase price) and by the exporter or his bank (from 15 per cent to 20 per cent). In addition, capital markets might be tapped through the sale of IDB obligations; the resale of export documents initially financed by IDB; or the placement of participation certificates issued against the combined portfolio of such documents, as has been the practice of the Export-Import Bank.

Private U.S. and European banks were also regarded as an important potential source of funds. They could underwrite a part of the loan transactions (as is already being done with respect to specific investment projects), or they might be willing to acquire the original export documents.

The Latin American central banks could also contribute, by depositing a small percentage of their gold and foreign-exchange reserves with the regional agency, which might pay them a modest return. Finally, some thought might be given to the utilization of Alliance for Progress resources, in the manner outlined in Title 4 of the Punta del Este Charter.

Another highly important aspect represents the need to bring uniformity to the system's operating rules. The European countries offer an instructive example of the difficulties that may be encountered in this connection, and of the disadvantages of a trade war waged on the basis of terms of financing. Some progress has already been made with the establishment of the so-called Bern Union, and the European Economic Community is studying a mechanism for coordinating and unifying rules applicable to export credits as well as credit insurance and other guarantees.

On the occasion of the seventh operational meeting of CEMLA, mentioned earlier, the opinion was expressed that member countries should be left at complete liberty to grant whatever terms they feel will promote their export trade with the region. The majority, however, was in favor of having the regional system impose discipline on regional export financing and make eligibility for refinancing contingent on compliance with export payment terms that the system defines as normal. Many observers maintain further that exports financed out of the exporter's own resources should conform to the general standards of discipline, so that uniform financing terms can be made effective throughout the regional system, whatever the origin of the export credit resources.

As indicated earlier, the consensus regarding an appropriate agency to undertake the regional functions was in favor of the Inter-American Development Bank. However, within this area of general agreement three alternatives were proposed: (1) the creation of a special export-financing fund, whose operational features would be patterned after the Fund for Special Operations already in operation in IDB; (2) the establishment of a subsidiary corporation to be administered by IDB, much in the manner that the World Bank has a hand in the affairs of the International Finance Corporation; and (3) the complete integration of the new agency within the Inter-American Development Bank's structure and patrimony.

The first two proposals offered certain operational advantages, but they also presented difficulties. In the case of the subsidiary corporation, for example, it would be necessary to construct a new juridical entity, whereas the special fund would have occasioned a modification of the IDB charter. In the majority of countries, either of the two alternatives would require legislative approval; and, as a result, the creation of the system might be delayed for several years. There was obviously little likelihood that the United States Congress would appropriate resources for financing the sale of capital goods in competition with those turned out by U.S. industry. From a national standpoint, the adverse effect of such competition on the U.S. would obviously be quite negligible, since the volume of Latin American purchases in that country does not depend on the area's export pattern but on the magnitude of over-all U.S. expenditures in the region; but everybody in Latin America understood that certain industrial sectors in the United States would offer resistance to support of the project.

Moreover, legislators in many countries in the region would be bound to encounter solid opposition to the channeling of domestic resources to the creation of a system whose benefits would apparently accrue only to the more industrially advanced countries. Although this allegation was completely baseless, as was fully recognized during the discussions on export financing, there was still the danger that some countries—particularly those that figure among the relatively less developed—would simply not be interested.

In the eventuality outlined above, the new institution would be stillborn. The absence of the United States would rule out any possibility of immediate recourse to international capital markets, and the failure of the U.S. or any other country in the region to join the new agency would undermine hemispheric unity. For all these reasons, the integration of the system within the structure of the Inter-American Development Bank was deemed the wisest solution and was duly approved at the Caracas meeting of the IDB Board of Governors.

The solid prestige gained by IDB, not only on the regional level but also in international financial centers, will obviously facilitate the mobilization of external resources under favorable terms at some future date. In addition, the assumption of this new function by IDB afforded the system the dual advantage of minimum operating costs—a factor of the utmost importance to its competitive position—and greater assurance of adequate coordination and distribution of available resources.

System for Protection Against Risks

Owing to its influence on both the availability and the cost of credit, a system to guarantee against risks, such as credit insurance, should, in practice, form an integral part of the mechanism for term financing of exports. An adequate guaranty system would enable exporters to expand their operations without endangering their financial position by virtue of excessive risk assumption.

In a draft resolution presented to the third meeting of the IDB Board of Governors, Argentina pointed out that the export trade of the individual Latin American countries would not be likely, within a reasonable period, to attain the magnitude and commodity composition that would enable a satisfactory premium structure for the operation of strictly national guaranty systems. For that reason, it was suggested that a study be made of the appropriate bases on which to found a regional export-credit-insurance system.

In a paper prepared in 1962 for the seventh operational meeting of CEMLA, Claudio Segré discussed the indubitable utility of establishing a regional system for multilateral reinsurance that would parallel the refinancing system.[7] At the same time, he directed attention to the considerable difficulties inherent in such a system, particularly insofar as concerns the key point of spreading the risk.

The need to make credit insurance, as well as export lending, a multilateral affair has been recognized and thoroughly discussed in European government circles in recent years. In 1960, for example, Xenophon Zolotas of the Bank of Greece proposed that an international export-credit-insurance agency be established in connection with the transformation of OEEC into OECD. The proposed institution might provide up to 90 per cent coverage in insuring credits extended in connection with capital-goods exports to all underdeveloped countries. The agency would function in close cooperation with other OECD departments and with other international bodies that lend technical or financial assistance to underdeveloped areas. It will be observed that Zolotas' credit-insurance plan is an approximate facsimile of the proposal elaborated by Rosenstein-Rodan for export financing.

The European Economic Community has set up a group for coordinating credit insurance and other financing guarantees. Dealing with the subject of harmonizing domestic export-credit-insurance systems, the group came to the conclusion that the mechanisms in oper-

[7] Claudio Segré, "El financiamiento de las exportaciones de los países de América Latina: bosquejo de una solución," *Cooperación financiera en América Latina* (Mexico City: CEMLA, 1963), pp. 243–68.

ation in EEC member nations are so markedly different that their instant amalgamation would be quite impossible. The group therefore proposed the gradual unification of the existing systems and has reached agreement concerning certain relatively minor aspects. During a later stage, the feasibility of establishing a reinsurance system will be explored.

The very nature of the insurance business suggests an additional argument in favor of multilateral methods. Insurance against commercial risks is founded primarily on actuarial calculations, and an increase in the number of policies written reduces the probable risk per policy and, consequently, lowers the premium rate. Here, the basic principle consists of combining a broad spread of the risk with a high volume of operations.

The launching of an export-financing system in Latin America could be accompanied to good advantage by the establishment of the bases for a regional credit-insurance agency, which might take the form of a Latin American reinsurance institute or consortium.

Domestic insurance institutions would have direct participation in an organization of this type, whose initial capital would comprise contributions from each of the participants, on whatever pro rata basis might be deemed advisable. Actually, the original cash contributions to the agency's capital would not have to be high. Members might be assigned a small paid-in quota plus another, larger amount, subject to payment only as and when necessary. Over time, normal operations should produce sufficient insurance-premium collections to provide the necessary resources for risk coverage.

As a first step, the domestic insurance institutions would have to be organized. Substantial government participation would appear to be highly advisable, not only from the standpoint of political and catastrophe risks, but also in connection with a given portion of risks classifiable as commercial.

It is entirely possible that private firms will undertake to insure the commercial risks involved. For example, the strictly commercial risk that the foreign importer may turn out to be insolvent is no different, in essence, from the credit risk implied when financing sales on the domestic market. Both instances call for strict observance of the same technical principles that govern the acceptance of normal credit transactions, i.e., client selection, complete information regarding the purchaser, ceilings on individual credit lines, etc.

Political risks surrounding export credit ordinarily stem from restrictive measures adopted by the government of the importing country, thus effectively blocking the corresponding foreign-exchange transfer. As classified by the Export-Import Bank, measures of this nature derive from economic-policy considerations, or others. Catastrophe risks have to do with natural phenomena such as floods, earthquakes, etc. Segré accurately observes that political and catastrophe risks are characterized by an element of great uncertainty; that is, their onset is sudden and unexpected, and the law of averages does not apply. Their economic effects on the exporter are serious in the extreme, and they cannot be measured in terms of financial resources on the insurance market. Given these circumstances, insurance against political and catastrophe risks obviously lies beyond the scope of the private insurance system.

By all indications, the organization of a national credit-insurance system should not be founded on a plurality of institutions operating in this specialized field. Ideally, all transactions would be concentrated in a single insurance enterprise.

Experience shows that only the state can assume the function of guaranteeing credits granted by an exporter to a foreign customer. In a majority of cases, collection claims do not involve a definitive loss but simply delayed payment. Owing to the state's ability to meet sporadic liquidity requirements without any very great difficulty, the government's role as an insurer does not imply a financial burden as such. Hence, in any country desiring to establish an export-financing system, credit grants to foreign importers should be guaranteed by the state.[8]

Prevailing conditions in Latin America according to several sources underscore the necessity of establishing two specialized institutions on the national level: one to offer facilities for the rediscount or direct purchase of export-credit documents, and the other to afford an insurance guarantee for such lending operations. Alternatively, in some respects, it would appear to be advisable to concentrate the credit and insurance functions within a single agency, on whose board of directors the central bank would be represented. Advocates of such a system urge that the export-credit-insurance department function on actuarial bases—except for political and catastrophe risks, where handling of that type is impracticable.

A national export-credit-insurance system may have a varied institutional base, ranging all the way from private companies to completely official agencies, but necessarily involving direct or indirect participation by the state. Systems of this type have already been organized in some countries in Latin America, and their present structure may enable them to function satisfactorily. In the nations in which such

[8] Raymond F. Mikesell, "Algunos problemas y posibles formas de abordar la solución del problema de pagos dentro de la ALALC," *Cooperación financiera en América Latina* (Mexico City: CEMLA, 1963), pp. 18–45.

mechanisms have yet to be established, a mixed solution would appear to be advisable, using existing private insurance firms as the base in each case.

One possibility would be the constitution of an export-credit-insurance consortium formed by the state, the national reinsurance institution (where such an agency exists), and private insurance firms authorized to operate in the basic areas of risk.

A consortium of this type of obviously to be recommended, in view of the limited size of the insurance market in Latin America and the region's relative inexperience in this field, plus the fact that certain individual transactions are of greater magnitude than any single organization, particularly a private one, could undertake to insure. By spreading the insurance function among a number of institutions, the consortium does not rule out, but rather reinforces, the advantages of unified management. Through its administrative organization, the consortium could concentrate all available statistics and other types of information on dealings with firms to whom insured credits are extended. Moreover, the consortium could readily maintain contact with sister institutions abroad, and with foreign banks and insurance companies, and thus obtain essential background knowledge covering prospective credit-insurance transactions.

Under a system of this type, political and catastrophe risks would be left exclusively to the state; and the consortium would assume commercial risks up to a cautious limit, taking into account the true financial capacity of the private insurance firms.[9]

The stipulation of a given limit for consortium operations was designed to prevent private companies from subscribing to a potentially excessive financial responsibility, particularly during the initial stages of operation of the system. During that period, before the consortium is properly capitalized, any pronounced deviation in the claim incidence would be likely to produce a violent contraction in the insurance market, apart from the dangers to which the companies would be exposed. On the other hand, since the imposition of inflexible limits on financial responsibility might discourage the more sizable export transactions, the portion of insurance coverage that is felt to exceed the bounds of prudence, from the domestic consortium's standpoint, might be turned over to the state or devolved on the regional consortium referred to earlier.

[9] In Brazil, where a system of this type was established, the limit has been set at U.S. $300,000, distributed as follows: Brazilian Treasury, $120,000; Brazilian Rediscount Institute (IRB), $60,000; and private insurance companies, $120,000. Coverage in excess of $300,000 may be absorbed by the Treasury.

XV

BARRY N. SIEGEL

Payments Systems for the Latin American Free Trade Association

My task is to survey and evaluate the various plans that have been proposed to meet the payments problems likely to result from the liberalization of Latin American trade. The Montevideo Treaty did not provide solutions to these problems, principally because of the opposition of the IMF and the United States Government to proposals that the Economic Commission for Latin America and others have sponsored for the establishment of a clearing and credit mechanism. Nevertheless, ECLA and other Latin American organizations and individuals continue to press for some scheme to complement the plans for free trade among the members of the Latin American Free Trade Association.

Elements of the Problem

LAFTA was conceived as a program to aid Latin America's economic development by removing barriers created by regional conditions. ECLA is convinced that a broad program of import substitution must be undertaken if Latin America is to grow at a satisfactory rate in the future. Furthermore, ECLA sees the need for import substitution as stemming from (1) the requirements for capital goods and other finished goods essential to economic development, and (2) a pessimistic outlook for foreign-exchange earnings from sales, outside the area, of traditional Latin American goods. Hence, ECLA reasons that, if Latin America is to achieve desired income levels by, for example, 1975, the region must undertake to supply itself with the goods essential to development.

Latin America has a decided disadvantage in manufacturing compared to low-cost producers in the United States and Europe. Therefore, in order to compete successfully in regional markets, Latin American producers must reduce costs and/or cause their governments to discriminate against outsiders. Since low costs presuppose large-scale production, and since large-scale production calls for extensive markets, a free-trade area for the whole of Latin America, protected from outside competition, is viewed as a necessary instrument to achieve import substitution.

Import substitution could cost Latin American countries dearly, particularly in the short run. The hope is that intra-Latin American trade will grow rapidly enough to allow the development of economies of scale that will reduce or eliminate the added costs arising from the purchase of Latin American goods. This hope is a crucial element in the position adopted by ECLA and other LAFTA proponents. It represents an acceptance of what is, in essence, the infant-industry argument applied to a region and, as such, provides the fundamental theoretical rebuttal to criticisms of ECLA plans. Indeed, the recent debates between ECLA, on the one hand, and United States officials and the International Monetary Fund, on the other, are very reminiscent of the classic controversies that arose in the nineteenth century between protection-minded young republics, such as the United States, and free-trade-oriented industrialized countries, such as Great Britain.

In any event, the Montevideo Treaty is now a fact. Those who advocate trade liberalization fear that the absence of a payments and credit mechanism will threaten the success of the treaty. This fear is based on the following reasoning:

1. Liberalization of trade will create balance-of-payments problems for countries within LAFTA. Since it is unrealistic, particularly at the outset, to expect imports of given countries to match their exports to other countries, a situation may arise in which some countries find themselves saddled with a chronic deficit, representing an indebtedness to other LAFTA countries.

2. Under the provisions of the Montevideo Treaty, such a situation is to be met by application of the principle of reciprocity. Under this principle, countries finding themselves with the area surplus must undertake negotiations with a view to speeding the elimination of barriers against imports from LAFTA members in a deficit position.

Conversely, countries with chronic deficits have the right to retard their barrier-dismantling process.

3. Negotiations are time-consuming. Furthermore, once they are concluded, still more time may pass before the effects of additional liberalization are felt. Therefore, deficit countries will be obliged to pay for their imports by means other than additional exports. If such other means are not available, they may find it necessary to take advantage of escape clauses in the treaty, which permit them temporarily to reinstitute import restrictions against LAFTA partners. A revival of these restrictions would, of course, hamper the treaty's effectiveness.

4. Such consequences would not ensue if deficit countries could use some means other than exports to finance their imports. Convertible currencies or gold could be employed, but these exchange media are in very short supply. For that reason, deficit countries would generally be unwilling to devote gold or foreign-exchange resources to paying for imports from the region—particularly since they would already be making sacrifices by accepting high-cost imports from their LAFTA associates instead of bringing in similar, low-cost goods from outside the area.

Creditor nations could, of course, accept payment either in the local currencies of debtors or in claims against them. If such currencies and claims could be used by the creditor to effect payments elsewhere, the problem would be solved. However, since the weak currencies of a number of Latin American countries cannot be so used, this route is also closed.

The only remaining source of financing to cover deficits on the international account is external assistance; and this assistance is contingent upon the willingness and ability of the IMF, the United States, and other external sources to provide the wherewithal. In the absence of aid of this type, many observers believe that some system of payments and credits must be created within LAFTA, or the whole treaty will be threatened.

The first task of a payments scheme, then, is the creation of an acceptable medium of exchange. Since a LAFTA plan could hardly be expected to create dollars, sterling, or gold out of thin air, any extra liquidity afforded by the system must be provided either by external borrowings or by devices to economize convertible currencies. There is the further possibility, of course, that the system could set up its own medium of exchange, limited to use within the region.

Having settled on a medium of exchange, the next step might be to install a clearing mechanism, which, after the fashion of similar expedients used by banking systems of individual countries, would increase the efficiency of settlements and hence lower their cost.

Finally, a third step might be the provision of credits to countries finding themselves in a debtor position. These credits may be: (1) negotiated or automatic; (2) provided *net* by the system or offset by countries having regional surplus positions; (3) carried in dollars or in some special monetary unit that is either limited to use within the system or convertible into dollars; (4) based upon *over-all* balance-of-payment positions or limited to intraregional positions; and (5) restricted to certain classes of transactions or made extensive to any and all.

Depending on its features, a particular payments and credit scheme can affect both the direction and level of trade. In judging a system, one must, therefore, examine both its proximate and ultimate goals. A smoothly functioning monetary system is one thing; it becomes quite another, however, if its collateral goals involve a change in the direction as well as the level of commerce.

Proposals by ECLA

An ECLA document prepared in 1949 by a panel of IMF experts considered and rejected the possibility of a payments system for Latin America.[1] The existence of a maze of bilateral accounts, exchange controls, and multiple exchange rates discouraged any rational plan. However, as the movement toward a free-trade area gathered momentum, and as the varied controls and bilateral agreements were gradually sloughed off, sentiment grew stronger in favor of some sort of payments system to complement trade liberalization. In a series of documents issued in late 1959 and early 1960, ECLA made and defended concrete proposals aimed at solving LAFTA payments problems.[2] As far as I can gather, ECLA's position that such problems are

[1] See ECLA, *Multilateral Compensation and International Payments* (mimeographed; Santiago, 1949; E/CN. 12/87).

[2] The documents are: "Payments and Credits in the Free Trade Area Projected by Latin American Countries: Possible Systems" (October 30, 1959); "Further Considerations on the System of Swing Credits in the Free Trade Area" (December 14, 1959); and "The Reciprocal Credits Systems for the Free Trade Area" (January, 1960). All of these documents are reprinted in *Papers on Financial Problems Prepared by the Secretariat of the Economic Commission for Latin America Free Trade Association* (Santiago: ECLA, 1961; E/CN. 12/569). Actually, discussions on payments problems date back to a 1956 meeting of the ECLA Trade Committee in Santiago. This gathering was followed by meetings of the working groups of central banks in Montevideo in 1957, and in Rio de Janeiro in 1958. The Rio meeting produced a draft protocol, which was submitted

susceptible of solution remains essentially the same today.[3]

ECLA proposed an international agency, endowed with a capital fund, whose threefold purpose would be: (1) to operate a clearing mechanism for payments between various LAFTA members; (2) to provide for the "multilateralization" within the area of bilateral payments between members; and (3) to provide a credit system to ease intra-LAFTA trade disequilibriums.

Each central bank would maintain with the agency an account denominated in U.S. dollars. At regular intervals—every sixty or ninety days—balances outstanding between banks would be determined and settled in convertible currencies and/or in credit according to some previously arranged formula. Rendering payments multilateral becomes a problem only when settlements are not effected in convertible currencies. The danger is that bilateral settlements may be made in currencies that will confine a surplus country's future imports to the goods and services of its debtors or to the few countries that may be willing to accept the currencies in question.

An ideal plan would be to multilateralize all bilateral settlements. A debt to a bilateral trading partner would be converted into a debt to the agency, while the creditor would receive agency credits, which could be devoted to the purchase of goods from any country within the area. ECLA, however, called for a more limited arrangement, whereby amounts in excess of predetermined swing credits or fixed percentages of bilateral balances (e.g., 20 per cent) would be transferred to the agency for multilateralization. In any event, this phase of the plan is somewhat academic, since bilateralism is in Latin America decidedly on the wane.

Another function of the system would be to provide a channel for credit grants. ECLA favors a mechanism that will provide *automatic credits* within pre-established margins. Deficit countries would automatically receive credits up to the limit of these margins, after which they would be required to pay in convertible currencies. Creditors would be obliged to grant credit until fixed limits are reached; therefore, they would be entitled to receive payment in convertible currencies. The agency would need a capital fund out of which to pay creditors whose margins have been fully utilized at a time when their debtors have not exhausted their own margins.

ECLA outlined two possible credit mechanisms. The first is a so-called a priori system, participated in by commercial banks especially

---

to the Trade Committee in Panama in May, 1959. No action was taken at the last-mentioned meeting.

[3] See *Realizaciones y perspectivas en el proceso del mercado regional* (Mar del Plata: ECLA, 1963; E/CN. 12/688), chap. iv.

designated for that purpose by each country's central banks. Internal credit would be supplied by banks in surplus countries during the duration of the accounting period, after which settlements would be made and net remaining balances with the agency determined. A portion of these balances would then be retained as automatic credits granted borrowers by surplus countries within previously fixed margins. In addition to furnishing credit, this plan would presumably reduce the need for convertible currencies as a medium of exchange for agency transactions.

With the second system, termed "a posteriori," transactions during the accounting period would be on a dollar or dollar-instrument basis, as is currently the case in most of Latin American trade. At the end of the accounting period, deficit countries would receive dollars to the level of their credit margins, and surplus countries would grant automatic credit in dollars, also within given margins.

The two systems would operate in identical fashion in the three respects: (1) automatic debits and credits would be established with the agency; (2) bilateral credits and debits would be eliminated; and (3) surplus countries would have an incentive to increase imports in order to reduce their credit grants. Under either system, the principal burden of liberalization would be thrown upon creditors. The a priori mechanism may be regarded as the more comprehensive of the two, in the sense that it would save on dollars; however, the a posteriori system has greater appeal for those convertible-currency countries desirous of continuing the use of dollar instruments in their commercial dealings.

Criticism of ECLA Proposals

ECLA's proposals have come under persistent criticism on the part of the IMF and the U.S. Government. The paragraphs following provide a composite of these objections with my own (not necessarily original) comments added.[4] First of all, there is concern lest ECLA's plans, if realized, would effectively deter the world-wide march toward

[4] IMF objections have been expressed on numerous occasions: at the ECLA Trade Committee meeting at Panama City in 1959; at the second meeting of the Intergovernmental Conference for the Establishment of a Latin American Free Trade Area, in February, 1960; and, more recently, at the seventh operational meeting of CEMLA, September, 1962. The U.S. position on these occasions has closely paralleled that of the IMF. For a review of some of the objections, and the answers they elicited, see the ECLA documents quoted in this paper, as well as Miguel S. Wionczek, "The Montevideo Treaty and Latin American Integration," *Quarterly Review* of the Banca Nazionale del Lavoro, June, 1961, and Gerardo M. Bueno, "La zona de libre comercio y el problema de pagos," *Comercio Exterior*, February, 1960.

convertibility. It is difficult to refute the claim that the mechanism suggested would limit the convertibility of the receipts of surplus countries within the area. Only by purchasing goods and services from within the area could such countries bring down their credit balances with the payments agency. For the few countries that still have bilateral ties, this would represent an advance. For others, however, whose currencies are convertible *de facto*, the system would be a backward step—although, viewed realistically, the weakness of some Latin American currencies would make the step backward not a very long one.

A similar objection has been raised to the proposal that credits be granted or received according to each country's regional surplus or deficit, without reference to its over-all position. Countries with regional surpluses might have larger deficits outside the area; conversely, countries having deficits within the region might have larger surpluses with outside countries. From a moralistic approach, one might object to the seeming inequity of such a situation. As ECLA points out, however, the surplus countries might have acquired that status as a result of liberalization measures taken by their trading partners within the area. Difficult, indeed, to strike a moral balance!

Be that as it may, the question of over-all positions has some serious economic implications. Countries with area surpluses and over-all deficits would be encouraged to reduce imports from abroad and increase purchases of regional goods. Hence, rather than creating *additional* trade only, the system might have the very different effect of diverting trade from abroad. Although the diversion might help solve the payments problems of the area creditor, the more costly LAFTA substitutes would certainly lower the country's general welfare.

In a similar vein, it might be argued that area debtors would have an incentive to accept credit and goods from the area, while beefing up their reserves or increasing outside imports by selling to other international markets. Moreover, the deficit countries would channel additional sales to area creditors in the measure that the creditors, under the principle of reciprocity, lowered their barriers to the deficit countries. Hence, the welfare impact of the system might be geared to a nation's debit or credit position vis-à-vis the others in the regional group: The deeper a nation goes into debt to its area trading partners, the higher the welfare returns it would be likely to reap.

It is likewise conceivable that a goal of intraregional balance might seriously impair the over-all balance-of-payments position of the area. The region's enhanced export trade might contain significant components purchased from outside the region. The net proceeds from such trade may be taken up in the margins set on the credits that surplus countries are obliged to extend to the region. Furthermore, because of the inability of countries within the area to supply crucial imports, the surplus countries may not be able to reduce their outside acquisitions for a considerable period. In both these cases, the over-all international payments position of the countries having a regional surplus would be worsened.

Indeed, countries with area deficits may also find that their over-all positions have deteriorated. Enhanced intraregional imports might induce stepped-up extraregional acquisitions—an especially serious threat if the added regional imports are capital goods and manufactured consumer goods whose production necessitates complementary imports available only outside the region. Moreover, there is nothing to prevent the diversion of the credit advanced by the surplus countries to financing additional outside imports, particularly if the a posteriori system is adopted; for, in that case, the loan funds would be furnished the deficit country in dollar form. If these dollar borrowings are expended on additional outside imports, the deficit country might be hard put to provide credit to other area countries when, in due course, the respective regional deficit and surplus positions are reversed as a consequence of the reciprocal tariff reductions.

If increased intraregional trade does, in fact, add significantly to the body of complementary imports from outside the area, as described above, LAFTA countries may face a very serious situation. Under these circumstances, liberalization will tend to drain the area of convertible currencies, unless LAFTA exports to other markets expand sufficiently to offset the outflow. The dearth of complementary industries within the area make such a contingency a very real one. Reactions to a situation of this sort are likely to include a weakened incentive for carrying out further intraregional trade liberalization and the erection of more barriers to trade with countries outside the area, in the form of higher duties, direct import restrictions, or exchange controls.

I hasten to say that the above argument applies to the liberalization program, as such, and should be made extensive to the particular payments and credit system adopted only insofar as the latter enhances liberalization. There is a strong implication, however, that unless accompanied by greater restrictions on imports from extraregional sources, a credit mechanism within the area would encourage increased dependence on outside credits, which would be needed to counteract the additional drain on LAFTA holdings of convertible currencies.

The need for economic complementarity, then, may turn out to be the Achilles' heel of import substitution. Whether this will occur in practice depends on the speed with which LAFTA countries industrialize and provide themselves with the necessary complementary goods. Domestic investment, technological change, education, and similar programs will all have a hand in the comparative success of this endeavor. It should not be forgotten, however, that the initial costs of liberalization will make the framework for regional complementary functioning more difficult to finance.

Another pitfall inherent in the ECLA plan was that it made no provision for the problem of the chronic debtor. Because of domestic monetary problems, or because of structural factors, certain countries may be unable to expand exports to their LAFTA creditors. Even with the best of intentions toward their free-trade-zone partners, such countries may not be able to control inflation or to produce reasonably priced goods of the type desired by the surplus countries. This problem defies solution, at least within the framework of the ECLA proposal. The principle of reciprocity can do only so much. It is entirely feasible that area creditors could remove all restrictions against their trading partners and still be in a surplus position.

This discussion merely stresses the important fact that LAFTA cannot aspire to complete regional autarky, a point which the defenders of the reciprocity principle often overlook. Once liberalization is achieved, LAFTA intraregional trade will undoubtedly be much expanded; however, LAFTA countries will still have to trade with the rest of the world. The ECLA plan for automatic credits is designed to provide incentives for speeding reciprocal liberalization. If chronic intraregional imbalances impair the effectiveness of the program, external sources may have to be called on to supplement regional loan transactions. Once liberalization is completed, however, automatic credits will no longer have any purpose. Chronic imbalance within the area can then be corrected through surplus earned outside the region. (ECLA somewhat sanguinely trusts that, by that time, LAFTA countries will be strong enough to earn such surpluses.)

One major criticism voiced to date is that both the principle of reciprocity and the regional-credit scheme designed to complement it imply considerable "distortion" of trade. If "distortion" can be read "trade diversion," then there is no question as to the truth of the charge. Creditor countries would have a definite incentive to reduce imports from abroad. Debtor countries might be prompted to divert exports away from extraregional markets to their LAFTA creditors. The limited selection offered creditors by debtors may force the former to accept commodities they do not want and, if their external balance is negative, to reduce imports of non-LAFTA goods that they do need.

In response to this charge, ECLA maintained that: (1) there is no "natural" trade pattern; (2) the existing pattern of trade works against the region's industrialization ambitions; (3) the present pattern is the result of historical forces that have biased Latin American trade in favor of exports of primary products and imports of manufactures;[5] and (4) to effect a change in this pattern is precisely the aim of the Montevideo Treaty. This is, I believe, a faithful outline of ECLA's basic position. Such a theoretical foundation has been persistently rejected by both the IMF and the United States Government. The latter, in particular, is opposed to any regional plan that serves to divert, rather than to create, trade. By the same token, the United States is also averse to payments regimes that encourage trade diversion by a system of bilateral or other restrictive settlement arrangements. Both of ECLA's proposed payments mechanisms fall in this category.[6]

While the foregoing discussion outlines what I deem to be the principal objections to ECLA's proposals, two additional critical allegations might be mentioned: (1) The credit system encourages inflation, since it allows debtors the luxury of raising internal prices without suffering the customary penalty of convertible-currency losses. Creditors, on the other hand, will find their export earnings locked up in area credits, and, since it will take time for effects of their liberalization efforts to make themselves felt, these countries, too, will be faced with an inflation problem. (2) In addition to encouraging and "exporting" inflation, the ECLA system will give rise to further controls, particularly if certain countries become persistent creditors or debtors. In such a case, central banks and governments will tend to keep a close watch over the system and resort to discriminatory techniques in an attempt to correct the situation.

There is some question in my mind as to just how serious these two criticisms are. LAFTA members conduct only about 10 per cent of their trade with zone partners. Even with a significant expansion in the future, the amount of automatic credit available within any prudently managed system would hardly be of a magnitude to stimulate inflation to any very great extent.

While, by virtue of its small size, zonal trade may not constitute a

[5] See Robert Triffin, "Una cámara de compensación y unión de pagos latinoamericana," in *Cooperación financiera en América Latina* (Mexico City: CEMLA, 1963), pp. 95–117. This paper was presented at the seventh operational meeting of CEMLA in 1962.

[6] The U.S. position is spelled out in a study by the National Planning Association, "United States and Latin American Policies Affecting Their Economic Relations," in *United States–Latin American Relations*, U.S. Senate Committee on Foreign Relations (August 31, 1960), especially pp. 466–70.

serious inflationary threat, it could nonetheless lead to a desire for reinstating intraregional controls. The Montevideo Treaty already contains escape clauses for countries having over-all balance-of-payments difficulties (Articles 23–26). While restrictions applied under these articles are not intended to be explicitly discriminatory, in actual application they may single out specific member countries. The only—and not too reassuring—safeguard against a revival of intraregional restrictions is the good will and determination of LAFTA's members.

Robert Triffin's Proposals

Robert Triffin has proposed a payments system, which resembles ECLA's plan in some respects, but is more limited in scope and more cautiously conceived.[7] Triffin envisages a gradual evolution, starting with a clearing house for Latin American central banks. In the very circumspect initial stage of operations, clearings of net deficits and surpluses would be limited to total and immediate payment in convertible currencies. Although such an arrangement might, in itself, yield limited advantages—lower settlement costs and stabilization of exchange arrangements[8]—Triffin believes that its successful operation could lead to the gradual granting of reciprocal credits and so reduce the need for convertible currency reserves.

Should a step be taken in the direction of multilateral loans, Triffin would relate them to the members' *over-all* reserves or reserve requirements and would limit them to definite credit lines pre-established by the participating countries. Credits would be expressed in terms of an international unit of account in order to avoid exchange risks. To minimize possible defaults, all member banks would agree to channel payments to a defaulting member through the clearing house until such time as the obligation was covered in full. The liabilities of the clearing house would be jointly guaranteed by all members.

Triffin, cafeteria-style, offers an array of credit possibilities to suit almost any taste. For the timorous, he would limit the system to reciprocal extensions of credit between monthly clearing dates, at which time full settlements in convertible currencies would be made. Next, at the request of debtors, small, short-term automatic credits might be granted, principally to allow time for the negotiation of longer-term discretionary credits. Finally, Triffin suggests the possibility of longer-

[7] Triffin, *op. cit.*

[8] Triffin does not explain how such advantages would arise in practice. Existing arrangements, even if expanded, might be more satisfactory than any provided by a clearing house.

term negotiated credits, extended to support debtor-country stabilization measures. The IMF could make these loans directly to member countries; however, requests for IMF assistance could be subjected to advance review by the clearing house and perhaps receive its endorsement. Triffin would leave for later consideration the granting of such credits by the clearing house itself.

Triffin's plan differs from that of the ECLA in two important respects: First, he advocates only *moderate* automatic credits. Second, he wants to relate those credits to the borrower's *over-all* balance-of-payments position. Raúl Prebisch, in an address delivered during CEMLA's seventh operational meeting, enthusiastically discovered "an extraordinary similarity between the animal envisaged by Professor Triffin and that envisaged by ECLA, except for one attribute which is very important to some animals, namely the length and size of the tail." Prebisch was, of course, referring to the volume and length of credits. Although Prebisch was not particularly insistent on the question of automatic functioning, he favored credits that are large-scale and long-term—characteristics that are requisite of such loans if they are going to be related to over-all deficit positions of member countries.

I believe Prebisch was a bit extreme in his appraisal of the degree of similarity between the plan outlined by Triffin and ECLA's proposals. Rather than seeking to encourage reciprocity, Triffin's plan for moderate automatic credits between monthly clearing dates, or for slightly longer periods, was designed principally to conserve LAFTA's store of convertible currencies. Moreover, if regional-surplus countries find little justification for extending credit to regional debtors, they almost certainly would be averse to granting credit to countries having over-all deficits, particularly when such deficits are accompanied by regional surpluses. Indeed, the whole idea of reciprocal long-term credits (i.e., in excess of one to three months) disintegrates when the loan transactions are governed by over-all positions, since it is quite possible for all members simultaneously to have deficits. Such a system would provide incentives for all countries to incur deficits, at least to the limit of their credit margins.

In consequence, I can only conclude that Prebisch's apparent enthusiasm for Triffin's plan was based upon the hope that, after having been put into operation, it could be expanded into something more akin to ECLA-sponsored proposals. This would be at cross purposes to Triffin's intentions, however, since he clearly sought to avoid the use of extensive automatic credits.[9]

[9] Triffin, *op. cit.*, pp. 105–6.

Raymond Mikesell's Proposals

An alternative solution to the payments problem has been proposed by Raymond F. Mikesell, in his capacity as consultant to the Organization of American States.[10] Mikesell's primary concern was the provision of additional liquidity to finance the extra expansion resulting from liberalization. Since, at present, most Latin American trade is financed by instruments drawn on New York or London banks, the additional credits might add considerably to the cost of such financing, if for no other reason than the fact that larger credit lines might be required. On the other hand, LAFTA countries are not equipped with a good system of bank-correspondent relationships, so in addition to the need for a more ample supply of convertible currencies for lending purposes, there is also the problem of providing a mechanism for their use.

Mikesell's proposal sought the dual goal of creating correspondent relationships and providing liquidity and credit. He suggested that a system of accounts quoted in convertible nonresident dollars (or a LAFTA monetary unit) be established in banks engaged in LAFTA trade. Not intended for use by the general public, these accounts would facilitate transactions between financial institutions. The deposits would accumulate from dollar collections made by banks on behalf of correspondents in other LAFTA countries, from interbank loans, or from payments on maturing drafts under letters of credit. Mikesell insisted on 100 per cent backing for such accounts, in the form of convertible deposits in U.S. banks, in a LAFTA credit agency, or in a designated central bank.

Although such a system would certainly improve trade relationships, and perhaps reduce some of the costs of financing, there is still the need to provide extra liquidity. This can be accomplished solely by recourse to external sources. For example, letters of credit issued by Latin American banks could be confirmed or guaranteed by a LAFTA credit agency and then sold in local or foreign money markets. Mikesell also suggested that the agency might make direct loans to LAFTA members for the purpose of financing regional trade, provided that such transactions would not be on an automatic basis and would be related to members' over-all balance-of-payments positions. Agency loans would supplement those available from IMF and might even be financed, to some extent, by the latter institution.

[10] Mikesell's paper, "Algunos problemas y posibles formas de abordar la solución del problema de pagos dentro de la ALALC," was presented at CEMLA's seventh meeting and published also in *Cooperación financiera en América Latina*, pp. 118–45.

Mikesell's plan has certain attractive features, especially with respect to the emphasis on strengthening or creating commercial and banking ties among Latin American countries. In addition, more extensive use of guaranteed trade instruments would reduce the need for convertible currencies within the area. Because of its convertible-currency base, the system would also guard against discrimination between LAFTA and non-LAFTA trade and, for this reason, would find favorable reception on the part of the United States and the IMF. ECLA, however, would object to the plan, primarily on the grounds that it is devoid of mechanisms for implementing or securing reciprocity. This omission was undoubtedly deliberate on Mikesell's part, judging from his known opposition to plans that attempt to enforce regional balance.[11]

Conclusions

The payments question continues in deadlock. The roots of the controversy go much deeper than the relative degree of technical superiority of one plan or another. ECLA personnel, in company with other Latin American experts, have adopted an essentially mercantilist point of view, while the thinking of both the IMF and the United States is colored by ideals of free trade and world-wide convertibility. The mercantilist stresses favorable payments positions; the free trader looks forward to international specialization and the gains from trade. The mercantilist concentrates on foreign exchange as the principal scarce resource to be economized. Money, to the free trader, is simply a lubricant that, through specialization and commercial interchange, contributes to savings in scarce real resources. The modern mercantilist relies on the teachings of Alexander Hamilton and Friedrich List; the free trader quotes Adam Smith and David Ricardo. Ships that pass in the night. . . .

It is not likely that any single payments plan can truly reconcile these divergent viewpoints. What, then, are the chances for compromise? The ECLA has little choice but to compromise, for LAFTA countries depend heavily upon both the IMF and the United States for assistance. Moreover, ECLA's proposals involve technical difficulties and uncertainties that warrant caution. This probably means giving up the idea of large automatic reciprocal credits, at least in the beginning. Under the Triffin or Mikesell plan, or some combination of the two, payments might initially be handled through a clearing house, with reciprocal or clearing-house credit made available between

[11] See, for example, his monograph, *Intra-Regional Trade and Economic Development* (Washington, D.C.: Organization of American States, 1958), chap. v.

settlement dates. Correspondent-bank relationships, with mutual dollar deposits along the lines suggested by Mikesell, would not be inconsistent with the operation of a clearing house. Both these measures might bring dollar savings and lower the cost of financing regional trade.[12] In addition, the clearing house might be expanded later to provide credit directly or to negotiate loan funds from international agencies.

I am well aware that the above compromise would be only half a loaf—and the small "half," at that—for ECLA and its supporters. This group seeks a payments mechanism that will provide an incentive for, if not enforce, reciprocity. My inclination would be to give such a system a chance, even though I entertain serious doubts as to the probability of success. Moreover, if Latin Americans are willing to bear the extra costs of import substitution in order to try to speed industrialization, that is their privilege. Viewed with objectivity, no strong case can be made against such an attempt. Since the cost of the undertaking would be quite modest, not a great deal would be lost, to my mind, if the gamble were to fail.

I cannot resist an obvious comment on the United States' position. The high ideals of free trade and convertibility have served U.S. policy well in the postwar years, with the possible exception of lapses that have occurred in such instances as the tying of dollar foreign aid to U.S. exports. However, these ideals are a luxury in which only a nation blessed with substantial reserves and a strong competitive position in international markets can indulge. As the recent measures to defend U.S. balance-of-payments indicate, even the United States is prepared to start slugging in the best mercantilist tradition when its international financial position is severely threatened. As a *norteamericano*, I must admit that the experience has been a humbling one.

My proclivity for gambling is not shared by the responsible authorities in the United States and the International Monetary Fund—a circumstance that may or may not be regrettable. Moreover, in contrast to those officials, I am in the complacent position of not having to answer to any constituency. One must also recognize the weight of the logic that argues in their favor. That is why I am convinced that compromise should be the order of the day. The minimum expectation would be a greater supply of credit than is presently available—an objective that the payments-plan proponents, whatever their other differences, should unanimously approve.

12 Triffin's minimum plan for a clearing house with immediate settlements scarcely merits consideration, for it would allow no real dollar savings and might not even reduce credit or transfer costs to any significant degree.

XVI

ROBERT TRIFFIN

Toward a Latin American Monetary Cooperation

The spectacular success of regional economic and monetary cooperation and integration in Western Europe since the end of World War II has long spurred similar efforts in other regions, particularly Latin America. Most of these efforts, however, have been thwarted so far by divided counsel, both among the countries concerned and on the part of international organizations and consultants.

In the monetary field, the opposition to regional organization sprang largely from the fear that regional agreements would weaken balance-of-payments barriers to domestic inflationary pressures and would involve discriminatory trading and settlements provisions, incompatible with world-wide currency convertibility and an economic allocation of the participating countries' productive resources.

These fears were by no means groundless, particularly as initial proposals tended to copy too slavishly the early provisions of the European Payments Agreement, based as they were on multilateral clearing and partial credit settlement of *bilateral* balances arising from a complex network of *bilateral* payments agreements. These initial EPU provisions were totally overhauled in later years, as Europe moved from bilateral shackles to near convertibility. Balances notified to the agent for compensation no longer arose from bilateral agreements, but from normal interventions of central banks on the foreign-exchange markets in support of exchange-rate stability. Convertible-currency settlements shifted from a 50 per cent to a 75 per cent basis, and would have progressed to 100 per cent if the EPU agreement had not been prematurely terminated at the insistence of the United Kingdom. Debtor balances were, moreover, regularly amortized, rather than left pending until the debtor country shifted to a surplus position within the region.[1]

The resurrection of the initial EPU provisions in the early proposals for a Latin American payments union were, indeed, a sheer anachronism in a world that had progressed, in the meantime, from early postwar bilateralism to substantial currency convertibility. Far less valid were the arguments leveled against Latin American integration and monetary cooperation on the basis of the admittedly low level of intraregional trade in Latin America. These arguments implicitly assumed that this low level of intraregional trade was a normal and desirable phenomenon (reflecting Adam Smith's invisible hand) and the most economic allocation of the area's production factors. Any regional integration measures could only—so the argument ran—disturb the natural pattern of trade, increase production costs, and lower economic welfare throughout the area.

Such views reflected, of course, a naïvely narrow economic viewpoint. The absurdly low level of trade within the region is very largely the product of an infrastructure—in such fields as transportation, banking, entrepreneurship, capital financing, etc.—historically developed by foreign interests, primarily European and U.S., to promote their own food and raw-material imports from the area and to seek outlets for their own exports. The resulting bias in favor of extra-area trade, and against intra-area trade, was no God-given phenomenon, but a by-product of history, calling for specific policy measures aimed at correcting the lopsidedness and uneconomic character of such a trade pattern.

Such correctives were all the more necessary in view of the additional bias resulting from national protectionist policies adopted by Latin American countries. Even when justifiable on the basis of an infant-industry argument, such policies should have been applied only against the more developed countries, but not against neighbors suffering from the same infant-industry handicap. Insofar as nondiscriminatory protection did not actually stave off *all* imports in favor of national production, it did actually discriminate in favor of exporters in the more highly developed countries and against exporters from other underdeveloped countries in the area.

The clarification of this issue, important as it may be for the aca-

[1] See Robert Triffin, *Europe and the Money Muddle* (New Haven: Yale University Press, 1959), pp. 218–20.

demic economist, probably had little influence on the governmental debate. Far more important, from this point of view, were (1) the drafting of new proposals, eschewing the pitfalls denounced above in the original ones;[2] and (2) the spectacular success achieved in Central America by the implementation of these proposals.

The new proposals established a sharper distinction between the clearing of compensable surpluses and deficits, on the one hand, and the settlement or financing of residual imbalances, on the other. A clearing mechanism for central banks could demonstrably shave off the unnecessary commissions and exchange costs now involved in triangular settlements via New York or other financial centers. Although such benefits would admittedly be very modest at the start, the clearing machinery would provide an institutional framework on which other, and far more significant, measures of cooperation could be grafted. The exchange guarantees implicit in the adoption of a joint unit of account could be supplemented by solidary guarantees, effective safeguards against default, etc., and could remove major obstacles to the granting of credits to a country in difficulties, both by other members and by countries outside the area. Clearing operations could also be facilitated by, and invite, the maintenance of some portion of each country's international reserves in the form of working deposits with the clearing institution, without decreasing in the least the liquidity of such reserves for balance-of-payments settlements. Such deposits would, in turn, provide the clearing agency with a mass of maneuvers that need not be permanently kept completely in foreign currencies, but could be used, in part, for short-term stabilization loans to member countries.

If one were to indulge in long-term dreams about a still distant future, one might even contemplate the ultimate development of such a system toward fuller monetary integration among the participating countries; just as central banks originally developed, on the national scale, from similar, and initially modest, deposit and clearing functions, through a natural and logical process of institutional growth.

The clearing, deposit, and credit mechanism briefly outlined above, and described in greater detail elsewhere in this volume,[3] escapes the major criticism leveled against *automatic and narrowly intraregional*

[2] See *Cooperación financiera en América Latina* (Mexico City: CEMLA, 1963); and *Problemas de pagos en América Latina* (Mexico City: CEMLA, 1964).

[3] See Barry N. Siegel, "Payments Systems for the Latin American Free Trade Association," (chap. xv).

credits, patterned upon the haphazard development of intraregional surpluses and deficits. Credits would, with minor exceptions, be discretionary, rather than automatic and would depend on mutual agreement regarding the borrowing country's monetary policies, internal as well as external. Credits would be granted to support over-all stabilization policies, rather than to finance intraregional deficits only. They would be derived from the deposits of all countries, *pro rata* of their actual reserve strength, rather than financed on a far less liquid basis, and only by countries in surplus within the region, regardless of their over-all balance-of-payments and reserve position.

To take a concrete example, automatic lending and borrowing criteria based on *regional* surpluses and deficits, if applied to the Central American area, would entail persistent lending by one of the poorest countries in that region, Honduras, to one of the richest, El Salvador. This situation would prevail merely because the most economic use of the two countries' factor endowment normally promotes a pattern of production and trade in which important Salvadoran foodstuff and raw-material import needs can best be satisfied by imports from Honduras, while fewer Honduran needs can be met economically from Salvadoran sources. There is no reason on earth why financial arrangements should be specifically designed to discourage such trade, desirable from both countries' point of view, as long as Honduras fully complies with its trade liberalization and preferential commitments under the Central American Integration Treaty.

Credit provisions under regional payments agreements should be geared to the over-all balance-of-payments and reserve needs and capabilities of the member countries, using temporary surpluses and unused reserves of some to help cushion temporary deficits of others. Such credits should, moreover, remain discretionary, rather than automatic, in order to promote the harmonization of national monetary policies indispensable to the correction of persistent balance-of-payments disequilibriums and to the successful implementation of member countries' trade and exchange liberalization commitments vis-à-vis one another.

The scope of such cooperation will, of course, be far more limited among underdeveloped countries with low levels of reserves and mutual trade than among the richer and more closely integrated economies of Western Europe. Much of the monetary stabilization assistance that they could profitably use will have to be sought, tomorrow as today, from outside sources, particularly from the International Monetary Fund. Mutual credit arrangements, modest as they have to be, could, nevertheless, prove of enormous value in improving relations between the Fund and the underdeveloped countries and avoiding unjustifiable policy conflicts and bitterness. The case of a country in need of assistance would normally be discussed first among the members of the regional organization, who would have to agree on the policies that the prospective borrower should pursue in order to justify the assistance required. If such agreement is reached, they would both risk their own lending resources in the proposed stabilization intervention and support jointly a request for complementary assistance of underwriting by the IMF.

This would strengthen the hand of the borrowing country in its negotiations with the Fund. It would also help the Fund formulate policy programs and conditions more acceptable to the members of the area and better adjusted to economic and political circumstances, which nonarea members may be less able to gauge correctly and realistically. On the other hand, the countries of the area would no longer be able to indulge in irresponsible criticism of the Fund for subordinating its assistance to reasonable conditions, on which they would also have to insist in order to minimize the risks attendant on their own participation in the stabilization program and to maximize its chances of success.

The recent weakening of long-standing prejudices against regional monetary cooperation and integration, however, can only be ascribed in part to the persuasiveness of such abstract arguments. As much, or more, influential has been the undeniable success of actual regional agreements devoid of the monetary discrimination features of the initial EPU agreement. The Central American Clearing House, which I helped draft in 1960–61, has been widely applauded as an undoubted success, not only by the participating central banks, but also by private bankers and traders in the area and by the IMF itself. The association of Mexico, in 1963, gave further evidence of the confidence so rapidly and deservedly gained by this institution, and this example of Mexico may be followed by other countries, such as Panama, Colombia, and Venezuela.

The meeting of Central Banks Technicians of the American Continent, held in Rio de Janeiro in October, 1963, witnessed, for the first time in twelve years of vain and sometimes bitter debates, a *unanimous* interest in the opening of concrete negotiations aiming at the creation of a Latin American clearing or payments union,[4] along the lines briefly summarized above and described in greater detail in the

[4] Documents and papers on Latin American payments problems, which originated in that meeting, form the volume published by CEMLA, *Problemas de pagos en América Latina.*

study I presented to the CEMLA meeting in Mexico City, in September of 1962.[5]

The unanimity achieved at the experts' level in Rio de Janeiro and the encouragement given to the participants by the IMF observers at that meeting create a new and promising climate for the negotiations among Latin American monetary authorities. Let us hope that they will attack the problem in a constructive spirit; eschew spectacular, but divisive and ultimately sterile, political sloganeering; and concentrate on laying, as rapidly and solidly as possible, the groundwork for future Latin American monetary cooperation and integration, within the world-wide framework of a more flexible, decentralized, and realistic IMF machinery. It would seem highly desirable, at this stage, to concentrate initial efforts on manageable areas, grouping only a small number of countries highly conscious of their interdependence and not too dissimilar in their economic and monetary policies and experience. This, I feel, is one of the lessons to be derived from the success of Central American integration efforts, as well as from those of the European Economic Community. Neither the former nor the latter would have made as much progress as they have, if they had waited for all other countries of Latin America or Europe to join them before taking any step toward closer cooperation and integration among themselves.

A *concentric, decentralized* approach toward Latin American monetary cooperation will remain necessary, for many years to come, in order to exploit fully the varying willingness and ability of different nations to merge some portions of their economic sovereignty for the sake of greater effectiveness in its very use. The existing Central American group, for instance, must retain its separate identity, if it is to implement as rapidly and efficiently as possible its plans for full monetary and economic union among its members. It could, however, participate with a less closely integrated group of other countries of Middle America and the Caribbean area in joint payments agreements. Finally, this broader group itself could join with other Latin American republics or, when and if it is formed, with a group of South American countries, in still more modest initial agreements. Only at a later stage, as and when each of these groups moves toward more intensive mutual agreements and commitments, could closer links be established also among them, so as to maximize the geographical extent as well as the actual content of feasible monetary and

[5] Robert Triffin, "Una cámara de compensación y unión de pagos latinoamericana," in *Cooperación financiera en América Latina* (Mexico City: CEMLA, 1963), pp. 95–117.

financial cooperation and integration in Latin America as a whole.

Many of the developments presently taking place in the international monetary field call for a reappraisal of the attitudes of Latin American governments and monetary authorities toward the problem of regional cooperation. One should note particularly the rapid recovery of European capital markets, both as an outlet for outside investment and as a source of funds; and, on the governmental level, the expansion of multilateral cooperation and even integration in respect to the cushioning of balance-of-payments disequilibrium. One should note, also, the mutual confrontation of monetary, fiscal, and economic policies bearing on such disequilibriums, within the OECD and the European Economic Community, among others. Finally, one should observe the current studies and planning of more ambitious institutional reforms aiming at the further broadening and consolidation of regional monetary cooperation mechanisms (the Committee of Multilateral Surveillance and the Study Group on the Creation of Reserve Assets, of the Group of Ten; the Council of Central Bank Governors and European Reserve Fund project, of the EEC countries; the Agreement for Establishment of the Central American Monetary Union; etc.).

These developments offer to the Latin American countries and their central banks new challenges and opportunities in various specific fields, such as joint investment of the central banks' reserves; Latin American security flotations in foreign markets in developed countries; arrangements by central banks, on a regional scale, in support of mutual trade; and arrangements among the region's monetary authorities in support of currency convertibility and stability.

Feasible regional agreements in the above-mentioned fields will often impose difficult, but inevitable, compromises between desirable geographical extension and desirable deepening of mutual commitments: the wider the extension, the shallower the depth is likely to be, and vice versa. Fortunately, the mutual benefits derived in the past from the coexistence of the International Monetary Fund, the OECD, the European Economic Community, and the Belgo-Luxemburg Economic Union amply demonstrate the complementarity, rather than incompatibility, of concentric regional approaches to world-wide economic cooperation. This is likely to prove true in Latin America, as well as in other parts of the world. Care should be taken from the very beginning, however, to keep open all avenues to the future broadening, as well as deepening, of the initial monetary agreements that prove feasible.

PART THREE

Central American Integration Program

XVII

JOSEPH MOSCARELLA[1]

Economic Integration in Central America

Among the economic blocs formed during the course of the past decade, the Central American endeavor is of particular interest since it is not limited to the establishment of a customs union, but also envisages joint planning for coordinating the development of the five member countries.

Following a brief description of the salient features of the Central American economy, the present essay examines the principal instruments used in the integration program and attempts to examine its results, in the measure permitted by available information and by the fact that the Central American Common Market has been in existence only a short time.

Characteristics of the Central American Economy and Integration-Program Objectives

The Central American economic-integration program is essentially an international cooperative effort aimed at surmounting the obstacles that stand in the way of the rapid development of five small countries, whose growth is largely dependent on the world market for a handful of commodities (coffee, bananas, cotton).

In the year 1952, which marked the initiation of the program, Central America's total population amounted to some 8.5 million inhabitants, occupying a territory that extends over almost 170,000 sq. mi.

[1] The author is a United Nations official, but the points of view expressed in this essay do not necessarily reflect the official U.N. position.

Expanding at an annual rate of more than 3 per cent, by 1963 this population had grown to nearly 12 million. The distribution of the population, concentrated in the highlands, shows very little relationship with the distribution of resources in the different regions of the individual republics or from one country to another. Population density ranges from a minimum of 10 inhabitants per square kilometer (0.4 square miles) in Nicaragua to a maximum of 122 in El Salvador, with intermediate levels of 35, 24, and 16, corresponding respectively to Guatemala, Costa Rica, and Honduras.[2]

These differences are even more pronounced as between zones on the isthmus: Some are overcrowded, while others have an abundance of agricultural and forest resources, which are not being worked. Thus, we find that only 4 million hectares (or 9 per cent of the total area) are under cultivation in the combined territory of the five countries; 4.5 million hectares are taken up in prairies and permanent pasture; and 22.8 million represent wooded tracts. The land area that is potentially productive, but at present not in use, is estimated at some 6 million hectares.[3]

Central American mineral resources have not been investigated to any very great extent, and activity in this field—mainly the extraction of lead, copper, zinc, and precious metals—is correspondingly modest. Exploratory work conducted in recent years turned up the possibility of commercial exploitation of iron-ore deposits in Honduras, and bauxite in Costa Rica. On the other hand, the search for oil, engaged in by almost every country in the area, has not as yet produced results worthy of mention.

During the last twenty years, industrial production has increased at a faster pace than the rest of the Central American economy, thanks to the impetus afforded by a number of circumstances: the restriction on imports during the war and the early postwar period; the active protective policy followed by most of the nations; and, until the mid-1950's, the rapid increase in export earnings.

Nevertheless, the industrialization process is still in the incipient stage in Central America. Manufacturing production accounts for a scant 12 per cent of the gross product of the region as a whole and

[2] See *Segundo Compendio Estadístico Centroamericano* (New York: United Nations; 63. II. G. 11), Table 1. Unless otherwise indicated, data cited in the remainder of the text were taken from this publication, or from the national government sources to which it makes reference.

[3] Except for Nicaragua (where an argicultural census was taken in 1958), the statistics shown are based on censuses and surveys carried out between 1950 and 1955. Additions, in subsequent years, to the area under cultivation—devoted mainly to cotton (in Nicaragua, El Salvador, and Guatemala)—have not substantially modified the general land-use pattern in the region as a whole.

provides employment for approximately 11 per cent of the economically active population. Although agriculture continues to absorb the bulk of that population (about 65 per cent), the contribution of agriculture to the gross regional product is less than 40 per cent.[4] This points up the relative inability of the Central American economy, within the restricted confines of the national and local markets, to absorb the portion of the labor force devoted to low-productivity pursuits and to cope with the rapid demographic growth. The low level of per capita product ($250 in 1960) attests to an insufficiency of investment capital and of technical progress in the region. Table 1 clearly indicates the small size of the national markets, evidently unequal to the task of supporting a satisfactory industrial structure and promoting the technological advancement of agriculture, which accounts for a major share of total economic activity.

TABLE 1
CENTRAL AMERICA: SOME INDICATORS OF THE SIZE OF THE NATIONAL MARKETS AND REGIONAL MARKET, 1960

		Gross Territorial Product		*Consumption of Manufactures*	
Country	Population (in thousands)	Total (in millions of dollars)	Per Capita (in dollars)	Total (in millions of dollars)	Per Capita (in dollars)
Guatemala	3,765	997	265	398	106
El Salvador	2,442	521	213	324	133
Honduras	1,958	378	194	168	86
Nicaragua	1,477	343	232	201	136
Costa Rica	1,206	469	389	251	208
Total for Central America	10,840	2,708	250	1,342	124

Sources: *Statistical Supplement to the Economic Bulletin for Latin America*, VII, No. 1 (Santiago: ECLA, 1962) and ECLA, *Segundo Compendio Estadístico Centroamericano*, 1961–1963. Data on gross territorial product and consumption of manufactured goods are ECLA estimates based on official statistics. Official exchange rates were used in converting to U.S. dollars.

In addition to its internal structural limitations, the isthmian economy had lost its principal stimulus to development as a result of the

[4] 1950 censuses show that 69 per cent of the economically active population in the region as a whole was devoted to agriculture in that year. This proportion ranged from 55 per cent in Costa Rica to 84 per cent in Honduras. Preliminary results of the population census taken in Honduras in 1961 would indicate an appreciable decline.

drop in export prices since the mid-1950's. Between 1955 and 1962, the unit value of Central American exports decreased by more than 25 per cent, largely as a result of the decline in prices on coffee, bananas, and cotton, which jointly account for three-fourths of the area's export trade. The total value of Central American exports to the rest of the world, which had increased steadily to a $445 million peak in 1957, fell off by more than 11 per cent on the average in the four years following (see Table 2). By 1962, it recovered its 1957 level; by 1963, it rose to $512 million, thanks mainly to a sizable increment in the volume of cotton sold abroad by Nicaragua, El Salvador, and Guatemala.

TABLE 2
CENTRAL AMERICA: VALUE OF EXTERNAL TRADE
1955–1963
(*In Millions of Dollars*)

	Trade with the Rest of the World		*Intra-Central American Trade*	
Year	Exports (f.o.b.)	Imports (c.i.f.)	*Value of exports*	Per cent of total exports
1955	401	401	13.0	3.1
1956	417	455	14.9	3.4
1957	445	508	17.6	3.8
1958	425	489	20.9	4.7
1959	339	445	28.7	7.8
1960	405	481	30.3	7.0
1961	413	458	36.8	8.2
1962	446	504	50.4	10.2
1963	514	579	68.0	11.7

Sources: ECLA, *Segundo Compendio Estadístico Centroamericano*, 1961–1963; IMF, *International Financial Statistics*; and Secretaría de Integración Económica Centroamericano (SIECA), *Carta Informativa No.* 36, Guatemala City, October 12, 1964.

The deterioration of the external sector tended to depress economic activity in general up to 1962. Compared with a 5 per cent rate recorded for 1950–57, the gross product of the region increased by only 3 per cent per year in the period 1957–62. The situation improved appreciably in 1963, as a result of the increased volume of cotton exports and a partial recovery of coffee prices. But, judging from the world-market outlook for these commodities, Central American exports are not likely in the next few years, to repeat the dynamic performance that characterized the first decade of the postwar period.

The foregoing sketch of the structural features of the Central American economy makes it evident that the formal expansion of the national markets, although a necessary condition, will not be sufficient to promote the economic development of the countries on the Isthmus. A series of joint efforts will also be needed, directed toward transportation, power, technical training, and modernization of the means of production, with a view to creating the productive activities that lend sustenance to free trade.

This broad design for the economic-integration program was conceived from the very start, as indicated in the corresponding resolution approved by ECLA in 1951, expressing the desire of the Central American governments to "develop agricultural and industrial production and the transport systems in their respective countries, so as to promote the integration of their economies and the expansion of markets by the exchange of their products, to coordinate their development programs, and to establish enterprises in which all or some of these countries have an interest." [5]

In pursuit of these aims, a Central American Economic Cooperation Committee was constituted in August of 1952. With a membership comprising the ministers of economy of the five countries, and assisted by several specialized subcommittees, this agency has been in charge of the integration program to date. Panama has participated in certain technical aspects of the program, but has refrained from formal adherence to the integration instruments as such. In March of 1963, in the Declaration of Central America, the presidents of all six countries in the region expressed their intention to link Panama with the integration program by means of a special agreement.[6]

Common Market

Formative stage. Although the general orientation of the integration program was established from the beginning, the formulation and negotiation of the instruments that brought the Central American Common Market into being turned out to be a rather lengthy process. During the first eight years, a large part of the activities of the Central American Economic Cooperation Committee were devoted to the study of problems connected with regional transportation, electric power, financing, technical training, and agricultural and industrial integration. Regional institutes were established (such as the Central American Institute for Industrial Research and the Central American College for Public Administration), and preliminary efforts

[5] Resolution 9, June 16, 1951.

[6] See SIECA, *Carta Informativa No. 21*, Guatemala, July 12, 1963.

were made in the direction of coordinating investment in the basic sectors of the economy. At the same time, work went forward on setting up the institutional framework for the common market. But it was not until 1960 that an effective formula was achieved to ensure free trade in the region and provide the instruments needed in promoting the industrial development that could give body and meaning to such interchange.

During the 1950's, intra-Central American trade channels were widened, to some extent, through the subscription of bilateral treaties, which, by 1958, took in almost all the countries in the area. In that year, the Multilateral Treaty on Free Trade and Economic Integration was signed, providing for the establishment of a free-trade zone, which was to be regional in scope and perfected over a ten-year period, with the ultimate aim of constituting a customs union. However, this instrument did not make provision for well-defined commitments with respect to the manner in which regional trade was to be freed and at what rate.

The treaty established a list of commodities on which all duties were eliminated, keeping certain quantitative restrictions. Initially quite limited, the list was intended to incorporate future additions, but was subject to the uncertainties of successive negotiations among the member governments. The member countries also undertook to equalize import duties with respect to third countries on the commodities included in the free-trade schedule, and to establish free transit as well as "national treatment" for individuals, investments, and goods within the region.

Designed for the coordinated promotion of new industries that will require access to the combined market, an agreement on the Regime of Central American Integration Industries was signed at the same time as the Multilateral Treaty.

In February of 1960, three countries—El Salvador, Guatemala, and Honduras—decided to step up the process of unifying their respective markets by entering into a Treaty of Economic Association. In contrast to the Multilateral Treaty, this instrument established immediate free trade in all goods manufactured or originating in any of the three contracting parties, other than those listed in an annexed schedule, which would be subject to quantitative restriction and to gradual tariff reductions during the transition period. It also provided for the creation of a full-fledged customs union within a maximum period of five years.

The coexistence of a series of treaties of varying geographic scope and prescribing different procedures with regard to the formation of the common market was an indication that, after eight years, the various countries had not yet agreed upon a clear-cut policy of free trade and economic integration in Central America.[7]

The situation changed rapidly during the course of 1960, the year in which the Economic Cooperation Committee undertook to re-evaluate the entire integration program and readjust its various elements. The result was the General Treaty for Central American Economic Integration, subscribed to in December, 1960, by four countries and in effect since June, 1961. Costa Rica rounded out the regional scope of the General Treaty (which has been ratified by all five countries) by signing in July of 1962.

Thus, the results of the previous bilateral and multilateral agreements were consolidated in a single instrument; and well-defined, fixed-term commitments were established for the adoption of a common tariff vis-à-vis third countries. In addition, the Central American Bank for Economic Integration (CABEI) was established, as well as the other agencies needed to administer the treaty and to provide policy guidance for the economic integration program: the Economic Council, the Executive Council, and the Permanent Secretariat of the General Treaty (SIECA).

As stipulated in Articles 1 and 2 of the General Treaty, the member countries undertake to establish a complete free-trade zone, in a period not to exceed five years from the treaty's effective date, and to adopt a common tariff, in the terms of the Central American Agreement on the Equalization of Import Duties and Charges, signed in September of 1959 at San José, Costa Rica. The General Treaty takes precedence over the Multilateral Treaty and any other free-trade instruments jointly subscribed to by such countries. These agreements all remain in effect, however, and their provisions may be applied in all matters not covered by the General Treaty.[8] In the future, no signatory country may unilaterally enter into treaty arrangements with non-Central American nations in matters affecting the principles of economic integration.

[7] See Víctor L. Urquidi, *Free Trade and Economic Integration in Latin America* (Berkeley and Los Angeles: University of California Press, 1962), chap. vii. For a detailed analysis of the differences between the Multilateral and Tripartite treaties, see ECLA, *El Programa de Integración Económica de Centroamérica y el Tratado de Asociación Económica suscrito por El Salvador, Guatemala y Honduras* (Managua, May, 1960; E/CN.12/CEE/212).

[8] The purpose of this clause was to ensure that during the period in which certain of the members had not yet ratified the General Treaty, or in the event of a subsequent decision to withdraw, regional trade relations would be governed by the commitments undertaken in the earlier agreements. See ECLA, *Informe de la Octava Reunión del Subcomité de Comercio Centroamericano* (E/CN.12/213; December, 1960), p. 5.

Free-trade system. In accordance with Chapter 2 of the General Treaty, the signatories reciprocally and immediately granted free trade on all goods originating in their respective territories, except for certain products enumerated in Annex A to the treaty. With very few exceptions, these commodities will be automatically subject to unrestricted free trade by the end of the five-year period, i.e., by June, 1966.

The list of exceptions comprises those products whose immediate liberation from trade restraints could seriously disrupt already established activities or occasion substantial losses in fiscal revenues, and the treatment established was adapted to the characteristics of each case. The first type entails the application, during a maximum period of five years, of a preferential tariff based on a fixed or progressively descending rate. Generally speaking, this treatment is accorded to consumer goods manufactured on a national scale and in need of sufficient time in which to adjust to new regional competitive conditions. Examples of this group are certain textile products, fats and oils, beer, paints, and soap. The second type of treatment establishes import or export controls or import quotas; and it conditions the application of free trade to the signing of special protocols designed to regulate commodity interchange, enable coordination of production policies, and ensure maximum freedom of trade. This treatment is applicable to basic foodstuffs, such as rice, corn, and wheat flour. Intended for temporary application—i.e., until such time as a special agreement is concluded in the matter—a third type of treatment provides for the imposition of duties on certain items corresponding to industrial plants designed for establishment on a regional scale.[9] Still a fourth type of treatment calls for customs equalization on the finished product, as well as on its raw materials, as a prior requisite to the concession of free trade. Application, in this instance, extends to the tobacco industry and to certain fibers, cloth, and other products of the textile industry.

Some commodities will be subject indefinitely to payment of duties or export and import controls, since their trade is regulated, at present, by international agreements or subject to internal fiscal monopolies. The products involved, in this case, are coffee and coffee extracts; alcohol and cane sugar spirits; cane sugar; and cotton.

It should be pointed out that the General Treaty contains no provision for special safeguards (escape clauses), since it was felt that the transitory-exception system allows enough flexibility for the contracting parties to impose restrictions in given products, whose immediate

[9] The reference here is to integration industries, whose establishment will be governed by the special agreement discussed later.

free trade might cause serious disruptions in domestic production. Had additional escape clauses been included, the process of the adaptation and specialization of internal production within the regional-market framework might have been indefinitely retarded.[10] In this connection, it is interesting to note that one of the functions of the Central American Bank is to facilitate this process by financing the adaptation of existing industries to the new conditions of common-market competition.

Common customs tariff. As regards the adoption of a common tariff for application to trade with third countries, the General Treaty served to accelerate the negotiations begun in 1959 with the signing of the Agreement on the Equalization of Import Duties and Charges. By means of protocols to that agreement, during the three years immediately following, uniform duties were established on 1,213 tariff items, or 95 per cent of the total.

Starting from national tariffs, designed to serve primarily fiscal purposes, the member countries have managed to build a uniform Central American tariff that fulfills the requirements of a selective policy aimed at stimulating the import-substitution process in a general setting of expanding foreign trade. According to a preliminary analysis, the average level of the new tariff is equivalent to 48 per cent, or 6 per cent higher than the average of the five national tariffs previously in effect.[11] On the other hand, the composition of the new tariff incorporates important changes by groups of products. Generally speaking, low duties have been fixed for capital goods and raw materials not currently produced in Central America, or not susceptible of production in the short term. Duties were set at relatively high rates on consumer goods (except for certain essential items not produced in the region), largely in response to fiscal criteria or the desire to protect and encourage regional industry.

Like the free-trade system, the common tariff makes provisions for flexible procedures to attenuate the effects that sudden changes in duty levels might have on the supply or prices of certain commodities or on fiscal revenues. In these instances, the desired duties are to be progressively arrived at over maximum periods of five years, beginning with the national duty in effect or some other specifically determined level. Gradual equalization has been adopted for a limited number of

[10] See *Informe de la Octava Reunión del Subcomité de Comercio Centroamericano*, pp. 7–8.

[11] See ECLA, *General Situation and Future Outlook of the Central American Integration Programme* (E/CN.12/CCE/265; February, 1963), pp. 18–19. The analysis referred to above covers tariff items accounting for imports valued at $372 million in 1960, equivalent to 72 per cent of the total Central American import trade in that year.

tariff items. In the vast majority of cases, the uniform duty agreed upon is applied as soon as the corresponding protocol goes into effect.

Evolution of intra-Central American trade. The expansion of trade among the Central American countries is a clear indication of the immediate results of the integration program. During the period 1955–63, this intraregional trade increased more than fivefold: from $13 million to $68 million. This achievement by the countries in the region—in contrast with the behavior of the rest of the economy, particularly the external sector—constitutes the most remarkable feature of the practical operation of economic integration during the period under review. In effect, the rapid growth of reciprocal trade coincided, during most of the eight-year span, with the price slump in the external sector, a relative stagnation of economic growth, and a diminishing export trade with the rest of the world. Thus it was that inter-Central American commerce, which in 1955 represented 3 per cent of the region's total foreign exports, had increased to nearly 12 per cent by 1963 (see Table 2).

Together with the expanded flow of merchandise among the five nations, there is evidence of a decided change in the commodity composition of that interchange, with an increasing share corresponding to industrial goods. To illustrate: Intraregional exports of manufactures increased at an annual rate of 22.5 per cent from 1955 to 1960, compared to only 5.2 per cent in the previous five-year period. In the case of nonmanufactured goods, exports expanded at approximately the same rate during the two periods under discussion (some 15 per cent per year). Judging from partial data, this trend appears to have continued.

The change in the composition of trade is attributable to the fact that the commercial agreements in effect among the Central American republics—initially limited to agricultural products—were gradually extended, in 1955 and thereafter, to include an increasing number of products turned out by the manufacturing industry. The mere existence of an economic-integration program and of the first multilateral treaties enhanced the market outlook for industry and thereby strengthened the trend in favor of the exportation of manufactures.

The new opportunities for interchange resulted primarily in the use of previously idle industrial productive capacity, rather than spurring new investment in this field to any very great extent. Ample support for this conclusion is derived from information available on the three countries that are the principal trading partners in the region: El Salvador, Guatemala, and Honduras. The total value of the Central American goods imported by these three countries in 1961 amounted to $30.6 million, of which $9.8 million corresponded to primary commodities, largely agricultural in origin, and $20.8 million to manufactures. In the last-mentioned group, less than $1 million of the imports were supplied by recently established industries: tires and tubes, and paints and varnishes.[12]

It is safe to assume that reciprocal trade will continue to expand at a rapid rate in the next few years, as a result of Nicaragua's full participation since 1961 and the more recent incorporation of Costa Rica into the common market. These circumstances will contribute to a broader geographic distribution of inter-Central American trade. Another favorable factor was the creation, in 1961, of the Central American Clearing House to facilitate intrazonal settlements.

The impetus afforded by the operation of the General Treaty will be offset in part, however, by several factors that will tend to retard the growth of intraregional trade. On the one hand, most of the formerly idle industrial productive capacity is already being utilized. On the other, the possibilities for further substitution of imports of the types of articles produced by the traditional industries in the Central American economies have been practically exhausted. The ratio of imports to total consumption of such articles is quite low, generally not more than 20 per cent. In those industries in which the margin of substitution is greater (textile manufacturing, for example), the expansion of trade and production presupposes substantial new investments in order to modernize equipment, enlarge plant facilities, and achieve a greater degree of specialization among the different countries of the region. Thus, the creation of new activities that do not conform to the traditional mold and a general strengthening of productive capacity constitute the point of departure for efforts aimed at sustaining the dynamic growth of inter-Central American commerce and taking advantage of the possibilities offered by the establishment of the common market.

Integrated Development

Industrial development. The possibilities for industrial development within the Central American Common Market are difficult to estimate. The process of integration, in itself, will imply important changes in the structure of production in the area by creating demand for new end-use products, intermediate goods, and raw materials. The magnitude of such demand cannot be forecast on the basis of the experience to date in the member countries, which has been limited to import substitution within the domestic markets.

[12] See Pan American Union, *Economic Survey of Latin America, 1962* (Washington, D.C.: Organization of American States, 1964), Table 73.

In a preliminary analysis of this problem, with the assumption that per capita income will increase in the coming years at an annual rate of 2.5 per cent, the ECLA Secretariat estimated that the regional demand for manufactures will have climbed from $1.342 million in 1960 to some $2.7 billion in 1970. On the basis of the projected increase in the region's capacity to import, it was estimated that manufacturing production in Central America would have to expand from $848 million to more than $1.8 billion in that period in order to be able to satisfy the portion of demand that could not be met out of imports.[13] This estimate, of course, is only intended to give an idea of the order of magnitude of the possibilities for import substitution within the common market. A more accurate calculation would call for a great deal more information than is presently available concerning potential supply conditions in the region.

Part of the increase in manufacturing output would result from the expansion and specialization of the existing industries, which can still look forward to a certain margin of import substitution at the regional level. With respect to new industries, the potential market in the region will not permit the establishment, in the foreseeable future, of large industrial complexes or plants for machinery and heavy equipment. That market is large enough, however, to give vigorous support in the coming decade to the production of intermediate goods, durable consumer goods, and even certain capital goods. By way of example, it has been estimated that the prospective market for iron and steel products in the next ten years would argue in favor of the installation of a plant to manufacture the items in greatest demand in this field: light reinforcement bars, shapes and rods, wire and welded tubing. Thus, the feasibility of a basic steel mill would depend, in the final analysis, on the possibilities for industrial exploitation of Central American iron-ore and coal resources. Exploratory work, to date, has not produced conclusive results. At least for the time being, however, there would be the possibility of installing semi-integrated plants—on the basis of local or imported scrap—for the manufacture of bars and rods and light structures; installations to turn out welded tubing made from imported steel strip; and wiredrawing facilities.

Preliminary studies on the present and potential market, and the minimum economic size in each case, indicate the possibility of establishing another ten industries within the common market: glass containers; sheet glass; light bulbs; caustic soda; chlorinated insecticides; petroleum derivatives; rayon; tires and tubes; fertilizers; and copper

[13] See *General Situation and Future Outlook of the Central American Integration Programme*, p. 35.

wire and cable.[14] Presently under investigation are several other industrial possibilities: sulphuric acid; electrolytic copper; plastic materials; and electric appliances.

It has been seen that the free-trade system and the common tariff are powerful stimuli for investment, and their effects are already making themselves felt in the region. Other instruments are also available to the program, for use in promoting industrial development and channeling investment toward regional-scale activities and toward the rehabilitation and improvement of existing plants: the Central American Bank for Economic Integration, the Central American Agreement on Fiscal Incentives for Industrial Development, the agreement on the Regime of Central American Integration Industries and the Central American Institute for Industrial Research mentioned earlier.

The CABEI was created in December of 1960, when the governments of Guatemala, El Salvador, Honduras, and Nicaragua signed the General Treaty for Economic Integration. The bank's charter went into effect May 8, 1961; and in September of that year the institution began operations, having established its headquarters in Tegucigalpa, Honduras.

Designed for the purpose of financing the economic integration of the countries on the isthmus, the bank channels its lending activities primarily to the following areas: (1) infrastructure projects that complete the existing regional system or correct basic sector disparities impeding balanced development in Central America; (2) long-term investment projects in industries that are regional in scope or particularly suited to the Central American market; (3) projects aimed at achieving agricultural specialization for purposes of adequate regional supply; (4) projects seeking to readjust given industries that have been adversely affected by the common market; and (5) any other activities closely connected with economic integration.

The CABEI's initial capital was subscribed by the governments in an amount equivalent to $4 million each. Half of the stipulated sum has been paid in each case, and the remainder is subject to call and may be increased by unanimous consent of the assembly of the board of governors. With Costa Rica's recent decision to join, the subscribed capital was increased to a total of $20 million. The institution will not earn interest, and its profits from fees and commissions will be devoted to constituting a capital reserve. Capital contributions are to be freely convertible, and the member governments are obliged to maintain the dollar value of local-currency holdings representing such contributions.

[14] See ECLA, *Possibilities of Integrated Industrial Development in Central America* (New York: United Nations, 1963; 63.II.G.10).

The bank is empowered to obtain loans and credit lines in any capital market and to accept funds deriving from any legal transaction. In mid-1963 the bank obtained a $5 million loan from the U.S. Government, through AID, and another $6 million from the Inter-American Development Bank, with both amounts being set aside for financing projects of regional interest. As of the same date, AID had also approved $2 million for loan operations and a further $1 million for basic research on Central American economic integration. The CABEI granted its first credit in December of 1961 and by June, 1963, had granted loans totaling $11 million, mostly for industrial development.[15]

With a view to unifying national industrial promotion laws, the member governments, in July, 1960, signed the Central American Agreement on Fiscal Incentives for Industrial Development. This instrument establishes a common base for company classification and the granting of tax concessions, and is to be applied to the creation or expansion of manufacturing industries that effectively contribute to Central American economic development. These are defined to include plants that produce goods necessary to the development of other productive activities, satisfy certain basic needs of the population, substitute for commodities presently imported in substantial amounts, or increase the export trade. With respect to assembly operations, the agreement provides that the contracting parties shall subscribe an additional protocol establishing the applicable fiscal incentives and, moreover, setting up procedures to be followed in the trade of assembled products in the common market. Intended for selective application, the agreement provides the greatest benefits for those industries of strategic importance to the region's industrial and economic development. Thus, for example (simply by virtue of being classifiable as such), industries producing goods and raw materials will receive the maximum concessions. The amount and periods fixed for benefits available to the remaining industries are established in a graduated scale that takes into account the use or nonuse of Central American raw materials, net benefits that may be expected to accrue to the balance of payments, and other elegibility factors.

The agreement on fiscal incentives is to be administered in each country by appropriate government authorities. In addition, a series of provisions were adopted for coordination at the Central American level, with a view to achieving complete "regionalization" of the application of fiscal incentives within a maximum period of seven years.

Benefits granted under the agreement include exemption from cus-

[15] See Banco Centroamericano de Integración Económica, *Segunda Memoria de Labores Año 1962–1963* (Tegucigalpa, Honduras, 1964), p. 18.

toms duties and similar charges on the importation of machinery and equipment, semiprocessed goods, containers, and fuel for industrial use, and exemption from taxes on income, profits, assets, and net worth. Exemptions vary in duration from three to ten years, depending on the beneficiary firm's classification.

The agreement on the Regime of the Central American Integration Industries, mentioned earlier, pursues the broad objective of promoting the establishment of regional-scale industries on an economic basis and avoiding the waste of scarce resources, while attempting, at the same time, to achieve an adequate balance from country to country as regards industrial location. The provisions of this agreement were adopted by the General Treaty for Central American Economic Integration and went into effect at the same time (June, 1961).

The so-called integration industries that are eligible under the agreement are defined as those comprising one or more plants that require access to the whole Central American market in order to operate under reasonably economic and competitive conditions even at minimum capacity. The products of plants designated as integration industries will enjoy free trade for a period of ten years; while those of plants not so designated would be granted annual customs-duty reductions of 10 per cent, beginning with the entry into operation of the first plant enjoying the benefits of the agreement.[16] The agreement also extends to integration enterprises the privileges and exemptions granted under the agreement on fiscal incentives.

The actual designation is to be made by special protocols for each industry, which will stipulate the minimum capacity and the location of the plants, as well as quality standards for the products; minimum-supply guarantee; and certain other conditions that will govern establishment and operation of the industries. January, 1963, marked the application of the first of such protocols, in accordance with which a tire and tube factory, in Guatemala, and a combined plant for the production of caustic soda, chlorine, and chlorinated insecticides, in Nicaragua, were incorporated into the integration system.

The instruments described above were designed to supplement and reinforce the stimulus that the broadened market provides for industrial development. They seek further to facilitate the adaptation of existing industries to the new conditions of competition and to ensure that the new investments will conform to sound economic principles.

[16] Thus, for example, the products of a second plant that is not eligible under the system and is established in the third year that the "integration" plant is in operation would enjoy an immediate customs-duty reduction of 30 per cent, and would obtain total free-trade status within seven years.

In the past, when operating in very small domestic markets, tariff protection on occasion led to high earnings unaccompanied by any improvement whatsoever in productive efficiency. The added competition within the expanded market will tend to eliminate present situations of inefficiency in the Central American economy. However, it should be kept in mind that the common tariff, inspired by development criteria, may at the same time work in the opposite direction, by offering greater opportunity for lucrative operation, even though a part of the installed capacity is not put to use. Thus, there is the danger that anti-economic forms of growth in industry will be transferred from the national to the Central American plane, with the resultant waste of resources and absence of effective competition.

In these circumstances, given the very incomplete knowledge of existing industrial opportunities, during the first few years new investment encouraged by the expanded market will tend to concentrate on consumer-goods industries or on processes that entail only a small degree of manufacture. Hence the plants producing raw materials, intermediate goods, and capital goods will more than likely be relegated to second place. It is here where deliberate and closely coordinated action will be called for on the part of the integration agencies, in order to channel investment to the larger-scale activities, which, because of their better long-run prospects, are in a position to supply the impetus necessary to advance to new stages of development.

Finally, it should be pointed out that the regional market is not large enough to support certain types of industrial activity for which local supply conditions are highly favorable. A case in point is the pulp and paper industry, for which ample forest resources are available in the region. For this reason, and owing to the fact that Central America suffers from a shortage of savings and technical skills, attention should be given the possibility of complementing the Central American market with that of other countries—particularly with that of the LAFTA group—in the case of certain industrial products, and of concluding agreements covering investments and transfers of technological know-how, as may be deemed desirable for the region's industrialization.

Coordinating development. In other areas of the integration effort, the work of the Central American Economic Cooperation Committee, mentioned earlier, has progressed to the stage of concrete accomplishments that constitute the first step in the direction of joint planning of the Isthmus' economies.

In this connection, mention should be made of the governments' recent decision to carry out a regional highway program by incorporating it within their national development plans and setting up a work schedule for the different parts of that program.[17] It forms a part of the Central American Highway Plan, which has been in the making since 1953, with a view to providing communication between the most important production and consumption centers throughout the region.

Work on the electrification program has been centered on a study of the possibilities for two or more countries to interconnect their power systems and undertake the combined development of hydraulic resources. An initial concrete result of the study project has been the approval, in principle, by the interested official agencies of the interconnection of the electrical systems of Honduras and El Salvador. Thorough feasibility studies are already under way in connection with this project, and a definitive decision has been taken. In comparison with the cost of independently developing each of the systems, this joint enterprise is expected to effect a net savings in investment of almost $30 million for the two countries.[18] A study is also being made of the possibility of interconnecting the Costa Rican and Nicaraguan electric-power systems, as well as those serving the border areas of Chiriquí, in Panama, and Golfito, in Costa Rica.

Currently in progress in the field of agriculture is a program to stabilize prices of basic foodstuffs (corn, rice, and beans), which includes coordinating the production and supply of these commodities and rationalizing their trade in the area. This program entails the construction of a regional network of silos and other installations for grain storage and preservation, and the constitution of sufficient working capital to finance the accumulation of reserve stocks against future contingencies.

Coordinated efforts are also being put forth in connection with a Central American cadastre, and studies have been undertaken concerning the installation of a Central American telecommunications network.

Concerted action in the different fields culminated, in 1962, with the decision by the Central American governments to coordinate the preparation of their national plans, with a view to the eventual formulation of an over-all regional plan. In addition to the other regional institutions, a Joint Mission for Central American Planning will assist in this project.[19] Having begun its advisory assignments in 1963, the

17 See *Informe de la Reunión de Ministros de Economía y de Obras Públicas de Centroamérica* (Guatemala, September 1, 1963; SIECA/NEOP-I/1).

18 See *Informe de la Segunda Reunión del Subcomité Centroamericano de Electrificación* (E/CN.12/CCE/306), June 18, 1963.

19 The mission comprises eighteen experts in the various planning fields who were appointed by the United Nations, the Inter-American Development Bank, the Organization of American States, SIECA, and the Central American Bank for Economic Integration.

mission works with the planning agencies in the five countries in connection with the preparation of national development plans for the period 1965–69 and their integration at the regional level.

Conclusion

The brief discussion contained in the preceding sections of this essay points up the fact that the Central American Integration Program has passed the formative stage. Free trade is clearing the way for the expansion of productive activity, which is also encouraged by a common tariff based on development criteria. In addition to the executive agencies created in connection with the functioning of the General Treaty, Central America has other regional institutions operating in the fields of finance and industrial technology. Other favorable factors include the prospect of intensive public investment in the immediate future and a greater availability of external sources of financing than has previously been the case.

All this would indicate the possibility of utilizing integration instruments to diversify economic activity as a means of offsetting the deteriorating influence of the external sector since the mid-1950's. Such compensatory action, however, would be only partially effective, since the structural factors responsible for Central America's slow rate of growth cannot be modified in the short run. It is therefore necessary to devise a more vigorous common-trade policy and to fortify the external sector by seeking economic ties with other countries or groups of countries. The present paper made no attempt to analyze this aspect, which was taken up for the first time at the most recent meeting of the Central American Economic Cooperation Committee.[20]

[20] For a preliminary discussion of this problem, see ECLA, *General Situation and Future Outlook of the Central American Integration Programme* (E/CN.12/666; May, 1963), pp. 10–12 and 24–30.

XVIII

JOSEPH C. MILLS*

Problems of Central American Industrialization

The Industrial Scene in Central America

Central America has a limited industrial market even when viewed on a regional basis. The combined population of the five countries was estimated at 12 million as of 1963; but in the view of one observer, the effective market is well under 30 per cent of that total.[1] Hence, although the region has one of the highest rates of population growth in the world (3.4 per cent annually from 1950 to 1960), the market will continue to be limited in size in industrial terms for many years to come. Dualism exists in the form of low productivity and poverty in the agricultural sector, illustrated by the fact that, in 1960, almost 65 per cent of the regional labor force was employed in agriculture, but produced less than half of the gross national product.

Where per capita income is concerned, Central America compares not unfavorably with other developing areas. At $250 a year in 1960, the regional level is two-thirds that for Latin America, but well above the Asian and African averages. The Central American figure, of

* The author, formerly with the Mexico City office of the Economic Commission for Latin America, is now with the United Nations Economic Commission for Africa. This article expresses his personal views.

[1] See Miguel S. Wionczek, "The Montevideo Treaty and Latin American Integration," *Quarterly Review* of the Banco Nazionale del Lavoro, June, 1961, p. 204 n.

course, does not disclose the wide intercountry disparities that are a further stumbling block of industrialization. The smallest nation in terms of population, Costa Rica, has a per capita income almost 60 per cent higher than the regional average.

Uneven distribution of income characterizes all five economies. The gravity of the situation is well illustrated in the words of a recent U.N. report:

> Indeed, the present distribution of income in the Central American countries constitutes what is perhaps one of the main obstacles to rapid industrialization of their economies, and to real integration. Being concentrated in certain sectors, and otherwise spread thinly as a result of the low income situation, the market available for manufactured goods is small and does not tend to grow with the same vigor as the economic system in general. The situation thus amounts to the existence of a sector with an income so high that any increases are spent on foreign goods instead of on goods manufactured in the region, while the remaining sector, consisting of the population as a whole, has so little income that its demand does not constitute an active factor, and is concentrated mainly on essential consumer goods.[2]

Central America at present is in a relatively favorable position, as compared with other underdeveloped areas, insofar as concerns possibilities for import substitution. Imports per capita amounted in 1960 to $47.50, indicating considerable possibilities in the hypothetical case where all foreign-exchange receipts were devoted to imports of machinery, equipment, and other goods directly facilitating economic growth. This level compares very well with the actual imports of India of $4.50 per capita and that of Africa of $29.[3] Import substitution, then, has a relatively high potential in Central America.

But the region has made little progress in recent years in altering the import coefficient.

> The expansion of the manufacturing sector observable during the fifties was not accompanied by any very substantial changes in the structure of production. Traditional manufactures, which in 1950 represented 80 per cent of the total product of the sector, still absorbed 77 per cent in 1960. This, in turn, has a bearing on the further circumstance that no signifi-

[2] ECLA, *General Situation and Future Outlook of the Central American Integration Program* (E/CN. 12/666; May, 1963), p. 8.

[3] The Central American estimate is based on population and import data found in the *Statistical Supplement to the Economic Bulletin for Latin America*, VII, No. 1. Data on Africa and India are from ECA, *Industrial Growth in Africa* (Addis Ababa: E/CN. 14/INR/1; December, 1962), p. 37.

cant progress was made in that period in the over-all import substitution process. The proportion of the total supply of manufactured goods represented by domestic production remained the same—about 63 per cent.[4]

In point of industrial resources, the Central American countries unfortunately do not possess either coal or oil, two of the common foundation stones of an industrial economy. Mining, once important, is no longer so; and mineral output forms only a small proportion of regional gross product. Certain industrial mineral deposits such as iron ore, copper, bauxite, etc., are known to exist, but in the main are not exploited. Agriculturally, a condition of self-sufficiency in staple foodstuffs a decade ago changed to one of shortage in more recent years. However, a reasonable increase in productivity should result in a regional surplus in all major food supplies within a few years. No adequate survey of the industrial raw materials of the five countries exists. It is evident, however, that the lack of certain readily exploitable industrial resources will undoubtedly influence the course of industrialization in this area.

Nor can Central America be said to be well endowed with industrial "growing points." Typical in the region are the usual small-sized consumer-goods manufactures usually found in the early stage of industrial growth, i.e., beer and soft drinks, bakery and dairy products, flour, cigarettes, leather footwear and tannery products, matches, soap and candles, etc. There are also a number of plants that supply national markets with various building materials, such as cement, lumber, and clay products. Really specialized production plants, such as the Guatemalan tire factory, which produces on a large scale for the regional economy, are very few in number. Hence, the area lacks both strategic industries and plants where economies of scale can readily be achieved. Labor-intensive techniques are widely used, as might be expected in the absence of large-scale operations, with, of course, adverse effects on the price levels. As a U.S. report has stated: "Since 'economies of scale' (i.e. cost advantages of large-scale production and marketing) are rarely achieved under circumstances governing most manufacturing activities in Central America, and production costs, especially capital costs, are high, there has been a tendency for prices of domestically produced items to approximate the high prices of competitive imports." [5]

[4] *General Situation* . . . , p. 31.

[5] Joseph Pincus, *The Central American Common Market* (Guatemala City: Regional Office for Central American and Panama Affairs, Agency for International Development, 1962), p. 18.

The entrepreneurial climate in Central America is difficult to assess, if only for lack of data. ECLA studies of the region are singularly reticent on the subject. The concentration of income in a relatively few hands suggests that the entrepreneurial group is a small one. (For example, a 1953 study by a U.N. technical assistance mission showed that as of three years previously, fewer than 8 per cent of the families of El Salvador were the recipients of more than half the national income.)

Entrepreneurs have been active, since private capital formation appears to have increased steadily in each country over the last decade, despite the fact that recent years have been somewhat unfavorable in terms of the general level of economic activity.[6] As one observer has stated: "Up to now, the entrepreneurial group has been small and the bulk of domestic private investment has been made by wealthy landholders who have selected the most promising and least risky situations in their respective countries usually for small-scale investments, while the bulk of their liquid funds has been invested or deposited abroad." [7]

The infrastructure in Central America cannot be termed impressive, either in quantity or quality, viewed in the context of probable industrial growth. Power facilities are reasonably adequate for the present, although, with almost half of the capacity being thermal power, rates vary sharply from country to country; e.g., they are several times as high in Honduras as in Costa Rica. All-weather-road mileage has sharply increased in recent years (8 per cent annually from 1952 to 1961) and now totals 21,000 kilometers. "Railway, inland waterway and coastal transport have lagged behind, and the development of the corresponding networks, equipment and operations has remained stationary. The railways have not enlarged their networks, nor have they renewed their equipment for more than ten years." [8] The economic infrastructure situation in Central America today may be summed up as follows: A basic system exists, but is oriented toward each country rather than the region; improvements in some, but not all, types of facilities are under way; and large expenditures are necessary if accelerated industrialization is to occur.

The Central American economies are characterized by heavy dependence on a few commodity exports. One commodity alone, coffee, accounted in 1960 for more than half the total value of exports; while two more, bananas and cotton, contributed another 23 per cent. Evi-

[6] See the previously cited issue of the *Statistical Supplement,* Table 10. Figures are given only for Costa Rica, Guatemala, and Honduras.

[7] Pincus, *op. cit.* p. 22.

[8] *General Situation* . . . , p. 40.

dently, the danger exists that industrialization could take place in such way as to cause adverse effects on these vital earners of foreign exchange. Similarly, the region is a good example of an underdeveloped area in which agriculture is the dominant economic activity and employs some two-thirds of the labor force. As usual, wide disparities existed among the five countries. In 1950, the concentration of the labor force in agriculture was highest in Honduras (84 per cent) and lowest in Costa Rica (55 per cent). Agriculture also led all sectors in contribution to national income, at 46 per cent for Central America as a whole, with the next largest contributor, manufacturing, accounting for only 16 per cent.[9] Later years are unlikely to have drastically altered this picture.

Within the industrial sector of the region, textiles constitute the most important single category in terms of value of production and employment. The textile industry, particularly cotton, was one of the first to be established in each country. Viewed on an area basis, some parts of the industry are quite modern and efficient, while others are the reverse. This may be the reason why cotton textile plants in the region currently supply less than 60 per cent of total domestic consumption, despite both the presence of raw cotton and a climate that favors use of this textile. Here, then, is what seems to be a clear example of a basic industry where additional resources would bring quick and impressive results in terms of lower production costs and reduced consumer prices. At the same time, however, even a highly efficient textile industry would not be likely to advance an industrial-development program to a marked extent.

One can only speculate that industrialists in the area entertain fears and suspicions regarding national and regional plans for industrialization, although it is impossible to determine just how deep-seated and widely held these beliefs are. One observer has stated: "Many Central American businessmen have had considerable misgivings concerning the benefits which might accrue from the integration program. . . . One of the missing elements in planning the integration program has been an analysis of the sectors of potential injury, the alternatives available to the injured concerns, and the financial resources that would be required for dealing with such cases." [10]

Until very recently, manufacturing has been very much oriented toward national markets, as demonstrated by the fact that, in 1950, intra-Central American trade represented less than 3 per cent of all the foreign trade of these countries. By 1963, the proportion had in-

[9] U.S. Department of Commerce, *Investment in Central America* (Washington, D.C.: Government Printing Office, 1956), p. 14.

[10] Pincus, *op. cit.*, p. 105.

creased to 12 per cent. The new trade openings within the region should have helped to allay the fears of established industrialists regarding changes in the embryo stage of industrial development now existing in Central America.

Central America cannot be regarded as a wealthy area in terms of available financial resources. It is noteworthy, however, that over the last decade the five countries have, on the average, managed to maintain a yearly gross capital formation approximating 15 per cent of gross national product—quite a respectable level in comparison either with Latin America as a whole or with the industrial nations.[11] Duplication of investment appears to be a prominent feature in the area. "Manufacturing in Central America consists largely of processing local agricultural products, together with imported raw materials, into consumer goods. Since the local agricultural products for the most part are similar in all five Central American States, their industries tend to be similar to one another." [12]

Overcoming the Obstacles to Industrialization

> The Central American Economic Integration Program is essentially a concerted international effort aimed at the removal of the main obstacles which prevent the accelerated economic development of five separate tiny countries which are largely dependent for their growth on stimuli received from the world economy. At the same time, it is an effort to achieve the maximum rate of economic growth compatible with their resources by putting the latter to the best possible use and securing the greatest yield from investments. . . . Given their limited capital resources and the slow rate of capital formation, it is essential to coordinate investments and achieve a degree of specialization and division of labour in the five countries. . . .[13]

The integration program has, of course, many aspects and is, indeed, global in nature, dealing with the use of resources in very different fields of activity.[14] For our purposes, we may properly concentrate on the industrialization measures that are designed to overcome, to the greatest extent possible, the industrial growth problems existing in

11 *Statistical Supplement*, VII, No. 1, Table 7.

12 Pincus, *op. cit.*, p. 32.

13 ECLA, "Central American Economic Integration Program: Evaluation and Prospects," *Economic Bulletin for Latin America*, IV, No. 2 (October, 1959), p. 33.

14 For a broader analysis of the economic implications of the integration program, particularly in terms of economic theory, see J. C. Mills, "La política de desarrollo y los convenios regionales de comercio: el caso de la América Latina," *El Trimestre Económico*, XXX, No. 119 (July–September, 1963), 382–96.

the region. At the same time, we must note briefly other activities that form a part of the integration program, such as the evolution of the free-trade area, tariff equalization, electrification, transport, etc., which have relevance to industrialization.

The planning stage of the Central American Economic Integration Program began in mid-1952, but, operationally, different parts of the program have proceeded at varying speeds. The free-trade area, for example, has evolved at a much more rapid pace than has industrialization. A considerable number of treaties with regional impact are in existence in Central America, but the basic one is the General Treaty for Central American Economic Integration, signed in Managua in December, 1960. This document, its protocols, and the collateral agreements or treaties on industry, tariffs, and the regional integration bank form the basis of the integration program.[15] The accession of Costa Rica in July, 1962, completed the coverage of the economic integration instruments.

The industrial treaty, known as the Central American Integration Industries Regime, gives encouragement and assistance to "integration plants," defined as those whose minimum economic size requires access to the regional market, rather than to any single national market. The integration plant (or plants, if transport charges are such as to make more than one advisable) will have free access to the Central American market for a period of ten years. Any national competitior attempting to sell regionally faces the tariffs existing in the five countries, while the integration plant sells on a tariff-free basis. The privilege is a decreasing one, since the tariffs faced by the competitor attempting to sell regionally faces the tariffs existing in the tenth year, the nonintegration plant enjoys full access to the free-trade area. Other benefits of integration status include tax incentives, and the right of free import of machinery, equipment, and raw materials, together with tariff protection against competition from outside the common market.

In turn, the treaty provides for the signing of a protocol between the integration plant and the five member countries, whereby the public interest is safeguarded in such matters as sufficient minimum capacity and provisions for expansion to meet future demand, location, quality standards, maximum prices, and so on. The philosophy behind the integration-industry concept is perhaps best described by the following quotation from an ECLA study: "While private enterprise will no doubt have to bear the main responsibility for industrial

[15] The text of the Managua Treaty and the related agreements on industry, etc., are to be found in *Multilateral Economic Cooperation in Latin America, I: Texts and Documents.*

growth, the Central American governments have taken the initiative of pointing out the sectors in which development requires the establishment of new plants and maintain, through a specific agreement, the right of coordination and general supervision in some essential sectors."[16]

Operation of the industrialization agreement from 1961 to 1963 has brought clarification and some modification of the original intent as stated in the Treaty. Early in 1963, the Executive Committee of the Central American Common Market met to specify in greater detail the privileges of integrated status outlined above. The minimum size of plant must be in excess of the needs of any single member's market. The arrangements for privileges and obligations are as described in the legislation, but the protocols will henceforth include such matters as the dates on which incorporation, construction, and production are to commence. Moreover, provision is made for offering a substantial, and preferably controlling, interest in the project to Central American investors. Integration status was accorded at the 1963 meeting to a caustic soda and insecticide plant to be established in Nicaragua, and to a rubber tire and tube factory already operating in Guatemala. Since the treaty provides for awarding one integration plant to each member country before any member receives two or more such industries, the privileged status will no doubt shortly be bestowed on projects in Costa Rica, El Salvador, and Honduras. ECLA, in recent years, has completed studies on a wide variety of possible integration industries, including oil refining, plate glass, glass containers, electric lamp bulbs, iron and steel, viscose and acetate for rayon, fertilizers, pharmaceutical products, paints and varnishes, steel pipe, pulp and paper, etc. However, the integration plants of the future need not necessarily come from among these industries; much depends on the initiative of the private sector.

The Executive Committee also adopted a new course of action not specifically referred to in the industrial treaty, namely a system to encourage new industries that do not qualify for integrated status. This will consist principally of a protective external tariff to become effective as soon as local production covers at least half the Central American demand. Since such tariffs were placed on window glass, lamp bulbs, and glass bottles and containers—three industries long thought to be likely candidates for integration status—it may well be that, in future years, there will be less emphasis on integration plants and more on industrialization via tariff protection alone.

Simultaneously, the regional economic-integration program has

[16] ECLA, *Central American Economic Integration and Development* (Santiago, 1961; E/CN. 12/586), p. 2.

been making rapid strides in other respects bearing on industrial growth. The common market is in operation, with all but a small number of "sensitive" products enjoying full free trade within the area. A common external tariff now applies to almost all of the region's imports. As part of the coordinated over-all approach to regional industrial-development problems, the five Central nations have agreed to standardize existing national legislation on tax exemptions and similar incentives to new industry. Since 1957, studies have been under way, through U.N. technical assistance, concerning the possibilities for specialized production of textiles. A Central American Industrial Initiatives Commission has been created with the aim of securing increased participation of private enterprise in the integration program. In 1962, a regional federation of industrial chambers of commerce came into being. An able, well-staffed secretariat for the integration program has been established, with headquarters in Guatemala City.

The Central American Institute for Industrial Research has been in operation for a number of years, performing market analysis and technological research for both government and private industry. Central American Bank for Economic Integration is active in financing both industries and infrastructural projects of a regional nature. In electrification, the main drive is toward the interconnection of existing hydroelectric systems, leading eventually to a regional grid. In transportation, as has been previously noted, substantial additions have been made to the national highways of regional interest, with rather less progress in maritime transport and ports and railways. Finally, in agriculture, where a considerable degree of specialization already exists, efforts are being made at the regional level to intensify specialization and increase output, so that the area may regain self-sufficiency in agricultural commodities.

All of the foregoing activity on the part of the Central American Common Market countries, assisted by ECLA, has not been accomplished without considerable controversy. This has tended to center on the question of whether the Central American Integration Industries Regime actually contributes to progress toward regional economic integration. Opponents of the regime are to be found both inside and outside of Central America. The industrial treaty itself is criticized as being uncertain and difficult to interpret, causing private enterprise, particularly from abroad, to be reluctant to invest. It is claimed that industrial concerns cannot be certain that one among them will not be designated as an integration plant to the detriment of all its competitors. From another point of view, integration status involves the reimposition of tariffs, thus restricting the free movement of goods and capital, which economic integration is designed to accomplish.

It is further argued that the regime is quite unnecessary, in that some of its basic objectives—such as attracting new industry, balanced industrial growth on a geographical basis, and avoiding duplication of investment—can be better secured by other means. For example, as mentioned earlier, an agreement exists among the five countries for the equalization of fiscal incentives. The Central American Bank for Economic Integration, by providing advantageous financing, could influence the geographical location of industries and, at the same time, look to the public safeguards, such as minimum capacity, quality standards, now contained in the protocols to the Regime of the Central American Integration Industries. As to the possibility of the waste of resources through duplication of investment, opponents of the regime contend that private enterprise is not likely to be so foolish as to establish economically unfeasible plants. But the most widely held objection relates to the monopoly provision of the industrial treaty. In this respect, antagonists put forward all of the standard arguments to be found in economics textbooks and maintain that the monopoly clause is both undesirable and unnecessary.

The Future

The Central American Economic Integration Program, from the industrial point of view, appears to be basically an attempt to overcome the obstacles to industrialization by emphasizing a type of development that will achieve the economies of larger scale production. As one U.N. study points out: "If the economies of scale to be expected from integration are important anywhere in the world, they must be important in Central America."[17] The common market as a means of widening the industrial market area, integration plants as growing points, and so on, are all obviously aimed at attacking the general problems of industrialization as these problems apply in greater or lesser degree in Central America.

Where the controversy as to the desirability of the industrial regime itself is concerned, there are limited indications that at least the monopoly clause is being modified in actual operation. However, the concept of exclusive rights to the regional market is a basic feature of the integration program, and it is much too soon to hazard any guess as to its future role.

The Alliance for Progress should undoubtedly prove of assistance to

[17] ECA, *The Significance of Recent Common Market Developments in Latin America* (Addis Ababa, 1960; E/CN. 14/64), p. 58.

the Central American countries in their drive toward economic integration. The Punta del Este meeting of August, 1961, commended Latin America's efforts in this respect, as represented by the Latin American Free Trade Area and the Central American Common Market. United States moral and financial support was emphasized by the late President Kennedy in his meetings in San José, Costa Rica, in March, 1963, with the presidents of Central American nations and Panama.

It appears unlikely that the members of the Central American Common Market will be in any haste, either individually or as a unit, to join the much larger LAFTA. The five nations have indicated that they may do so in time, but only as a single entity. Meanwhile, there are numerous problems connected with the regional integration program, which require solution before consideration can be given to membership in an all-Latin American trading bloc. More probable is the expansion of the Central American Common Market itself, possibly to include Panama and/or the creation of links with some Caribbean trade scheme.

While progress to date under the industrial regime may appear slow (e.g., there are only a few integration plants to date), new industrial projects are being attracted to the area in steadily increasing numbers, thus serving one of the basic objectives of that regime. An incomplete list shows the following industries built in the early 1960's: El Salvador—business forms and equipment, margarine and detergents, plastics, toothpaste, shirts, motorcycle assembly; Costa Rica—chemical fertilizers, refrigerators and washing machines, concrete products; Nicaragua—powdered milk, caustic soda and insecticides, flour milling; Guatemala—rubber tires, electrical equipment, ladies clothing; Honduras—pineapple canning and packing, plywood. Such a list could not have been compiled a few years earlier and, significantly, contains various examples of larger-scale industries. Similarly, trade among common market members is increasing rapidly and, in 1963, amounted to $68 million, or more than six times the 1950 level.

The future will surely see changes in emphasis within the integration program. Removal of tariff barriers and creation of a common external tariff nears completion. In the immediate future, it would be logical to emphasize implementation of the industrial regime, as is, or as amended. In similar fashion, substantial investments will be needed in the regional infrastructure, with funds probably being obtained from the Alliance for Progress. In time, perhaps, less attention will be placed on a balanced geographical distribution of industrial growth. In this event, Guatemala, El Salvador, and Costa Rica, given the greater advantages they offer new industries as compared to Honduras and Nicaragua, will obtain the lion's share of new investment. Much of the progress in industrialization will depend on the state of world commodity markets, on which these countries will continue to rely heavily for a long time to come.

In summary, few will deny that the economic integration program is a step in the right direction—in fact, a giant step in terms of its potential effects on the countries concerned. There may be serious differences of opinion as to the techniques used, particularly in promoting industry, but in some cases, at any rate, the differences concern emphasis rather than the fundamental aspects. Central Americans have reason to be proud of their regional integration program as one means of overcoming, at least in part, the obstacles to industrialization in the area.

XIX

JORGE GONZÁLEZ DEL VALLE

The Intra-Central American Payments System and Trade

Although, in a strictly formal sense, there was a ten-year lag between the initiation of the Central American Economic Integration Program and the establishment of an intraregional payments mechanism, in actual fact the preliminary stages of Central American monetary integration followed almost immediately on the early development of the common market.

It is generally conceded today that it was not until the beginning of 1961 that real impetus was given to the creation of the Central American Common Market, by the implementation of the treaties signed in Managua in December, 1960. For their part, the five central banks in the region, in July of 1961, undertook to create a multilateral clearing system, whose structure and evolution form the central theme of the present essay. It should be remembered, however, that what is regarded as the "accelerated stage" of Central American economic integration began to take shape as early as the year 1958.

Between 1951 (which marked the formal initiation of the integration endeavor) and 1958, inter-Central American commerce increased at an accumulative annual rate of 10 per cent on the average. From 1958 on, the Central American countries have expanded their trade dealings with one another by an average 25 per cent yearly. The evolution of concrete mechanisms for monetary integration purposes has been considerably slower, although as far back as 1953 the Central American central banks had considered setting up multilateral clearing arrangements. At the present time, the far-reaching effects of a progressively improved common market and the accelerated development of other economic-integration instruments are exerting pressure in the direction of more rapid and decisive progress in the monetary field.

The General Treaty for Central American Economic Integration—the master plan in current application to bring about the region's economic union—does not definitively spell out the monetary and financial objectives of the integration program. The treaty's sole reference to this matter is contained in Article 10, which recommends that the central banks cooperate "so as to prevent monetary speculation that can adversely affect exchange rates, and to maintain convertibility of the respective countries' currencies, on a basis that will, within a system of normalcy, guarantee exchange freedom, uniformity and stability."

This policy definition is incomplete, to say the least, and probably somewhat less fundamental than its authors believed back in 1960. Generally speaking, the Central American exchange experience has been highly satisfactory in the last two or three decades. For many years, the currencies that figure most importantly in the region's foreign trade have been freely convertible and quite stable. The occasional application of exchange restrictions has not seriously obstructed the development of intraregional trade. The central banks have cooperated closely in exchange matters, particularly since 1952, when they instituted the practice of holding periodic meetings for purposes of consultation and the exchange of information.

Prior to the establishment, in 1961, of the Central American Clearing House, relations between the central banks in the area evolved in slow but satisfactory fashion on the basis of bilateral agreements. This fact notwithstanding, the bulk of the commercial and financial dealings among the Central American countries were settled in U.S. dollars. Although it was customary to use local currencies in border trade, particularly as regards cash transactions, there was no concerted effort to take advantage of the benefits afforded by multilateral clearings. In contrast, at the present time, it is estimated that 90 per cent of the payments originating in intra-Central American commodity commerce are effected in the member countries' currencies.

From a strictly technical point of view, however, it would be a mistake to exaggerate the importance of the above-mentioned gains. Economic integration, especially insofar as the development of the common market is concerned, has given rise to numerous and complex financial problems that can be solved only by means of a more coherent and vigorous effort in the future in behalf of monetary integration. For example, there is a need for efficient mechanisms to encourage financing of intraregional trade, capital mobilization within the area, and the economic organization of the region's commerce with the rest of the world.

The coordination of domestic monetary policies as a prior requisite to Central American monetary union is very probably the most important objective in this field. The operation of the Central American Clearing House has been useful in promoting the exchange of ideas on the subject, and it has been possible to schedule desirable step-by-step progress in policy coordination for achievement in the near future. With all due regard for the importance of the multilateral clearing system, it is in the area of policy coordination where the results of Central American monetary and financial integration will make themselves most solidly and permanently felt. Monetary union as an ultimate aim of integration will not be feasible until all the still largely experimental stages of domestic-policy harmonization have been successfully completed.

Central American Clearing House

Although the idea of establishing a multilateral clearing system in Central America was conceived in 1953, difficulties of various types blocked realization of this project until 1960. Prompted by the accelerated stage of economic integration, the matter came up for reconsideration toward the end of that year (at the sixth meeting of Technicians of Central Banks of the American Continent, held in Guatamala City). After a series of negotiations at the technical level, the five Central American central banks eventually (in July, 1961) signed the agreement creating the Central American Clearing House.

The new agency began operations on October 1, 1961, with the participation of the central banks from Guatemala, El Salvador, and Honduras. The central bank of Nicaragua joined the Clearing House on May 1, 1962, while the Costa Rican central bank acquired membership on June 16, 1963.

The structure and operating principles of the Central American Clearing House are patterned after the well-known practices of the local clearing houses that function in practically every country of the world. In other words, mutual claims are settled multilaterally, through credit and debit entries, as the case may be, on the member banks' accounts, which together form a common fund. However, multilateral clearing among the Central American central banks involves the utilization of small automatic credits to reduce the need for too frequent recourse to cash settlement of outstanding balances.

This is particularly important because the international nature of the clearing arrangement makes it necessary for cash settlements to be made in foreign currency—in this case, U.S. dollars.

Clearing credits. From the beginning of its operations until December 31, 1963, the Central American Clearing House was financed by member-bank capital subscriptions amounting to the equivalent of $300,000 each. Twenty-five per cent of these subscriptions represented dollar contributions for use in constituting a Guaranty Fund, earmarked for settling whatever "excess" credit balances might be accumulated by members in a creditor position. The remaining 75 per cent made up the Current Operating Fund, comprising amounts paid in by each member institution in its own national currency.

Local-currency contributions to the Current Operating Fund represented the normal credit line that each member central bank agreed to make available to the others in the course of the Clearing House's regular operations. Any amount in excess of the automatic credit thus provided was immediately due and payable to the banks having a net balance in their favor following the multilateral clearing process. In practice, the Current Operating Fund constituted the central clearing mechanism, since the Guaranty Fund did not have to be used. By mutual agreement between the debtor and creditor banks, dollar settlements were made on a direct basis instead of having recourse to that fund.

As of January 1, 1964, a new Central American Clearing House agreement went into effect, which eliminated the capital subscriptions in favor of credit lines that each member central bank is committed to grant the others, jointly. These credit lines are equivalent to $500,000 per individual member, or a total of $2.5 million. Credits are extended solely in the respective local currency of each of the participating institutions. As in the case of the earlier mechanism, creditor banks may demand immediate payment in U.S. dollars of any "excess" lending (i.e., beyond the limits of the automatic $500,000 credit line).

The Central American Clearing House concentrates the individual accounts of its central bank members and makes debit or credit entries, respectively, corresponding to remittances received and remittances sent by each. These accounts also reflect the dollar settlements between debtor and creditor members resulting from loan grants in excess of the normal credit-line limits. Documents for clearing are exchanged directly between member central banks, and the clearing house bases its operations on the corresponding notices of remittance.

Exchange media eligible for clearing. In the terms of the Clearing House agreement, the following exchange media may enter the clearing process: bills and coins, bank drafts, personal checks, bills of exchange, and other types of payment deriving from commercial dealings. In practice, the Clearing House has found that approximately 75 per cent of the total value of settlements is taken up in bank drafts and personal checks. Although cash clearings still account for 20 per cent of the total, the increasing use of checks and drafts in Central American currencies is tending to limit the employment of paper money to the relatively modest border-trade transactions and tourism.

The existence of exchange controls in some of the Central American countries has made it necessary to impose certain requisites and restrictions on the clearance of drafts, checks, and cash. The Clearing House agreement provides, in a general way, for multilateral cooperation in this area; but the adoption and implementation of specific regulations has been accomplished by means of protocols that the member central banks subscribe to and revise as often as necessary. The most recent of these multilateral conventions was signed June 16, 1963, in San José, Costa Rica, and set up regulations for the clearance of drafts, checks, and cash in Guatemalan and Salvadoran currencies —the only two currencies in the region that were subject to exchange controls at that time.

In order to be eligible for clearance, checks and drafts in the Guatemalan and Salvadoran currencies are currently subject to certain validity requirements. The principal requisite, in this connection, is prior authorization by the respective exchange-control offices of all bank drafts and personal checks for amounts in excess of a given limit (at this writing, the equivalent of $200). Although documents that fail to comply with this requirement are ineligible for automatic clearing, they may nonetheless be accepted for collection. In all other respects the clearance of checks and drafts does not involve any very great delay, with the natural exception of uncertified personal checks that the honoring banks will customarily accept only with the normal collection reservation.

In the matter of cash clearance, the central banks of Guatemala and El Salvador have set up monthly quotas for the other members, limiting the amount of paper-money remittances that are acceptable for automatic conversion within the multilateral clearing process. This measure seeks to prevent speculative capital movements and to hold the volume of transactions in bills to a level in line with legitimate cash requirements. The establishment of the monthly quotas for each of the central banks has obliged them, in turn, to introduce concurrent restrictions in their respective banking systems.

It should be pointed out that, although remittances of documents eligible for clearance are effected directly between the member central banks, in practice the private commercial banks are the ones who negotiate with the public most of the exchange media that go through the regional Clearing House. To cover documents expressed in other Central American currencies and channeled through their local clearing houses, the private commercial banks ordinarily obtain a credit to their account with their respective central banks. Hence, the central banks, in their capacity as agents of the Central American Clearing House, centralize all exchange media eligible for clearance that have been negotiated by the domestic banking system in each case.

Exchange rates and unit of account. All the transactions handled by the Central American Clearing House are recorded and settled at fixed rates of exchange for the Central American currencies, based on the par value of each in terms of the U.S. dollar. The Clearing House agreement stipulates that each member bank must declare the rate of exchange of its local currency at the time of joining and prior to initiating clearing operations.

Although advance consultation on the part of member banks is not required in the event of a variation in their local currency-exchange rates, they must notify the Clearing House and the other members immediately of such action. The primary reason for this ruling is to enable an accurate valuation of the members' obligations to the Clearing House, with particular emphasis on a readjustment of the balance corresponding to the central banking institution whose national currency external value has been modified, so that its capital contribution to the agency will remain unchanged. Remittances in transit and cash on hand in the banking systems under the jurisdiction of the other central banks are subject to settlement at the rate of exchange filed with the Clearing House prior to the most recent rate change.

The Central American Clearing House has adopted its own unit of account for use in recording all transactions conducted in the currencies of the member central banks. This unit of account is called the "Central American peso" and has been assigned a par value equivalent to U.S. $1.[1] The "Central American peso" is significant only in an accounting sense since the exchange media eligible for clearance and the corresponding accounts carried by each of the member banks are expressed in the Central American countries' local currencies.

Apart from the exchange-rate stability characterizing Clearing House operations, the member central banks have given one another an unconditional guarantee of convertibility of debit balances that

[1] Hence, the official par value of the "Central American peso" is equivalent at present to: 1 Guatemalan quetzal, 2 Honduran lempiras, 2.5 Salvadoran colons, 6.625 Costa Rican colons, and 7 Nicaraguan córdobas.

may accumulate on their accounts with the Clearing House in excess of their local-currency capital contributions. The sole exception to this rule—and a relative one, at that—would stem from the restrictions mentioned earlier, applicable to the automatic clearing of exchange media expressed in currencies of countries that are currently imposing exchange controls. Automatic and unconditional convertibility into dollars would presumably not apply to those portions of balances chargeable to the central banks of Guatemala and El Salvador and representing checks or drafts that have not been authorized by the exchange-control authorities, or to remittances of paper money in excess of the stipulated monthly quotas.

Settlements and interest charges. For purposes of periodically reestablishing the original position of each member central bank and canceling the automatic credits provided for in the system, the Clearing House agreement makes it compulsory for regular accounts to be settled twice yearly. According to present practice, the settlement dates are June 15 and December 15. Debtor banks are given a period of one week in which to effect payment in U.S. dollars of any outstanding balances chargeable to their account.

As indicated earlier, the automatic credits are so small in comparison with the total clearance volume that "extraordinary" settlements to cancel excess credits are actually more frequent and important than the ordinary semiannual settlements. In effect, the central banks have raised no objection to the Clearing House practice of making a weekly calculation of the debtor or creditor position of each member in order to determine the excess credit balances payable immediately in dollars. In most instances, these extraordinary weekly settlements occasion direct payments by debtor to creditor institutions in the manner outlined before.

In accordance with the Central American Clearing House agreement, all balances resulting from the multilateral clearances earn interest, which the debtor central banks are required to pay to the creditors. The applicable interest rate is set periodically by the Clearing House Board of Directors, which ordinarily takes into consideration various internal, as well as external, factors, including the international market rate on short-term dollar investments. The interest presently chargeable on Clearing House operations amounts to 3.5 per cent per annum.

Multilateral Clearance Experience

Notwithstanding the fact that the Central American Clearing House has been in operation for only slightly more than four years, the experience accumulated to date has been very valuable for the central banks in the region. In terms of volume, as well as direction and composition, the transactions cleared through the regional agency have given evidence of a dynamic process at work within the framework of Central American economic integration.

In the twenty-seven months from October 1, 1961, to December 31, 1963, the total clearance volume handled by the Clearing House reached the equivalent of $78.7 million. Average monthly clearings expanded gradually from $1.8 million during the first six months of 1962 to $5 million in the last half of 1963. In the calendar year 1962, clearings totaled the equivalent of $24.6 million, compared to $50.7 million in 1963.

In evaluating the significance of the foregoing figures, one should keep in mind that, despite the intensification of the integration process, the level of intra-Central American commerce is still relatively low and accounts for only 10 per cent to 12 per cent of the total value of the region's foreign trade as a whole (thus testifying to the limited degree of complementary functioning of the Central American domestic economies).[2] The importance of the multilateral clearance operations can best be gauged by comparing the rate of growth in intra-Central American trade between 1961 and 1963 (approximately 62 per cent) with the fact that clearings during the same period doubled in value.

An appraisal of Central America's experience with multilateral clearing may be focused on three fundamental aspects: (1) the degree to which the settlement pattern reflects the structure of intra-Central American trade; (2) the influence of exchange restrictions on the direction of multilateral clearances; and (3) the quantitative importance of the "self-liquidating" factors implicit in the multilateral payments system.

Trade and payments pattern. As mentioned earlier, the accelerated formation of the common market has had a direct impact on the growth of inter-Central American trade. In the five-year period from 1953 to 1957, regional interchange increased by 60 per cent in value terms, compared to an over-all expansion from 1958 to 1962 amounting to almost 140 per cent. However, the intra-Central American trade pattern has remained practically unchanged with respect to concentration of commerce in certain of the countries in the area.

It is estimated that the value of the import and export trade of Guatemala, El Salvador, and Honduras together represent approximately 90 per cent of the total intra-Central American trade. However, Nica-

[2] Intra-Central American trade was estimated at $50.4 million in 1962, and $68.0 million in 1963.

raguan and Costa Rican participation in regional interchange has increased gradually in the last ten years. Guatemala and Honduras, at present, have a favorable regional-trade position, while El Salvador and Nicaragua are showing a deficit, and Costa Rica's intraregional commercial situation is one of relative balance.

The multilateral clearing system appears to have adapted itself quite well to the structure of intra-Central American commerce. In 1963, 90 per cent of total exchange media for clearing by the Central American Clearing House corresponded to Guatemala, El Salvador, and Honduras. Except for Guatemala, each country's clearings closely parallel its balance on intraregional trade account.

Table 1 compares total trade transactions and Clearing House settlements during the first six months of 1963:

TABLE 1
TOTAL VALUE OF INTER-CENTRAL AMERICAN TRADE AND PAYMENTS
JANUARY–JUNE, 1963[a]
(In Millions of Dollars)

	Guatemala	El Salvador	Honduras	Nicaragua
Exports	8.1	7.9	5.8	1.6
Imports	−4.1	−13.1	−3.8	−2.4
Balance	4.0	−5.2	2.0	−0.8
Settlement credit	5.8	7.7	6.4	0.9
Settlement debit	−7.7	−8.5	−2.7	−1.9
Balance	−1.9	−0.8	+3.7	−1.0

Sources: SIECA, *Carta Informativa*, October, 1963; and the Central American Clearing House.

[a] Exclusive of Costa Rica, whose central bank joined the Clearing House in June of 1963.

Despite the fact that the pattern of multilateral clearings closely follows the composition of trade between the countries in the area, it should be pointed out that the amount and direction of intra-Central American payments were influenced, in 1962, by abnormal factors deriving from the exchange restrictions in effect in El Salvador, Guatemala, and Nicaragua.[3] Exchange controls directly encourage greater utilization of local currency in meeting payments in other common-market countries, owing to restrictions placed on the substitution of local currency for the dollar. This explains why, in the year 1962, debit clearings chargeable to Guatemala and El Salvador jointly repre-

[3] Clearing House settlements in quetzals and Salvadoran colons jointly represented almost 85 per cent of total clearings in 1962.

sented 70 per cent of the value of their imports, while payments chargeable to Honduras (with its freedom of exchange) accounted for only 30 per cent of that nation's import trade.

Adaptation to exchange restrictions. The above analysis would indicate that the existence of exchange controls had an appreciable effect on the development of the multilateral clearing system in 1962. When the Central American Clearing House began operations in October, 1961, exchange restrictions were already in effect in El Salvador; but no immediate action was taken to curb the flow of funds to countries that, in the interest of freedom of exchange, might be disposed to permit the flight of capital through multilateral clearings. The adverse effects of this lack of foresight began to be felt late in 1961 and led to the hurried adoption of a protocol to regulate clearing transactions in Salvadoran colons.

To render the existence of exchange controls compatible with the multilateral settlements system, the central banks comprising the Clearing House membership agreed to require special authorization of checks and drafts for clearance and to fix monthly quotas covering settlements in bills and coins. The adoption of these measures necessitated the institution of certain regulations in the banking systems of countries enjoying freedom of exchange. These rulings, however, could be made effective only gradually: It is estimated that it was not until April, 1962, that a high degree of efficiency was achieved in the internal regulations adopted by the Guatemalan and Honduran central banks to keep transactions in Salvadoran colons from facilitating speculative capital movements.

The successful outcome of this experience encouraged the Nicaraguan central bank to join the Clearing House in May, 1962. (Nicaraguan exchange controls had previously stood in the way of such action, since the central banking institution was unable to perceive any real advantage in actively participating in the settlement system as originally designed.) When exchange restrictions were established in Guatemala in October, 1962, the multilateral agreement regulating clearings in other controlled-currency checks, drafts, and cash was fully operative and hence could be readily adapted to transactions for clearance in quetzals.

It will be observed from the foregoing discussion that, although multilateral clearances were initially exposed to speculative pressures, the situation was fortunately only temporary and at the present time in no way threatens the normal functioning of the system. Although cash clearings continue to imply certain risks for countries having exchange controls, since the monthly quotas for the conversion of bills in quetzals and Salvadoran colons are relatively liberal, the member banks have deemed it unwise to introduce stricter regulations, because of their possible adverse effects on border trade and tourism.

The recent elimination of exchange controls in Nicaragua and Costa Rica constitutes significant progress in consolidating the gradual expansion and improvement of the multilateral clearing system in Central America. As a matter of fact, participation by the Nicaraguan and Costa Rican central banks would have been curtailed had the exchange controls been allowed to remain in effect. Exchange controls in Guatemala were simplified in May of 1963; in El Salvador, such restrictions continue to be circumscribed to speculative capital movements. Consequently, it is fairly safe to assume that regulations in effect covering clearings in quetzals and Salvadoran colons will not obstruct the development of the Central American Clearing House and that active participation by the central banks of Nicaragua and Costa Rica will work in favor of extending and perfecting the system.

Clearing House settlements. As indicated earlier, the Guaranty Fund that formed a part of the Central American Clearing House mechanism up to December 31, 1963, was designed to effect automatic reimbursement to creditor members of credits granted in excess of their local currency contributions. From the very beginning, however, the Guaranty Fund was too small to be operative, in the face of the large volume of settlements handled by the Clearing House. For this reason, the member banks decided in favor of the practice of direct dollar payments by debtor to creditor banks. These payments were initially quite frequent and sizable, but the improvement of the system has increased the settlement of claims through the clearing mechanism proper.

The frequency and magnitude of direct dollar settlements in the early stage of Clearing House operations reflected the existence of a very marked bilateral relationship between Honduras and El Salvador, since Guatemala's participation in the multilateral clearing arrangement was relatively small and customarily resulted in a position of equilibrium as regards remittances sent and received. Membership taken out by the Nicaraguan central bank, in May of 1962, and the institution of exchange controls in Guatemala, in October of that year, were decisive factors in the improvement of the multilateral system and, at the same time, made it possible to reduce dependence on direct dollar payments.

Table 2 below summarizes Clearing House settlements, breaking the data down into four successive six-month periods to illustrate the structural changes that have taken place:

TABLE 2
BY-TYPE BREAKDOWN OF CLEARING HOUSE SETTLEMENTS
OCTOBER, 1961–SEPTEMBER, 1963

(*In Millions of Dollars*)

Type	*Oct., 1961– March, 1962*	*April, 1962– Sept., 1962*	*Oct., 1962– March, 1963*	*April, 1963– Sept., 1963*
Direct payments in dollars	3.6	4.9	3.3	4.1
Multilateral clearances	3.8	6.6	13.6	18.9
Temporary investment in securities	...	...	...	1.1
Net credits at end of period	1.1	0.5	0.6	1.4
Total Settlements:	8.5	12.0	17.5	25.5

Source: Central American Clearing House.

It will be observed that, in the Clearing House's initial stage of operations (October, 1961, to March, 1962), multilateral clearances (i.e., debits offset against credits on the members' accounts) represented only 44 per cent of total settlements, with direct dollar payments (deriving mainly from the Honduras–El Salvador bilateral relationship mentioned earlier) taking up 42 per cent. In contrast, during the last six-month period analyzed (April to September, 1963), multilateral clearances constituted 74 per cent of the total, while dollar payments shrank to only 16 per cent. Allowing for settlements via reciprocal investments in securities—an innovation in the last-mentioned period—internal clearings represented almost 80 per cent of total settlements effected during that half-year span.

The success of the multilateral payments systems in Central America should be measured in terms of its ability to settle account differences without having recourse to payments in dollars or in other convertible, non-Central American currencies. If the mechanism is to be consolidated and perfected, direct settlement of mutual claims by offsetting debits against credits on the member bank accounts should represent an increasingly substantial portion of the total settlement operations. The automatic credits provided for in the multilateral arrangement are quite small in relation to total settlements. In like manner, direct dollar payments to cover credit grants that exceed the automatic credit-line limits should be reduced to a minimum. Theoretically, of course, the ideal operating plan for any multilateral clearing system requires that 100 per cent of the mutual claims be settled by means of debit and credit entries on the members' accounts.

Toward a Central American Monetary Union

Apart from the specific accomplishments growing out of cooperation among the Central American central banks (which have centered on the development of the multilateral payments system and exchange-policy coordination), plans have been under consideration since mid-1962 for creating the bases for a broad Central American monetary union. These efforts have taken on added coherence and emphasis recently, to some extent in response to the exhortation that the Central American Economic Council [4] addressed to the region's central banks in a resolution issued August 16, 1962.

The Board of Directors of the Central American Clearing House, made up of the major officials of the member central banks, serves as an advisory and cooperative body. The board has not limited its discussions to payments problems, as such, but has directed its attention also to regional coordination of central-bank action and policy in other, broader fields. Moreover, the Clearing House has promoted frequent meetings for direct consultation between the presidents and managers of the Central American central banks, and, from these, important regional-level policy decisions have emerged on occasion.

Among the achievements scored by the Clearing House Board of Directors in the matter of inter-Central American payments, special mention should be made of the creation of the "Central American draft," which, in time, may well turn out to be the embryonic forebear of a sole currency for the region. The Central American draft was conceived as a uniform, low-cost bank draft expressed in the local currency of the issuer and payable at par in the payer's local currency. Although this document does not preclude the use of traditional instruments such as cashier's checks and certified personal checks, its introduction into the multilateral payments system is expected to have a favorable psychological effect and to contribute to generalized use of Central American currencies in the monetary transactions conducted in the region.[5]

The idea of establishing in Central America a broader and more formal monetary organization than the Clearing House was brought up for discussion in the Clearing House itself in October of 1962. A committee of experts from the five Central American central banks was appointed in mid-1963, with the assignment of studying all as-

[4] The chief organ of the General Treaty for Central American Economic Integration, whose membership comprises the member countries' ministers of economy.

[5] Operating rules for the Central American draft were approved in July, 1963, with practical application having started at the beginning of 1964.

pects of the problem and drafting a legal instrument to enable establishment of an appropriate regional agency. The creation of such an agency was agreed to in principle by the central banks late in 1963 and formally ratified in a convention signed at the end of February, 1964.

The convention was designed to promote the coordination and harmonization of Central American monetary, exchange, and credit policies, and progressively to establish the bases for the Central American Monetary Union to be created in some as yet undetermined future. By means of the exchange of information, technical investigations, consultation and research in general, it is anticipated that, within a few years, monetary integration goals—i.e., the unification of all the monetary systems in Central America—will have been attained. Implementation of the agreement will fall to the Central American Central Banking System, which has been equipped with the following subordinate agencies for that purpose: the Central American Monetary Council, the Advisory Committee, the Action Committee, and Executive Secretariat. As one of its functions the Monetary Council is to propose whatever agreements may be necessary for signature at the government level in order to create the Central American Monetary Union.

In its broader and more significant implications the Central American Monetary Union would contribute to the harmonious and well-balanced development of Central American monetary and financial policies aimed at furthering economic integration. It is often forgotten that economic integration is a process that does not end, but rather begins, with the formation of a common market and a customs union. The field of financial policy action within the over-all economic integration endeavor is therefore vast and complex. The exchange problem on which so much emphasis is being placed is, in the long run, simply a partial reflection of the way in which all money and credit structures and movements respond to the application of central-bank policies.

The economic unification process that is beginning to take shape in Central America will inevitably involve the interrelation of monetary, exchange, and fiscal policies. The enforcement of domestic financial policies having divergent or even contradictory means and ends would be inconceivable. It may, therefore, be concluded that the harmonization and eventual integration of the financial policies of the Central American countries are essential to the ultimate success of the structural policies already adopted in the fields of free trade, the customs union, industrial integration, uniform taxation, and the balanced development of the economic infrastructure.

Selected Bibliography*

ASSOCIATION OF THE BAR OF THE CITY OF NEW YORK (Committee on Foreign Law). *Economic Integration in Latin America.* New York, 1962.

BUSINESS INTERNATIONAL. *Latin America's Merging Market.* New York, 1964.

COCHRANE, J. D. "United States Attitude towards Central American Economic Integration," *Inter-American Economic Affairs* (Washington, D.C.), Autumn, 1964.

DELL, SIDNEY. *Trade Blocs and Common Markets.* New York: Alfred A. Knopf, 1963.

FEDERAL RESERVE BANK OF NEW YORK. "The Emerging Common Markets in Latin America," *Monthly Review* (New York), September, 1960.

GRIFFIN, KEITH, and FRENCH-DAVIS, RICARDO. "Customs Unions and Latin American Integration," *Journal of Common Market Studies* (Oxford), October, 1965.

HAAS, ERNEST B., and SCHMITTER, PHILIPPE C. *Mexico and Latin American Economic Integration.* Berkeley, Calif.: University of California, Institute of International Studies, 1964.

———. *The Politics of Economics in Latin American Regionalism.* Denver, Colo.: University of Denver, 1965.

LINDEMAN, JOHN. *Preferential Trading Systems in Latin America.* Washington, D.C.: International Economic Consultants, 1960.

LOWER, MILTON D. "Economic Integration in Latin America: A Dynamic Assessment," in LOWER, MILTON D., HANNIGAN, RAYMOND R.,

* Includes English-language titles only.

and JANSEN, RUDOLF K. *Some Aspects of Latin American Trade Policies.* Austin, Texas: University of Texas, Bureau of Economic Research, 1964.

MIKESELL, RAYMOND F. *Liberalization of Inter-Latin American Trade.* Washington, D.C.: Pan American Union, 1957.

———. "The Movement toward Regional Trading Groups in Latin America," in ALBERT O. HIRSCHMAN (ed.). *Latin American Issues: Essays and Comments.* New York: Twentieth Century Fund, 1961.

PERLOFF, HARVEY S., and ALMEIDA, ROMULO. "Regional Economic Integration in the Development of Latin America," *Economía Latinoamericana* (Pan American Union, Washington, D.C.), November, 1963.

PINCUS, JOSEPH. *The Central American Common Market.* Mexico City: Agency for International Development, 1962.

PLAZA, GALO. "For a Regional Common Market in Latin America," *Foreign Affairs* (New York), July, 1959.

TRIFFIN, ROBERT. "International Monetary Arrangements, Capital Markets and Economic Integration in Latin America," *Journal of Common Market Studies* (Oxford), October, 1965.

UNITED NATIONS. *Towards a New Trade Policy for Development.* Report by the Secretary General of the United Nations Conference on Trade and Development. New York, 1964.

UNITED NATIONS ECONOMIC COMMISSION FOR LATIN AMERICA. *The Latin American Common Market.* New York: United Nations, 1959.

———. *Multilateral Economic Co-operation in Latin America.* Vol. I: *Texts and Documents.* New York: United Nations, 1962.

———. *Possibilities for Integrated Industrial Development in Central America.* New York: United Nations, 1964.

———. *Towards a Dynamic Development Policy for Latin America.* New York: United Nations, 1963.

URQUIDI, VÍCTOR L. "The Common Market as a Tool of Economic Development," in ALBERT O. HIRSCHMAN (ed.). *Latin American Issues: Essays and Comments.*

———. *Free Trade and Economic Integration in Latin America.* Berkeley and Los Angeles, Calif.: University of California Press, 1962.

WIONCZEK, MIGUEL S. *Latin American Free Trade Association.* New York: Carnegie Endowment for International Peace, January, 1965.

———. "The Montevideo Treaty and Latin American Integration," *Banco Nazionale del Lavoro Quarterly Review* (Rome), June, 1961.

The Contributors

ENRIQUE ANGULO H. is Head of the Information Service, Center for Latin American Monetary Studies, Mexico City.

BELA BALASSA is Associate Professor of Economics at Yale University. He is the author of *The Theory of Economic Integration* and edited *Changing Patterns in Foreign Trade and Payments.*

SIDNEY S. DELL is Director of the New York office of the United Nations Conference on Trade and Development. He is the author of *Problemas de un mercado común en América Latina* and *Trade Blocs and Common Markets.*

ERNANE GALVEAS is Adviser to the Brazilian Ministry of Merchant Marine. In 1962–63, he was a member of the Inter-American Development Bank working group on export financing.

PLÁCIDO GARCÍA REYNOSO is Mexico's Deputy Minister of Industry and Commerce and Chairman of the Governing Board of the Latin American Economic and Social Planning Institute.

JORGE GONZÁLEZ DEL VALLE is Alternate Executive Director of the International Monetary Fund and a former Director of the Central American Clearing House.

FELIPE HERRERA is President of the Inter-American Development Bank.

HIROSHI KITAMURA, of Tokyo University, is Chief of the Economic Development Branch, United Nations Economic Commission for Asia and the Far East, Bangkok.

STAFFAN BURENSTAM LINDER is Professor of Economics at Stockholm University. He is the author of *An Essay on Trade and Transformation* and *Teoría del Comercio y política commercial para el desarrollo.*

GUSTAVO MAGARIÑOS is Deputy Executive Secretary of the Latin American Free Trade Association.

Raymond F. Mikesell is W. E. Miner Professor of Economics at the University of Oregon. He is the author of *Intra-Regional Trade and Economic Development* and the editor of *U.S. Private and Government Investment Abroad.*

Joseph C. Mills, formerly with the United Nations Economic Commission for Africa, Addis Ababa, is Visiting Professor of Economics at Waterloo Lutheran University (Canada).

Joseph Moscarella is Deputy Director of the Mexico City office of the United Nations Economic Commission for Latin America.

Raúl Prebisch is the Secretary General of the United Nations Conference on Trade and Development.

Barry N. Siegel is Associate Professor of Economics at the University of Oregon. He is the author of *Economic Aggregates and Public Policy.*

Jan Tinbergen is Director of the Netherlands Economic Institute. He is the author, among other books, of *International Economic Integration* and *Shaping the World Economy.*

Robert Triffin is Professor of Economics at Yale University. His works include *Europe and the Money Muddle* and *Gold and the Dollar Crisis.*

Miguel S. Wionczek is Adviser, Center for Latin American Monetary Studies, Mexico City. He is the co-author of *Planning Economic Development* and *Public Policy and Private Enterprise in Mexico.*